PERTH &
KINROSS
COUNCIL

thelibrary
or words

Tel 017   .gov.uk/library

D0765978

Please return/renew this item by the last date shown
Items may also be renewed by phone or internet

Donated by **The Crockart Foundation**

Sam and Chester

How a mischievous pig transformed
the life of my autistic son

JO BAILEY
with RUTH KELLY

CORGI BOOKS

TRANSWORLD PUBLISHERS
61–63 Uxbridge Road, London W5 5SA
www.penguin.co.uk

Transworld is part of the Penguin Random House group of companies
whose addresses can be found at global.penguinrandomhouse.com

First published in Great Britain in 2016 by Bantam Press
an imprint of Transworld Publishers
Corgi edition published 2017

This book is a work of non-fiction based on the life, experiences and
recollections of the author. In some cases names have been changed solely
to protect the privacy of others.

A CIP catalogue record for this book
is available from the British Library.

ISBN 9780552173261

Typeset in 11.4/14.39pt Minion by
Jouve (UK), Milton Keynes.
Printed and bound by Clays Ltd, Bungay, Suffolk

Penguin Random House is committed to a sustainable
future for our business, our readers and our planet. This book
is made from Forest Stewardship Council® certified paper.

1 3 5 7 9 10 8 6 4 2

Contents

Contents

Prologue

Devon, England, January 2009

The barn was full of scents as we entered: a mixture of fresh straw, dung and the farm animals themselves. We could hear the pigs oinking softly, a constant hum of noise that seemed to suggest contentment and happiness. Intrigued, we walked over to the pen and looked inside.

He was so small that I didn't spot him at first, but tucked away in the corner of the pigsty was the only ginger piglet of the litter. He looked sad and lonely, like my son Sam, who had autism, often did. He looked tiny and lost.

Neither that little piglet, nor I, realised it then. But in that moment, both he and I were found.

Life had just changed for ever.

CHAPTER ONE

Shattered Dreams

Benalmádena Pueblo, Spain, Summer 2005

I CLOSED MY EYES AND ENJOYED THE SENSATION OF THE COOLING Mediterranean breeze on my face.

I was sheltering from the searing midday sun on our veranda. Luckily for me, I wasn't on holiday: I lived full-time in Spain, and had done for fourteen years, ever since I'd finished university. I worked in Málaga as a translator and also in operations at Málaga airport. Not what you might call a typical 'Brit Abroad' on the Costa del Sol, I was fully integrated into Spanish life, for most of my friends were Spanish and my husband, Jaime, was too – in fact he barely spoke a word of English.

Our two-and-a-half-year-old son, Sam, was currently at the supermarket with my mum, who also lived in Spain, while our eleven-month-old boy, Will, was having a nap. Consequently, I had a rare five minutes to myself. I was very tempted to follow Will's lead – it was hard to stay awake in such heat.

Every now and again, sitting there on the veranda, I caught the zesty scent of the nearby orange groves, which sweetened the air and added to my somnolence. The wicker chair creaked beneath me as I sank further into the padded cushions. Kicking off my flip-flops, I eased my feet up on to the coffee table. I couldn't put a price on how nice it was to snatch

1

a few moments to myself; being a mum-of-two didn't give me much time to relax. My eyelids grew heavy and rolled sleepily down as I gave in to the heat and my exhaustion. It was, after all, the time of day when most people took a siesta. Nonetheless, I kept half an ear listening out for Will's cries in case he woke, not quite allowing myself to drop off fully.

We lived only twenty minutes from Spain's party city of Málaga, but the view from our veranda couldn't have been more different. There were no bars, clubs or skyscrapers rising from the water's edge here – Benalmádena Pueblo was a sleepy seaside village with picture-postcard white-washed buildings tangled in vines and brightly coloured flowers. The village centre was called the Plaza de España: it amounted to a fountain, circled by a series of cafe tables set out under the orange trees. It was peaceful – it was a place you would want to raise your family, just as we intended to do with our boys.

Our house was on a quiet street, roughly a fifteen-minute walk from the beach. It was a dream home that Jaime and I had designed and built from scratch. Spread over four floors, it was spacious and had a garden with a pool, palm trees and a stone gazebo smothered in jasmine and bougainvillea. You could see the sea from our bedroom balcony, as well as the dozens of swimming pools that paved the way down to the sea. At night, the sky would glow like the northern lights from all the family-run restaurants stretching along the bay.

As I sat sleepily on the veranda, drifting somewhere between a doze and sleep, the peace of the afternoon was suddenly shattered. I was jolted firmly awake by the screeching noise of a car pulling into my drive.

'Jo, Jo!' I heard my mum crying out.

I was out of my seat instantly and had just reached the

front of the house when my mum and Sam came hurrying through the door. My mum was clearly distressed and carrying Sam in her arms. Tears were streaming down my little boy's face as he clutched his eye.

'Something awful has happened to Sam,' Mum spluttered.

'What?' I panicked, chasing after them into the living room.

'He smacked his head against a concrete pillar in the supermarket.'

She passed Sam into my arms and I cradled him against my chest. His eye was swollen and already turning blue.

'You silly sausage, what have you done?' I pushed his blond, tear-soaked hair back from his eyes. Sam didn't reply, he just buried his face into my warm body.

I glanced up at my mum for answers. She was shaking.

'He didn't half take a knock, Jo,' Mum said, her voice quivering with shock.

She explained how Sam had been running up and down the supermarket aisle with his head bent over the refrigerators, trying to get his eye as close to the counter as he could without touching it. Sam had recently developed an obsession with straight lines – it was most peculiar – and he'd been trying to line up his eye with the horizontal lines of the fridges.

'He was so preoccupied that he ran full speed into a concrete column and fell on his back. He didn't even see it.'

She said that the staff in the supermarket had been very helpful – but when they'd tried to cool the bump with a cold flannel, Sam had lashed out at them.

'He just would not have it, he was screaming. I couldn't calm him down, he was almost hysterical.' Mum's voice cracked at the memory of seeing her grandson so distressed.

Looking down at Sam, it was hard to imagine he was the

same boy my mum was describing. He was calm and content now as he rested in my arms. My mum handed me a bag of frozen peas and I carefully placed a corner on Sam's bump. He didn't even flinch. As I stroked his soft blond hair, Sam reached his little arm up to my ear and started to stroke my lobe.

I'll never forget the look my mum had on her face that day. She looked at Sam with a worried expression etched into her features. And as she watched her grandson stroke my earlobe, over and over again, she slowly shook her head and turned to me.

'There's something not quite right here.'

'I know,' I snapped at her, the words shooting out before I had a chance to stop them. And they took me by surprise as much as Mum, for up until that point it hadn't consciously occurred to me that there was something *wrong* with Sam. I had noticed some small changes in his behaviour recently, but I'd put them down to Sam developing.

Shakily, I took a deep breath and regained my composure. 'I'm sorry, Mum, I didn't mean to have a go. I just don't know what to make of it all,' I explained weakly.

I thought over his recent behaviour. A few months before, Sam had taken to lying on his belly and running his favourite toy car backwards and forwards in front of his eyes; he would sometimes replay this action for hours on end. He also insisted on watching the same episode of *Thomas the Tank Engine* again and again. He craved repetition, which was a little odd, but I didn't think anything was 'wrong' with him as such.

Yet I'd also noticed that Sam liked to flap his hands, as though they were a bird's wings, when he was excited – for example, when Tinky-Winky appeared on *Teletubbies* or when Thomas the Tank Engine did something silly – or when he was particularly anxious about something. Was it normal? I thought it must be, for he seemed a happy enough toddler, bouncing and dancing to his favourite television shows. Perhaps if Will had been older than Sam I would have noticed differences in their development but, as it was, I was just a young mum learning as I went along.

But my mum, who had two grown-up daughters, knew better. Sensing my stress at her comment, Mum now softened her gaze and joined me on the sofa. She was a beautiful, well-dressed and elegant woman with high cheekbones and youthful skin. My dad had left her when I was little, but she'd never let that get her down. Mum had moved from London to Málaga not long after my older sister, Sarah, and I had relocated there. She was the heart and soul of her expat community: a regular at the British Legion Club and always out doing things with her friends.

'Jo, love,' she now said, delicately, 'this obsession Sam has with straight lines, it's not normal. I think you should take him to see someone, if only for your own peace of mind.' She smiled at me, reassuringly.

I was grateful to have my mum there for support. But in a way her presence made me sad. For as wonderful as my family was, their solicitude reminded me that the one person I really wanted to talk to about Sam, I couldn't reach.

My husband Jaime: Sam's dad.

To my intense sorrow, my marriage with Jaime was breaking down. We'd been drifting apart for some time, but things had become even more difficult since he'd moved to Seville last November for work. My husband was gone all week, as he had to be, and the geographical distance had put an added strain on our already faltering marriage. In recent months, our communication had deteriorated to just a handful of phone calls in between seeing each other at the weekends. The more we drifted apart, the more needy I became. I had this beautiful dream home, but no husband to share it with. And now our son Sam seemed to need our help, but we weren't a team any more, ready to leap into action.

I told my mum I would think about what she'd said, and she then headed back to her villa in nearby Torremolinos. I was left alone with just the boys and the sound of the Mediterranean for company.

That evening, I tucked Sam into bed next to Will's cot. Their room was so cheerful, with bright yellow walls and shelves filled with cuddly toys and children's books. Yet it hardly reflected how I was feeling at that moment, as my brain whirred unstoppably over my mum's words.

'Sleep well, boys.' I kissed them both goodnight and slipped out of the room. I'd be checking on Sam throughout the evening to make sure his bump wasn't bothering him but, for now, I returned to the breeze out on the veranda and became lost in my thoughts.

As dusk settled over Benalmádena Pueblo, I listened to the hypnotic chirping of the cicadas. My mind replayed everything that had happened that day. Who can I ask about Sam's behaviour? I wondered. Up until that point, we'd only needed to see the doctor for coughs or colds. This was one of the rare moments since I'd moved to Spain that I felt like a foreigner.

I decided I'd start with Sam's nursery. Sam went there five

days a week; it was only a five-minute drive away in Benalmádena. *I'll ask them about it*, I thought, *when I drop the boys
off tomorrow morning.*

But the nursery manager had only reassuring words for
me when I spoke to her the next day. 'We haven't noticed
anything strange with Sam,' she said cheerily. 'He's very
well-behaved. A beautiful blond blue-eyed boy!'

I felt a wave of relief wash over me. *Maybe I don't have anything to worry about.* I took the name of a child psychologist
from the manager anyway, as Mum was right: I should see it
through for peace of mind.

Just as I was leaving, though, the manager added: 'There is
one thing we have noticed . . . Sam doesn't talk to any of the
other children.'

'Oh.' I was taken aback. It was another alarm bell.

I booked an appointment with the child psychologist as
soon as I could, but he couldn't see us for another week. In
that time, my anxiety levels rocketed. In the days leading up to
our appointment, I spent a lot of my time scrutinising Sam's
behaviour. His latest 'thing' was to sit in front of the washing
machine holding our pink oven glove. When the cycle started,
Sam waved the glove. When it stopped, Sam stared vacantly at
the drum. He would sit, cross-legged, on the kitchen floor for
the whole washing cycle if I didn't pull him away. I was desperately worried and so wanted to help him but I just didn't know
how. Something was not right with my boy, I knew that – but
I didn't know exactly what was wrong. I needed someone to
give it a name so that I could start to deal with it. Night after
night, I went to bed hoping that our upcoming appointment
would show us the way forward.

When the day arrived, Sam and I headed into the waiting

room of the child psychologist's office in Torremolinos. I was clutching the notes I'd made on my son, the papers crinkling in my hands as we waited to see the psychologist. The room was crammed with games, books and a climbing frame with a slide – everything you might need to keep a child amused. I fanned myself against the sticky Spanish heat while Sam played quietly in the corner with a toy fire engine. The bump on his brow had gone down, but there was still a nasty bruise: a visible reminder of his peculiar behaviour, and how it could get him badly hurt.

A door opened abruptly and a short, slightly round man appeared, proffering an outstretched hand. The doctor ushered me into an equally busy room, only this time it was packed floor to ceiling with medical books. The fan on the ceiling was whirring at such velocity that the paperwork on his desk looked like it was about to take off, save for the paperweight pressing it down.

'Shall I fetch Sam?' I looked back at my son in the waiting room.

'No, let him play.' The doctor eased himself into the chair behind his desk and gestured for me to sit too. He had warm, hazel eyes and smiled broadly at me. He seemed kind. I hoped he could help.

Yet as the appointment progressed, I felt as if I was in some sort of therapy session rather than there to get help for my son. I chatted about the changes I'd noticed in Sam while the doctor listened and nodded whenever I paused for breath. I peered back at my son in the adjacent room as I described his behaviour, feeling increasingly frustrated that the doctor wasn't looking at him. The next thing I knew, the hour was up and the doctor hadn't offered any explanation as to what could be wrong with Sam – or even examined him. Instead, he suggested buying some picture cards and asked me to work with Sam to encourage him to predict what might happen next after the scene shown, as well as to say what the people in the cards might be feeling. With hindsight, I can see the doctor had a diagnosis in mind and was asking me to work with Sam on things that he might find difficult, should the doctor's suspicions prove correct – but at the time I didn't know any of that. I walked away still none the wiser about what was going on with Sam.

'Mum, it's useless. The doctor's visits don't seem to be helping.' I recounted what had happened to my mum. She told me to try and stay calm but it wasn't easy. For fourteen years I'd loved living abroad but now, faced with trying to get a diagnosis for Sam, I realised just what a difficult position I was in. For I was based in a country where I didn't know the ins and outs of the national health system – and not knowing where or who to turn to for help was frightening.

Over the next few weeks, as I tried to get my head around the Spanish health system and Sam and I began his 'homework', my son's condition rapidly deteriorated. It soon became clear that the picture cards were a non-starter because, almost overnight, Sam started to shut down.

The first big change concerned his eyes. Sam wouldn't look at me, his dad or his baby brother any more.

'Sam, baby, I'm over here!' I would wave my hands in front of his face.

Nothing. He stared through me as if I wasn't there.

'SAM!' I tried again, and again. Nothing. He stared obsessively at his own fingers rather than at us, holding them close to his face or flickering them in front of his eyes.

'Sam, stop.' I pulled them away. He was scaring me.

But a minute later, there he was, 'flickering' again. His eyes had turned cold and vacant, as though there was nobody home.

Previously, Sam had been able to feed himself and to point to the things he wanted to eat. But, now, as the 'shutdown' accelerated, he couldn't even do that any more. If he wanted some food, he would take my hand and lead me to the fridge to show me he was hungry, but he seemed to have lost the power of choice, the power of communication.

Sam lost all interest in his brother. He didn't want to play with him or look at him. Will was as good as invisible to Sam.

It made my heart ache. Only weeks before, the boys had been messing around in the sandpit together – Sam sprinkling sand into Will's hair and me getting cross because Will's baby hair was so fine that I could never get the stuff out. How I longed to have those moments back again now. I kept a picture of Sam kissing and cuddling Will in a frame by my bedside but, these days, I didn't even recognise the boy in the photograph.

Perhaps the most distressing thing of all was that Sam stopped speaking. He had been able to say about forty words in both Spanish and English. He had sung and clapped along to nursery rhymes. Now, he could barely utter a single word.

'Sam, would you like a yoghurt?'

He stared into space as he twizzled the spoon around in his mouth.

'Yoghurt,' he repeated carefully: the last word of the sentence. That was the most I'd get out of him – my last word was his only word. He couldn't even say 'Mummy' any more. It was heartbreaking. I cuddled him, I sang to him, but nothing I did could revive him.

The one thing he hadn't lost was his ability to sleep – though that was probably because he was unresponsive most of the time. While Sam was sleeping, I, on the other hand, would be lying wide awake two rooms away, terrified to fall asleep for fear of how I'd find Sam in the morning.

How much further was he going to regress? Would he soon lose the ability to walk as well as talk? Was he going to end up in a wheelchair or even on a life-support machine? I thought a disability like cerebral palsy or Parkinson's disease was taking him over, destroying his body and his mind.

I couldn't seem to get through to my husband about how serious things had become. On his visits home, Jaime treated Sam as though nothing had changed.

Jaime would ask Sam to eat up his food, as he always had done, and something Sam had done so easily just a few weeks before. But Sam simply stared down at the table, blankly, as though his dad hadn't spoken.

'He won't eat; he won't do anything any more.' I couldn't help what happened next. I rushed out of the room so Sam didn't see me upset, and promptly burst into tears.

It's almost impossible to put into words how desperate I felt. Sam's fate ate away at me and kept me up at night as I wracked my brains for a way to bring him back to me. I worried constantly about where this downward spiral would end. Despite my attempts to stay positive for Sam in the daytime, in the wee small hours I couldn't help but imagine my poor boy eventually ending up on a psychiatric ward, his eyes glazed over as he stared into space.

And, scarily, it wasn't even that much of an exaggeration or a leap for my frightened mind to make. For just three weeks after I'd first seen the doctor, my son had regressed beyond all recognition.

And I had reached breaking point.

Things came to a head one sunny day. The Spanish heat that I'd once loved now seemed cloying and I hadn't been out in it, enjoying its warmth. Instead, I'd spent the morning trawling the internet, doing as much research as I could to try to figure out what was wrong with Sam. Pausing for a minute as I tapped away at my computer, I turned to look at my boy who was lying, completely withdrawn, on the sofa. He'd been in the same position for hours, just stroking his earlobe, his eyes locked on a single spot on the rug.

I stopped what I was doing. Though none of my previous efforts had borne fruit, I went over to him to see if I could lift him out of his trance. I wanted to shake whatever it was that had taken hold of my son out of him, but you wouldn't have known it from my touch. Instead, I scooped him into my arms and gently rocked him back and forth.

'You're beautiful,' I sang to him; James Blunt's song. And Sam *was* beautiful. I loved him so much. I closed my eyes and tried to remember Sam as he once had been. As I rocked him and sang to him, my mind drifted back to one of my happiest memories . . .

We'd just moved into the house. I was heavily pregnant with Will, and Sam was eighteen months old. He was sitting at the head of the kitchen table, raised up on a pile of cushions so that he could see the stack of picture cards in front of him. Jaime had turned the top card over and placed it in front of Sam. Our son had paused for a moment as he digested the drawing. With a cheeky, proud smile, he'd turned to me and said, 'Cat,' and then looked at Jaime and announced: '*Gato!*' We'd cheered and clapped and Sam had beamed as he'd patted his little chubby hands together, cleverly mimicking us. Then on we went to the next card. There were at least twenty pictures and Sam could say them all in both Spanish and English. I know every mum thinks her child is a genius, but we were genuinely convinced he was.

Now look at him, I thought, as I stared down at his sad little face, his body limp and unresponsive in my arms.

My thoughts were broken by the sound of something crashing to the ground. I gently lay Sam back down on the sofa and ran into the kitchen – to find that Will had pulled everything out of the cupboard and tipped the box of dishwasher tablets all across the tiled floor.

'Will,' I sighed, dropping to my knees to clear up the mess. Will was almost crawling and he had become very good at shuffling himself around on one knee, using his back leg as a rudder to steer.

Just as I had finished putting everything back, I turned around to find that Will had pulled out every baby wipe from a packet and strewn them across the floor. He was just as dextrous with his hands as he was at getting around.

I tidied up once again and returned to Sam in the living room, but what seemed like only two seconds later Will was back in the kitchen, pulling out the contents of the saucepan cupboard. The irony was not lost on me: I had one little boy who was very much present and letting me know it, and another who was disappearing before me on the sofa. The contrast was too much and I felt a sob rising in my chest. I was mentally, physically and emotionally exhausted. I just wanted to run away and hide.

I made sure the boys were safe – and Will distracted with a toy – and then took myself off to our study, a cosy little room at the bottom of the house far away from the heat. It was my home from home, a little piece of England, for moments such as these when everything got too much. It had a thick blue carpet, bookcases packed floor to ceiling with my favourite reads and family photos all over the walls. It even contained my grandmother's old fireplace, which we'd had shipped over from the UK. It smelt comforting – old and musty, like a library. I felt safe and secure there and the feel of the soft carpet under my bare feet had never felt so soothing. The room had a desk and a swivel chair, which I now collapsed into.

Trying not to cry, I picked up the phone and rang my mum. Who else do you turn to when you've nowhere left to go?

'I just don't know what to do, I just don't know what to do,' I kept saying, over and over. What was happening to Sam seemed like a bad dream, but I couldn't wake up. This was all too real, and at that moment it felt all too much.

'Oh love, I wish I knew what to say to you,' Mum replied, feeling helpless.

I wanted to say more but the words were caught in my throat.

'I'm so sorry,' Mum carried on. I could hear her voice cracking now too. She was really upset and worried as well, for she adored both my boys. I was losing my son, and Mum was losing her grandson. But neither of us was prepared to let that happen.

'Listen to me, Jo,' Mum went on now. 'Whatever it costs, we'll get him right, we *will* sort it out.' She promised me: 'We'll go private, we won't mess around, we will get him back.'

It was exactly what I needed to hear. One way or the other, we were going to get this straightened out.

I only hoped we weren't too late.

CHAPTER TWO

The A Word

THE NEXT DAY I LAUNCHED STRAIGHT INTO ACTION. WE WERE on a mission to save Sam. My mum was a rock and my sister, Sarah, was also brilliant – she started taking my boys to nursery with her sons, Tom and Dan, so that I could concentrate on finding the right paediatrician to help Sam. My whole family pulled together.

I turned to my friend Inma, who is a lawyer and has a little girl, for guidance. She recommended her own paediatrician and I managed to get an appointment with him in the city that same week. Jaime was away in Seville as usual – he was due back late on the day of the appointment – so my mum came with me for support.

It had been weeks by now since I'd left my house; after the consultation with the doctor and then Sam's sudden decline, I hadn't ventured out, focusing solely on Sam and his needs. I didn't normally look forward to travelling into Málaga but I found I was now gasping for noise and contact with other people, even if they were strangers.

Mum drove us to the doctor's office in her little blue Ford Fiesta. Sam was sleeping in the back – my sister Sarah was babysitting Will – and I rested my tired head against the window, watching the quiet streets of our sleepy seaside village morph into towering skyscrapers, hotels and holiday apartments. The sunburnt grass that lined the road became replaced with concrete buildings topped with flashing neon signs trying to lure people to beach restaurants and bars. We met a sea of tourists in the city centre, moving lazily through the midday heat, so deeply immersed in the holiday spirit that they seemed to have forgotten basic road safety. Mum honked the horn as they stepped carelessly into the road.

The clinic was in a high-rise on the east side of Málaga. We found a parking space in a multi-storey car park nearby and then took the lift in the doctor's building all the way to the top floor. Sam was in my arms, his head drooping over my shoulder. Ever since his shutdown had begun, he'd lost all interest in the world around him and didn't even look up as the elevator doors opened with a *ping*.

The waiting room was filled with children, all sitting on their parents' laps. I felt sick with anticipation. I was absolutely convinced the specialist was going to tell me my son had some sort of degenerative disease. What else could it be?

I steeled myself for the worst as we were called into his office.

The paediatrician was in his fifties. For some reason I'd imagined he would be wearing a white overcoat but he was dressed smartly in cream chinos and a shirt with the top button unfastened. He was very pleasant and instantly earned my confidence. The whole set-up had a much more professional feel to it when compared to my frustrating experience with the previous doctor.

Sam sat quietly on my mum's knee as the doctor listened intently to what I had to say.

'Hmmm.' He arched one eyebrow. I looked at Mum – what did *that* mean? He scribbled something down on a piece of paper and then slid it across the desk:

SYMPTOMS COMPATIBLE WITH
ASPERGER'S SYNDROME.

It was written in capitals, as if it wasn't a shocking enough message as it was.

'Asperger's?' I asked, uncertainly. I'd heard of it, but I couldn't have told you what it was.

He handed me another piece of paper: written on this was the address of a clinical psychologist in Fuengirola, which was about twenty miles away. Finally, he spoke: 'This is what I think it is.' He tapped the second piece of paper. 'And this is who you should see for an official diagnosis.'

And that was it.

Despite the brevity of the meeting, I felt strangely relieved on the journey home. At that time, I thought Asperger's meant that you were a bit socially awkward, but very gifted. There had been a lot of coverage of the book *The Curious Incident of the Dog in the Night-time*, which is narrated by a boy with Asperger's, and I guess my thinking came from there. *It's going to be OK*, I reassured myself.

Jaime was already home and in the kitchen when we got back. I broke the news to him at once.

His interpretation of the diagnosis was similar to mine, only he seemed more positive. That was typical Jaime – take it as it comes, take it all in his stride, super laid-back and unflustered – whereas I was left with dozens of questions . . . and I wanted answers.

I turned to my computer for research. I needed to know more about this Asperger's syndrome. I spent hours trawling the internet and very quickly became much more informed about the condition.

What is Asperger's? I typed, my fingers flying across the keyboard.

The answer came back right away: *It's a neurobiological disorder.*

What are the symptoms?

People with the condition display unusual nonverbal communication, such as lack of eye contact, few facial expressions or awkward body postures and gestures.

Yes, I thought, *that's Sam.*

They may strongly prefer repetitive routines or rituals and become upset at any small changes.

Yes, that was Sam too.

They may perform repetitive movements, such as hand or finger flapping and may also 'daydream' or 'zone out' when overstimulated.

Yes, that indeed was Sam too.

Many of the symptoms I read about married up with Sam's behaviour – however, there were also a worrying amount that didn't. For example, Sam's speech: if he had Asperger's, he should have developed a style of speaking that was advanced for his age. But Sam had gone the opposite way. I also learned that in many cases Asperger's can't be properly identified until the child is around seven years old.

I put the boys to bed and kept researching until I was so tired that the words on the screen blurred before my eyes. I woke up with my head in my arms and a crooked neck – and a realisation that things had changed. For the tears I'd been crying before our appointment were now long gone. Instead, I had a purpose: I was now channelling all my energy into finding out exactly what was wrong with Sam and how I could get him better. I needed to see this woman in Fuengi-rola as soon as I could.

I instantly liked her when Sam and I entered her waiting room just a few days later. Dr Mariángeles Kalis looked typ-ically Spanish – she had long dark glossy hair, tied neatly in a bun, and beautiful dark eyes framed by meticulously pruned eyebrows. I found her friendly and kind, and she clearly tried to make Sam feel like he was the most special child in the room, despite him being unreceptive to her efforts.

Mariángeles explained that at this first appointment she would spend some time alone with Sam, watching him play, and would call me in at the end to give me her initial diagno-sis. An hour later, I anxiously returned to the playroom to find Sam in the corner, driving a yellow toy car backwards and forwards across the bright green carpet.

'Sam, sweetie, I'm back.' I crouched down beside him. Nothing. There was no response, not even the flicker of an eyelash.

Mariángeles smiled at me sympathetically. She'd clearly been here before with many other heartbroken parents whose children failed to acknowledge their existence. Talking over Sam's pointed silence, she outlined to me the significance of the yellow car he was clutching.

'I asked Sam to pick a car out of the toy box,' she explained, recalling the game they'd been playing. 'Sam chose the yel-low one. I took it off him, put it back in the box, mixed it up and asked him to pick out another car. He picked out the yellow one. He repeated this half a dozen times.'

I stared at her blankly.

'It's a sign of autism,' she revealed.

Autism – I had heard of that. Thanks to my hours of internet research, I knew that Asperger's was a form of autism, part of what experts call the Autistic Spectrum. People with 'classic' autism and those with Asperger's shared similar characteristics but there were also differences.

Mariángeles's announcement didn't sit well with me, though, because I had also read that 'classic' autism could be much more challenging than Asperger's.

'What's autism?' I asked nervously, wanting to hear the doctor's take on it. My knowledge was, after all, based only on an internet search.

Mariángeles explained that autism was a developmental condition that affects how a person communicates with, and relates to, other people. It also affects how they make sense of the world around them.

'People with autism have described the world as a mass of people, places and events which they struggle to make sense of, which causes them considerable anxiety,' she revealed.

I must have looked worried, for she went on to reassure me: 'Some people with autism are able to live relatively independent lives.'

'But others?' I asked. My own anxiety was increasing with every question.

'Others may have accompanying learning disabilities and need a lifetime of specialist support.' I let that sink in as Mariángeles kept talking, describing more symptoms. 'People with autism may also experience over- or under-sensitivity to sounds, touch, tastes, smells, light or colours.'

My mind was busy racing over the last six months, searching my memories, trying to recall if Sam had exhibited these telltale signs of autism.

Knowing of the paediatrician's initial diagnosis on his scrap of paper, Mariángeles went on to explain that Asperger's syndrome was widely known as a mild form of autism.

'People with Asperger's have fewer problems with speaking and do not usually have the accompanying learning disabilities associated with autism,' she explained.

As she said the words, I was horribly, horribly aware that Sam had regressed to being completely nonverbal. He definitely *did* have problems with speaking – did that mean he had autism and not Asperger's? The concern in my eyes must have been clear as Mariángeles now said cheerily, 'He's very young, it could be a number of things.' She smiled sweetly at Sam, who ignored her.

As the consultation drew to a close, Mariángeles told me that we would have to wait for a year to find out if Sam was actually autistic, or had Asperger's, or had something else that was causing his regression. She wanted to continue to monitor him before issuing a formal and official diagnosis.

I don't have a year! I wanted to scream. What if after twelve months Mariángeles came back and said, 'He's not autistic'? What if what was wrong with my son was what I'd feared at first, something life-threatening – like a brain tumour?

I left her clinic feeling anxious and afraid. As soon as I was home I picked up the phone and called my mum.

'Mum, I can't sit back and wait – because that's a year I could lose curing Sam from something else!'

Mum told me to stay calm. She told me we were going to work through this together, that no price was too much to help her grandson. I don't know what I would have done without my mum.

Mariángeles was going to work with Sam every week for the next year. From that moment on, I was on two journeys: the diagnostic one with Mariángeles, and my own path searching for a cure for Sam – maybe a cure for whatever disease might be plaguing him, or simply some other way to make him better. I would not rest until I'd found the answer. Every night after the boys had gone to bed I researched for hours online and ordered books for further reading. I was absolutely determined to be as informed as I possibly could be in order to help Sam.

The first thing I had to do was rule out if Sam had a brain tumour, which involved him having an MRI scan. Jaime came with us to the hospital in Los Alamos, near Torremolinos. The MRI machine was tucked away in the basement. As the three of us headed down into the gloom, it was like walking into a cave – and in the middle of the room was a huge machine that was making an ear-splitting noise.

In order to perform the scan, the doctors needed to encase Sam inside this loud, coffin-like machine for five minutes – but he had other ideas. Sam, who had been lying quietly in my arms up until this point, now started thrashing wildly, thumping his fists into my chest.

'Jaime, help!' I cried out. I couldn't hold on to him.

The MRI scanner boomed as the electromagnet fired up.

Sam was crying and thrashing and hitting at anything he could reach. Every time Jaime carried him over to the MRI machine, he'd become increasingly distressed.

Eventually, the doctor stepped in.

'This isn't going to work. Take him outside and we'll turn the machine off and try again,' he instructed.

We made several attempts to go back into the room, to try and get Sam to lie down on the bed, but every time he got close to the machine, he'd become distraught all over again. It was tearing me apart watching him suffer. How awful this must be for him.

'We are going to have to give him a general anaesthetic,' the doctor directed, asking for our help to keep him pinned down while he administered the drugs.

He sedated Sam but, twenty minutes later, my son was still wide awake. Part of me now wanted to abort the whole thing because my poor baby was so distressed, but the other half of me couldn't give up. I needed to know why he was behaving like this.

'I've got an idea: let's get in the car,' I told Jaime.

There was a road outside, lined with palm trees, which led to the seafront: a two-mile stretch of sandy beach. I thought if we drove up and down the sea front, over and over, the motion would rock Sam off to sleep.

I sat in the backseat cradling my son's head on my lap. But poor Sam couldn't stomach the anaesthetic and was throwing up all over me.

The atmosphere in the car had become intense. Sam was unwell, we were becoming increasingly agitated and I was feeling so guilty for putting my baby through all this.

'I love you,' I whispered, stroking Sam's cheek, trying to calm him.

Eventually, he did nod off. I carried his limp body back down into the treatment room and lay him down on the scanner bed. Thank God the anaesthetic had taken hold: he didn't wake up even through the noise of the MRI machine.

They told us the results straight away. It was one of the few moments I felt reconnected to Jaime as we both braced ourselves for the worst. I really wanted answers, and unless I had the answers I couldn't help Sam – but waiting to hear if my son had a tumour was horrific. I swallowed the dread that was inching up my throat.

'Normal,' the doctor announced, clipping the pictures of my son's brain on to the lightbox.

I closed my eyes with relief.

The peace didn't last for long, though. As soon as we left the hospital, I was thinking about what I needed to do next. *Is Sam deaf?* was my first thought once we knew he didn't have a brain tumour. *Maybe the reason Sam won't answer me is because he can't hear what I'm saying?*

I booked Sam in to see an otolaryngologist: an ear specialist. My baby was put under anaesthetic again; he was enclosed in another dark, coffin-like box. Electrodes were placed all over his head and in his ears. It was horrible for him, but we needed to know.

'Normal,' the doctor said afterwards.

Relief.

I felt like I was riding an emotional roller-coaster, it was such a strange and confusing mixture of feelings that I was experiencing at that time. I was happy that the results of all the tests were coming back negative, but I was also anxious because with each clear result I was running out of possibilities as to what might be wrong with Sam. He didn't have a brain tumour. He wasn't deaf. So what *was* wrong with him? We still had over half a year to wait for Mariángeles's official diagnosis.

Next, I started trying things like blood tests for gluten allergies and adding omega-3 fish oils to Sam's milk to aid his brain development.

Negative; nothing worked.

I remembered that Sam had never crawled, just gone straight to walking. Perhaps that meant part of his brain was undeveloped? I started doing 'brain gym' exercises with him, encouraging him to join me in playing indoor football on all fours, hoping to strengthen his brain so that this regression would stop.

I read a book that said certain foods and flavourings could bring out morphine-like substances in the brain. If Sam was allergic to these substances, could that explain why he was spaced out all the time?

I turned our cupboards upside down, drawing a big black cross on any tin or food packet that contained casein, mono-sodium glutamate or aspartame. Our kitchen looked like a biological hazard zone by the end of the day – you'd open the cupboard to find a sea of black crosses. With these restrictions in place, there was very little Sam could eat but somehow I concocted a two-week menu for the whole family; I thought it would only be fair to Sam if we all embarked on the new regime with him, because I thought it would be unfair if, for example, Will had a biscuit when Sam couldn't. So we all ate the same food: healthy, raw things like tuna and gluten-free pasta, fruit and vegetables.

I noticed a slight change in Sam's behaviour – he seemed a bit more 'with it' after a few weeks – but I wasn't sure if it was just my imagination because I knew I was desperate to see a positive change in him.

And each night, after Sam had gone to bed, I read every single bit of literature on autism that I could – to prepare myself in case Mariángeles came back with a positive diagnosis.

I was a woman possessed. My resolve was driving me forward, but it wasn't necessarily strength that drove me on. For there was a part of me that was afraid to stop, for fear the loss of momentum would bring me to a grinding halt and I wouldn't be able to pick myself back up again.

I needed to keep going. I needed to fix Sam.

Sadly, I couldn't fix my marriage. As the year went on, we spoke less frequently on the phone; maybe once a week, if that. I only rang Jaime if I had a problem.

Despite feeling desperately unhappy, I still wanted to make my marriage work. We had a very challenging boy on our hands and I was terrified I wouldn't be able to cope without my husband, even though him working away during the week meant that in many ways I was already doing that. In addition, I'd never given up on anything in my life and I wasn't about to start now. I was fighting for Sam and I was fighting for my marriage.

But by the September of 2006, it had become clear that there was very little left for us to fight for.

Perhaps if things had been different I would have spoken up more, tried to figure out exactly what the cracks were and how to mend them, but I felt so ground down by the worry about Sam that I'd lost my voice.

It was October 2006 when things finally came to a head. The boys were in bed, and Jaime and I were in the living room, sat on the low-slung green sofa that I'd bought in Habitat in the 1980s. I loved it so much that I'd gone to the trouble of shipping it out to Spain. But not even its familiarity could offer me any comfort now.

We talked things through, but there comes a point, no matter how hard you battle or how hard you try and kid yourself, when a realisation hits you. And sat there, together on the sofa but a million miles apart, I knew our marriage was over. And Jaime knew it too.

He stood up, running his hands over his face and through his jet-black hair.

He said that he would be the one to leave, to give us a clean break.

It was over.

And, seven weeks after he left, in December 2006, my year-long quest to find answers for Sam was over too. Just before Sam's fourth birthday, Mariángeles called us back to her office and there, with Sam on my lap and my mother by my side, she told me the news I'd been dreading since the day I first met her.

It was official, she told me. My little boy had autism.

'Classic' autism.

Our lives would never be the same again.

CHAPTER THREE

Castaway

I OPENED THE FRONT DOOR AND WALKED INTO THE KITCHEN — but soon realised Sam hadn't followed me in. I turned around to see him still hovering in the doorway, standing awkwardly in a puddle of his own urine.

'Oh, Sam.' My heart went out to him. This was the third day in a row that he'd wet himself after I had picked him up from school.

He was staring at the ground, looking sad and helpless. I didn't draw attention to his accident; it wasn't his fault, the poor thing. I just took his hand and led him upstairs where I could change him into some fresh clothes.

I was increasingly concerned about Sam and school. Though Mariángeles's diagnosis had given me the answer I'd long been looking for as to what was wrong with Sam, it soon became clear that it didn't make much difference on a day-to-day level to have that 'label' for him, mostly because the primary school he'd been going to for the past five months wasn't making any time or allowances for his condition. They didn't seem to have an understanding of autism, which perhaps wasn't that surprising. When I'd been sent away from the clinic that had diagnosed Sam, I felt I'd been given very little explanation about what autism was and how to cope with it. I could hardly expect teachers who didn't specialise in the condition to know much more than I did.

'Show him language,' Mariángeles had advised. So I'd booked Sam to see a speech and language therapist twice a week. But it seemed the rest was up to me to figure out – and I was like a blind person, feeling my way in the dark for answers. It was an incredibly frustrating and lonely mission.

Thanks to all my reading, I now knew, above all, that Sam needed structure and predictability. If Sam had a regular and consistent routine and knew what was coming next, he was much less likely to become anxious and upset. The way to help Sam achieve this knowledge was to map out his day for him in a storyboard type of way. Mariángeles had given me some picture cards with Velcro backs that I could arrange in a sequence. For school it would look something like this:

Reading. Fruit time. Painting. Lunchtime.
Toys. Home time.

The aim being for Sam to visualise his day, because if he could predict how it would pan out, he wouldn't be so worried about going to school.

But his teacher did not use the cards. 'He doesn't need them,' she said airily, brushing away my concerns.

Moreover, Sam had no continuity in his school life. I had made a friend in one of the dinner ladies, and she used to tell me how Sam was being seated on a different chair every lunchtime.

The fallout of all this was on my porch – Sam wetting himself. He'd spend the day bottling up his anxiety and his fears so that when he finally got home, somewhere safe, he couldn't control his muscles for a second longer and had to let it all out. Even though he couldn't speak to tell me, I knew Sam must have felt as awful wetting himself as I did watching him and not being able to help.

Another big problem at school was the noise. Autistic brains have a much higher number of nerve cells than 'neurotypical' brains. This means that autistic people can suffer from sensory overloads – where noise, light, tastes or colours become overwhelming, and painfully so. It was impossible to predict what might trigger a sensory overload or how much it would hurt Sam. With hindsight, it was no wonder Sam had had a meltdown when he'd heard the banging of the MRI machine – it must have sounded like a shotgun in his ear, and we'd been trying to put him inside the contraption that was making all the racket!

But the screaming and shouting of the loud Spanish children was just as deafening for Sam and became impossible for him to cope with. The noise of the dining hall was horrendous. The teachers reported how Sam spent all his time in class with his hands clamped over his ears and his head on the desk.

I was back and forth to the school constantly, dealing with phone calls from frustrated teachers.

'Sam is trying to block out the noise,' I told them, as I tried to explain why he was pretending to sleep through his lessons.

But my best medical summarising didn't help – they couldn't understand Sam's behaviour. It wasn't out of malice, it was just a small provincial school and they had no experience of autism.

Every morning I'd drop Will off at the nursery and then wind my way up to the top of the mountain with Sam, to where the school overlooked the bullring and our village of Benalmádena Pueblo. The location was nothing short of beautiful, with its sea view and mountain backdrop, only I was too preoccupied to take it all in.

There was a main staircase running through the centre of the school, from which branched lots of classrooms. On the ground floor was the dining hall, which opened out on to the playground. To the right of the dining hall was a big room where I dropped Sam off in the morning. All 300-odd children would be in there with the dinner ladies, screaming and shouting, as kids do. Every morning, Sam would look so lost, so withdrawn and so obviously frightened and overwhelmed by everything that was going on around him. His eyes were big and watery. I hated walking away and leaving him there.

I didn't know what else to do, though. I presumed I'd be prosecuted if I didn't take him to school. Moving him to a new school didn't seem to be an option, as new routines could do more harm than good. The only consolation, and the main reason I didn't pull Sam out, was that his cousins, Tom and Dan, also went there. Tom was five and Dan four; Dan was in the same year as Sam but not in the same class, which was such a shame as I think it would really have helped Sam to see a familiar face in his lessons.

I would have picked Sam up at lunchtimes to feed him at home – so that he could avoid the dining hall – if I hadn't had to work, but now I was a single mum I had assumed the economic responsibility of running the household. My sister's ex-husband had stepped in to help by giving me a new job in sales at his property development company. It had eased the financial worry, but I was barely holding it together.

After all, I was trying to come to terms with the fact that my husband and I had split up and that one of my sons had special needs. It was a fraught time, to say the least.

I experienced so many different emotions; among them shame. What sort of monster must *I* be for my husband to leave me? Though Jaime still saw the children every other weekend, I blamed myself for us not making it work as a family. I felt ugly and unlovable.

My mum and sister tried to reassure me, telling me that I was beautiful, but their pep talks were just words to me and I couldn't take them in. Every time I looked in the mirror I saw an overweight 'thing'. I hated my red hair, I hated my pale freckly skin; I wished I could be bronzed and slim like all the beautiful Spanish women walking along the promenade. I wanted to be anyone but me.

I felt so lonely that I even turned to virtual strangers for help.

One evening I was sitting on the veranda, staring blankly at the moonlight on the pool. I was alone – the boys were at my sister's house and Mum was at the British Legion club. I was getting more and more depressed that I would be on my own for ever. It wasn't even for me that I felt down; I desperately wanted my boys to have a father figure in their life. I'd grown up without a dad and I didn't want Sam and Will to have to do the same.

As my thoughts swirled round and round in my head, my gut twisted into an unbearable knot and I felt an immediate and intense need to escape from the fears that were closing in on me.

I knocked on my neighbour's door.

'Jo!' Leslie exclaimed in surprise as she opened the door to my teary face.

'I'm sorry, I just didn't know who else to turn to,' I said weakly, my voice catching in my throat.

Leslie was an English lady in her fifties. She'd been married to a Spaniard, Diego, for years. Of course, she'd heard that Jaime and I had separated; everyone in the street had. Being a close-knit community, the news had spread like wild fire. She invited me in and my flip-flops crunched across the dry Mediterranean grass of her garden as she led me to a table and chairs which looked out on to the ocean.

'Have this,' she said, handing me a very large glass of wine.

Leslie had a pretty, sweet face. Softly spoken, she was a motherly figure who had grown-up children of her own. Seeing the sympathy in her expression, I couldn't hold the words in a second longer.

'I'm going to be alone for ever,' I blurted out. 'I'm thirty-eight; no one is going to want to be with me.'

I didn't have the courage to say what I was also thinking: no one is going to want to take on my autistic son.

Leslie threw her arms around me and gave me a squeeze. 'What rubbish, that's not going to happen.'

'How do you know?' I asked, tears streaming down my cheeks by now. I felt like a little child asking her mum for all the answers.

'A beautiful woman like you will be snapped up soon!' She gave me another squeeze.

But in my heart of hearts it wasn't my single status that was really getting me down. It was the fear of being a single mum to Sam, and the knowledge of how challenging Sam's autism could become, that was terrifying me now. I couldn't see how anyone would want to take us on as a package and I was worried that I wouldn't be strong enough to cope on my own; that I wouldn't be enough for Sam.

Leslie's encouragement, like that of my family, was hugely appreciated, but it didn't stop me from becoming an emotional wreck. The slightest thing would set me off and start the tears welling in my eyes, such as Will putting a flannel down the toilet. It was just another thing to deal with and when things like that happened, I would physically feel the stress grip my body. I would have to stop what I was doing and remember to breathe – it was almost like having a panic attack. It's silly, really, because there are loads of mums out there with difficult children, but I wasn't coping very well at all.

In truth, Will was probably behaving so mischievously because he had lost his playmate. He would entertain himself now, as if Sam didn't exist. Will would even crawl over Sam, like he was just another bit of the furniture. And that's exactly what Sam had become as he spent hours lying lifelessly on the sofa. Only one thing seemed to give him any spark of life: drawing. One day he picked up a blue felt-tip pen and drew a huge smiley sun with eyes and ears on it. He had never drawn anything before and the huge smile on the sun's face gave me a faint glimmer of hope; a rare highlight in those dark days (I still have that drawing in a frame today). From that moment on, Sam's drawing became more and more a part of his life, but he didn't draw that often. He spent most of his time zoned out, not interacting with the world – not with me, not with my mum, and definitely not with his brother, who had seemed to cut all ties and dismissed Sam entirely as he charged about the house. It was all too evident that one of my sons was blossoming while the other was wilting.

I'm embarrassed to admit this, but I turned to wine to numb the pain. Towards the end of the day, I was so exhausted and so down that I would have a glass or two to calm my nerves. I'd relax and then I'd have another one, and then another one . . . and the next thing I knew I'd had a whole bottle. Never more than that, and I never drank spirits – always a rosé wine called Peñascal. Life in Spain was very much about drinking in the sunshine, so when you are used to socialising with wine, it's easy to turn to it when things go wrong. I wouldn't be the first frazzled mum to hit the bottle, but my own mum was quick to pull me back from the brink.

It was a Saturday afternoon when she realised how very low I'd become; we'd all just been to the supermarket in Torremolinos. Sam had been quiet and withdrawn throughout the trip to the shops, while Will had been as inquisitive as ever, wanting to pick all the fruit and vegetables out of the buckets and touch everything and anything. We were all worn out by the end.

'Let's go get a coffee,' Mum said, pointing to the cafe across the street.

It was a very traditional-looking place with brightly coloured ceramic tiles. There were jugs mounted on the walls, chorizo hanging above the counter and Spanish music playing. The waitress was just a little curt as she told me that Will's pushchair was in the way . . .

I burst into tears. Mum looked at me the same way she had looked at Sam two years ago, out of the corner of her eye, shaking her head with worry and concern.

'Oh, Jo, we've got to get you sorted out.' She cupped her hand over mine.

'I just don't know what to do,' I cried. 'Sam can't cope with being in school, the school won't help him, I have no real idea if what I'm doing is making him better or worse, and I'm scared. I'm so scared.'

My mum could see that I was close to breaking point. Rather than telling me simply to get a grip, however, she helped me through the worst of it by looking after me. And she wasted not a minute before sending in the troops.

The first thing my mum did was to get her cleaner to blitz my house from top to bottom – and just having my house spruced up gave me a massive lift. Mum appeared at my house with bags full of groceries. She also sent me over to her best friend, Fran, for a pick-me-up.

Fran lived in the UK most of the time, but she had a gorgeous penthouse holiday home on the beach. She loved the sun-and-sangria lifestyle of the Mediterranean. Like my mum, Fran, who was in her sixties, always looked immaculate. She was mad about fashion and loved make-up and clothes. Her outfits were always ironed, her hair was always perfectly coiffed and her nails always mani-cured. She put me to shame! Fran also has the most magnetic personality – really vivacious, full of laughter – and is the sort of woman who brightens a room when she walks into it. When she talks to you, she is so interested and asks loads of questions – she really knows how to make you feel special.

I took the boys with me to see her and we all sat out on the terrace. Fran had put on a lovely spread with champagne and salmon bites. She could tell I was really down, especially when I shared my fears about the future. 'This is it for me,' I mumbled glumly into my champagne flute.

'Right!' She suddenly stood up, her highlighted chestnut hair bouncing with her. Fran wasn't the sort of woman who cried into her pillow at night and she was determined to ensure that I wouldn't be either.

'We are going to get you a new wardrobe,' she declared, and directed me towards her bedroom. Fran started pulling out dresses, tops, bikinis, and throwing them across her perfectly ironed bedsheets. She told me that I could keep anything I liked: here was my brand-new wardrobe. It was so generous of her.

And not only did she do that for me, but when I emerged from her bedroom after trying on all her clothes, she had a hamper waiting by the door, full of wine, cheese, biscuits – even nappies. She probably knew I was struggling, so it was incredibly kind and thoughtful of her.

Being around her gave me the lift I needed – and the confidence to say 'yes' when one of my other neighbours, Barbara, asked me if I'd go on a blind date with a man she knew. By then it was July 2007 and Jaime had been gone for nine long months – and in fact, our relationship towards the end had been so distant that I felt I'd been on my own for twice that time – so I was more than ready for this next step. The man was called Darren, he was British and he worked on the oil rigs. That's all I knew about him when Mum dropped me off to meet him in the square in Benalmádena Pueblo.

'I'm so nervous,' I said, buttoning up my white cardigan. I was wearing one of Fran's dresses – a purple Grecian-style sundress – and was suddenly worried it was a bit revealing for a first date.

'You've got a beautiful figure, go and show it off,' Mum said as she batted my hands away from my chest. I took a deep breath and opened the car door. Given it was the height of summer, I was grateful for the sea breeze that swept through the village.

I'd seen a picture of Darren, so I knew who to look out for as I approached the tables and chairs scattered outside Fidel's, a beautiful little seafood and meat restaurant where we'd arranged to meet. My heart was beating hard as the usual first-date questions filled my head: *will Darren like me? Have I worn the wrong dress? Should I have worn more make-up?* My critical thoughts were interrupted as a tall, athletic man rose up from behind a table.

'You must be Darren,' I said with a shy smile, recognising him from his photograph.

'That's me.' He grinned back, his soft Yorkshire accent coming through even in those two short words.

I was so nervous that I must have been babbling at a hundred miles an hour, as well as playing with my hair and pulling at my cardigan. But I didn't think I was alone in my nerves as Darren also looked worried. Indeed, he suddenly blurted out: 'You're really disappointed, aren't you?'

'No!' I was taken aback. He was a really good-looking man, tall, muscly – a silver fox. It was something of a relief to know that I wasn't the only one feeling insecure, though; perhaps we were more alike than I knew.

One of the great things about where I lived in Spain was being able to spend so much time outdoors: it meant you were forever exposed to a wonderful array of scents. As Darren and I dined, the smells of mimosa, jasmine and the sea wafted over us, helping to calm our nerves and relax us into our conversation.

Over a plateful of tapas, Darren told me how he worked half the year on the oil rigs as a safety officer and spent the other half at his house in Valencia. He was a year older than me, he had a teenage daughter with his ex-wife, and he would soon be returning to South Korea, where he was building a ship for the next oil excavation. With unforgiving work rotas, he explained that it was hard for him to meet someone. I was fascinated by his stories of life on the rigs, dicing with death, but Darren was much more interested in finding out about me.

Having a man offer to listen to me was a new experience, and I found myself opening up to Darren. I broke every rule in the dating book and told him my life story. I described what had happened with Jaime, and revealed I had a son who had autism. If I'm honest, I thought that as soon as I told Darren I had a child with special needs, he would run for the hills, so I wanted to get it out in the open straight away.

But Darren didn't seem the least bit fazed. He was so calm and rational and, above all, kind and decent. It was a pleasure to be spending the evening with him.

We had a laugh, too; so much so that I didn't even notice we were the last people sitting on the terrace at Fidel's. I found I was glad of the solitude, though, when Darren leaned over to kiss me. I kissed him back, but I didn't let my emotions run away with me. For as much as I liked him, I wasn't ready for a full-on new relationship just yet. My focus had to be on Sam.

As we said goodnight, Darren mentioned that he couldn't wait to set up another date for when he was back from Korea.

'Just give me time,' I said, a little hesitantly, reluctant to set

a date so far in the future – Darren would be away for
months – but equally worried that he would be put off by my
desire to take things slowly.

'Take as much time as you need,' he said, understandingly.

As I hailed a taxi, I experienced something I hadn't felt in
a long time.

Hope.

CHAPTER FOUR

Back in the Ring

'YOUR SON HAS BEEN REPORTED TO THE HEADMASTER.'

'What for?' I stared at my friend, the dinner lady, in disbelief.

She told me that Sam had attacked the boy sitting next to him in the dinner hall, scratching his face, before ripping a framed painting from the wall and hurling it at the staff who had rushed to separate the children. I clasped my hand over my mouth, struggling to believe what I was hearing: firstly, because it was so completely out of character for Sam – he was usually very placid – and secondly because only the previous day I had pleaded with his teacher to keep him out of the dining hall. I had said before that the noise of three hundred children was too much for him to cope with; it must have sounded like thunderclaps to his sensitive little ears, those really loud ones which come out of nowhere and are right above you and make you jump out of your skin with shock. The sensory overload was causing him to lash out, much like a frightened animal does when it's cornered. I was starting to realise that he couldn't cope with being pushed to these limits.

'Is the other boy OK?' I checked.

'The other boy is fine, but his father has made a complaint to the headmaster.' She raised her eyebrow.

I felt like the talk of the playground as all the other mums came to collect their children. One mum steered her child away from Sam as she whispered something under her breath. I just wanted to get Sam out of there as quickly as possible. I felt awful for him, my poor boy. But Sam didn't notice the stares. He was staring at the ground, lost in his own little world as usual – it was hard to believe what had just happened.

I found myself becoming increasingly angry as I drove back down the mountain. I smacked the steering wheel in annoyance and, as I glanced in the rear-view mirror, the sight of my boys brought with it the now-familiar sensation of tears pricking at my eyes. Yet they weren't tears of upset, but of frustration. Sam's teachers just didn't seem to be listening to my advice about how to help him. Sam needed to have his visual aids to guide him through the day. He needed to be somewhere quiet – he should never have been in that dining hall in the first place. It sometimes felt like I was hitting my head against a brick wall trying to show the school what he needed. And I felt guilty too. *What Sam must be going through*, I thought, *to make him do something like that, to lash out at the world when normally he ignored it* . . . I was his mum, I wanted to protect him from any kind of hurt or upset. But I couldn't help but feel that no matter what I did, I was failing.

By the time we got home, I had worked myself into a real state and immediately ran to the phone.

This time, the first person I called was not my mum, but Darren.

We'd been emailing every day for the past month, ever since he'd left for Korea, and he'd become a constant in my life. No problem seemed too great for him; he was always ready to offer kindness and support – as a friend, with no expectation of anything more.

'Hello?' He sounded half asleep and his voice was gravelly.

I was so overwhelmed with what had just happened, I'd completely forgotten the time difference – it was 11 p.m. in South Korea.

'Oh my goodness, Darren, I'm so sorry,' I said apologetically.

'It's no bother,' Darren replied as he cleared his throat.

As I had been so many times in the past month, I was touched by his understanding. We barely knew each other yet he was prepared to get up for me, and my problems, really late at night. I wouldn't have bothered him if I hadn't felt so utterly helpless, though. I just didn't know what to do or where to turn. I felt trapped.

'There's only one thing you can do,' he said, having listened to the drama of Sam lashing out in the dining hall and my concerns about the sensory overload he was enduring every single lunchtime. 'You'll have to change your work hours and take him home for lunch.'

Just like that – he solved it.

It must have seemed like the most obvious solution to an outsider but I was so caught up in all the turmoil that I couldn't think clearly. I needed a problem-solver like Darren to show me the way.

My boss, my sister's ex-husband, was incredibly understanding and agreed to me having the afternoons off work. And as soon as Sam started coming home for lunch, he improved. He was calm and content as he ate his sandwiches at the kitchen table. Sam still had the noise and disorder of the classroom to contend with, but at least he didn't have to deal with the mayhem of the dining hall at lunchtime any more.

I'd overcome a small hurdle, and it was thanks to Darren.

Every day we chatted on Messenger. We'd usually be in contact around lunchtime in Spain because of the seven-hour time difference and then Darren and I would put the world to rights. There were many moments when I felt down but Darren was always there to cheer me up. He even listened to me cry when Jaime filed for divorce that same summer. I wasn't shedding tears because I wanted my husband back, but more because of the finality of it all. Nine years together, but now it was over.

Darren made sense of my muddled thoughts. He would reassure me that things would look different after I'd had a chance to sleep on them and that a new day always brought a fresh start. It was comforting, and for the first time in my life I felt like I could really put my trust in a man.

Darren gave me the strength and conviction to decide what I had to do next. It wasn't going to be easy. It was going to call on all of my courage for it was a decision that would take my boys away from everything they had known up until now.

But I had no alternative: I needed to bring my sons back to England where I could find the medical and educational provisions to help Sam.

I knew it wouldn't be easy breaking the news to my mum and sister. We had all made our lives in Spain, and now I was breaking up the party. We were all sat around the dining-room table at my sister's house when the time came to tell them. I nursed a cup of tea between my hands as I struggled to find the words. In the end, I just came out with it.

'I'm moving back to England. Spain can't give Sam the help he desperately needs,' I blurted in one breath.

My mum seemed OK; maybe she had been half expecting the news. My sister, on the other hand, didn't hold back.

'No, you can't!' she cried out.

I explained that it wasn't an easy decision because I didn't want to leave my family behind. I didn't want to separate the boys from their cousins because they were like brothers, but what choice did I have?

Sarah turned to look at Will, Sam, Tom and Dan. 'You have to remember that the boys love each other – Sam will be fine because they all love him,' she announced confidently.

It was a convincing argument, but once I'd left my sister's house I knew that my head had to rule my heart. Family simply *wasn't* enough. After all, I loved Sam desperately, but all the love in the world couldn't protect him and make things right for him. I knew that the best thing for Sam was to be in England.

Darren was 100 per cent in favour of the move. He told me he wanted to carry on our blossoming relationship wherever in the world I was. Perhaps because he was so used to travelling long distances, an extra few thousand miles between us didn't really make much difference. The strength and support I got from Darren was all very new to me – and it felt wonderful.

The moment I made my decision to leave, I closed the door on my Spanish life and started to dream about the English countryside and all the things I missed about my home.

The first thing I did was to find a lawyer in the city: Jaime and I were partway through our divorce and I knew such a major decision about the children's future would need professional handling. Thank goodness I acted so quickly as the woman I hired, Juana, advised me that if I wanted to go to the UK at any point in the future, I had to apply to do so now, during the divorce proceedings. All decisions regarding the children, such as visitation rights, maintenance costs and – crucially – where we would live, had to be established in this one court order, which would be issued at the point of our formal divorce. If I missed this window of opportunity, I might never get my boys to the UK.

My stomach clenched. I had just over a month to build my case. The divorce hearing was due to take place in September 2007.

'What do I need to do?' I asked my lawyer.

Juana warned me that the judge was likely to rule in favour of the children staying in Spain. After all, I spoke the language, had been here for almost two decades and had a network of support with my family living in the country. Plus, of course, Spain was where the boys' father lived. Juana told me I had a real battle on my hands: the only way I could win was to prove that Spain couldn't offer Sam the provisions he needed.

I launched into action. First I gathered lists of schools in the UK that specialised in autism, such as Treehouse in London, and mainstream primary schools that catered for children with assisted needs. I wanted to prove that the UK was decades ahead of Spain in the treatment of autism. I also lined up two jobs in the UK to demonstrate that I could afford to look after the boys: my cousin and my best friend's brother both offered me work. I even drew up a list of all the things Britain has to enhance the life of a child with autism, such as the Donkey Sanctuary Assisted Riding Therapy, sensory rooms and no end of other therapies, including art, music and occupational therapy, aromatherapy, reflexology, and speech and language therapy.

I wanted to prove that I had a support network as soon as

I landed, so I also drew up a list of UK-based friends I knew who had children with autism. I approached the National Autistic Society for brochures and explanations about autism so that I could show the judge I knew what I was talking about. I collected brochure after brochure, documents, magazines . . . I had a massive pile of paperwork towering on my desk. I was channelling the same determination I'd put into finding out what was wrong with Sam into putting together a watertight case. I was a woman on a mission.

And my next mission was to show that Spain *lacked* the provisions to help Sam.

I asked one autism charity for their help. Their reply? 'God gave you a son like Sam because he needed a mother like you.' Although very kind, their response angered me and just added fuel to my fire.

I approached three state schools and two fee-paying international schools in the area – these were the schools most likely to provide Sam with his secondary-school education, if we remained in Spain. The first three said no to Sam outright: they wouldn't even admit him. One of the international schools said that I would need to employ a speech and language therapist to accompany Sam to every class – so I'd be paying school fees as well as the salary of the specialist. The final international school had the most straightforward approach.

I didn't walk in thinking it would be a lost cause – far from it, as from the outside the school looked magnificent. It was clean, neat and orderly. There was a nice playground with hanging ropes and slides to the right as you walked in.

I was shown into the headmaster's office, which was huge. The headmaster was sitting behind a giant glass desk.

'How do you do?' He held out his hand.

I explained my situation. How Sam had been rejected from three Spanish state schools, how I hadn't even received replies from schools further afield and how the other international school had told me I would need to employ an additional therapist every day of Sam's school life.

'Would you be able to provide an education for my son?' I asked, breathless from all my explanations.

The headmaster leant forward across his desk.

'There is nothing to discuss,' he stated bluntly. 'I think you should return to the UK.'

Yes! I thought. For it was another weapon in my arsenal. It was also incredibly reassuring. For an education professional such as him to say categorically that my son would be better off leaving the country cemented what I had felt all along.

Every time I got another email from a school, or something to further my case, I forwarded it to my mum.

'You must be so proud of yourself,' she often replied. Mum was always encouraging me, telling me to believe in myself. She was also incredibly self-sacrificing – for she had told me that she would also move back to the UK if it helped to strengthen my case.

'Mum, you can't do that!' I had exclaimed. 'All your friends are here, you have such a busy social life! I wouldn't want you to say goodbye to all that.'

But Mum had lifted Sam on to her knees and combed her fingers through his blond hair. Both Sam and Will adored my mum. She kissed his little head and looked up at me. 'He needs help and if you can prove to the judge that you have a family network back in the UK, that could swing the decision,' she explained simply.

My eyes welled up. 'I love you,' I said. There were no other words.

All the incredible support I was receiving made it feel like I had an army behind me as the court date approached: 12 September 2007. Nonetheless, I was a bag of nerves the night before as I studied my prepared documents from cover to cover, memorising all the answers to all the questions my lawyer would be asking. My stomach was full of butterflies as I ran through all the possible outcomes.

I was also dreading seeing Jaime again. We hadn't spoken in weeks, while the only time I'd seen him was when I'd spied him from the kitchen window as he dropped the boys off outside the house one weekend. I was worried that he would think I was doing this out of revenge, which couldn't be further from the truth: it was all about helping Sam.

Yet it wasn't just Jaime's opinion I was worried about. I was very concerned about how the judge and everyone in the courtroom would view me – would they think I was some kind of monster who made Jaime leave me and his children, and was now robbing a father of his boys? I still carried that irrational feeling of shame for the family breaking up wherever I went.

I tried to calm myself by laying out my outfit on the bed. It didn't help much but it focused my mind: in the end, I settled for an all-black shirt-and-trousers combination.

I then called Darren. By now, I couldn't go a day without chatting to him on Messenger or on the phone; we sometimes chatted for up to three hours straight. We hadn't seen each other in two months but our constant contact had helped us build up a strong relationship – perhaps stronger than if we had been going out on actual dates because we had laid the foundations for a friendship first. I couldn't wait to see him when he returned from the rig in October. But, for now, I just had to focus on getting through the next twenty-four hours. I couldn't mess this up – Sam's future rested in my hands.

'Don't be so hard on yourself,' Darren said as I poured out all my worries to him. 'You've chosen a good lawyer, you've researched all you possibly can on the subject. There is nothing more you can do. Try and get some sleep.'

Of course, I didn't catch a wink.

It didn't seem to matter, though. I had so much adrenaline pumping around my body that I practically sprang out of bed the next morning and raced around the house getting myself dressed and the boys ready for school.

We all bundled into my Jeep Cherokee and I drove up the mountainside. This was Will's second week at primary school (in Spain children start school at three years old) and he seemed to be settling in fine. As I walked my boys to the school gates I felt a wave of dread wash up my throat. It occurred to me that by the time I returned to pick them up, their fate would be out of my hands and in those of the judge. I cuddled and kissed them until María took Sam and Will by the hand and led them towards the big hall.

Sam turned back once to look at me. It was the first time he had looked me in the eye for ages. *Does he know that today is an important day?* I wondered.

Once I was back in the car, I felt the all-too-familiar tears welling up. But I told myself firmly that this was no time for crying: it was time to be strong for Sam. I looked in the rear-view mirror to check my make-up, dabbed my tears away and turned the keys in the ignition. It was time to save Sam.

I'd had the same CD stuck in my player for weeks. It was a really naff pop compilation from 2001, but there was one song on it that was particularly significant for me.

'All rise, all rise,' I sang, cranking up Blue's smash hit. The words were apt considering my impending court case, but it had more meaning than that. It had been the soundtrack to my research mission and over the past few weeks it had become my fight song. I wound down the window and drove back down the mountain to the courthouse in Torremolinos with the song blaring out. I had butterflies in my stomach and my heart was pounding. I had to keep telling myself that I was going to win, that we would get through this.

It didn't help that I didn't have a clue what to expect when I got to the court – I didn't know if it would just be me and Jaime and a judge across a desk, or a full-blown courtroom like in the movies. All I knew for sure was that I'd be meeting my lawyer and my mum down there.

It was an overcast, windy day so as I got out of the car and made my way to the courthouse, I couldn't quite work out if I was trembling because of my nerves or because of the chill sweeping through the side streets. I crossed my arms protectively and leant into the breeze.

The courthouse was a beautiful, grand old building with four huge colonnades holding up the sandstone architecture. There were two Spanish flags marking the entrance. I took a deep breath and stepped into the unknown.

I hadn't expected the waiting room to be so small. It was a tiny narrow room with four plastic seats lined up against either wall, forming a corridor into the courtroom. My lawyer and her assistant were sitting on one side, mirrored by Jaime's lawyer and her assistant on the other. We were only feet apart from each other; it couldn't have been more claustrophobic.

Juana dipped her head and started to whisper instructions in my ear. My mum was also going to be giving a testimonial, so Juana filled me in on what questions she planned to ask her, such as, 'What are Sam and Will like?' 'What's Joanna like as a mother?' 'What's Jaime like as a father?'

And then Jaime himself walked in. My whole stomach heaved.

'*Buenos días*,' he greeted the room confidently in his deep voice.

Everyone stopped what they were doing and looked up at him. He had always possessed a great deal of charisma. I couldn't bring myself to say hello, even though I knew it was rude; my eyes were glued to the floor. My hands were trembling so much I was clutching my notes to stop them falling out of my hands.

My mum was the next person to appear. I immediately felt stronger having another ally there: it was four–three to me. Then the interpreter for my mum turned up, so the room was really beginning to fill up. Every time I looked up, Jaime's lawyer's eyes were on me. Jaime was leaning against the wall in a nonchalant way. I couldn't even force myself to look at him due to my feeling of shame. The whole situation felt incredibly tense.

I spent the final moments before we were called in testing myself in my head on what I was going to say. I had prepared for the judge a very simple explanation of what autism was and how Sam behaved. I imagined myself on the stand, and mentally drew up a list of all the possible questions they might ask me and my respective answers. I felt as if I was revising for an exam, but at least I was prepared.

I wasn't ready, however, for so many people to be in the courtroom when the doors finally opened. It was packed with at least a dozen ushers, legal staff and some members of the public. Benches branched off the aisle that led to a giant wooden table, which stretched the breadth of the room. Mounted on the wall were gold-framed portraits of the King and Queen of Spain. In the far left-hand corner was a tripod with a camera. Not only was I under the watchful eye of the Royals but I was also being filmed.

Come on, Jo, you can do it. I pumped myself up.

I was shown to a bench right next to Jaime and took a seat just along from him. There were only about three feet between us but it felt like a mile – we'd become that detached from each other. It was crazy to think how close we once were. Jaime felt like a stranger now.

'All rise,' announced the clerk as the judge swooshed in with his draping robes. He had bushy silver hair and half-moon spectacles that he wore halfway down his nose. He took a seat on his throne-like engraved chair.

I could hear my heart pounding in my ears and glanced across at Jaime. Even he was looking stressed. From his body language I surmised that, like me, he hadn't expected so many people to be present for a divorce hearing.

The judge peered over his spectacles at each of us in turn. I suddenly became very conscious of the way I was sitting. *Is the judge evaluating me on my posture?* I wondered. I straightened my back, crossed my legs and folded my hands neatly into my lap. I tried to look as prim and proper as I possibly could to make a good impression.

The judge cleared his throat and then rattled off a list of formalities, including the reason he would be filming us – he would look at the evidence again when making his final decision. Luckily I was fluent in Spanish or I wouldn't have been able to follow a word of what was going on.

'Would Joanna Bailey please stand up!' the usher bellowed.

My heart almost stopped as I heard my name being called. I had to squeeze past Jaime's knees to get to the stand, which was awkward, to say the least. Fortunately my lawyer, Juana, started off the proceedings, which put me at ease.

'How long have you lived in Spain? How old are the boys?' Our rehearsed questions flew thick and fast as she warmed me up for the main event: the challenge of explaining what autism was to a room full of people who had probably never heard the term before. And all in Spanish!

At the appropriate moment, I launched into my spiel. Midway through, I looked up to find everyone watching me intently as I described all the impairments associated with autism and how they affected Sam. I could tell they were fascinated by what I was saying. I carried on, determined to get through every bullet point marked in my memory.

Eventually I stopped, took a breath and turned to my lawyer. 'Is that sufficient?'

'That's sufficient.' She nodded, and there was a rumble of laughter across the courtroom. I think those in attendance could tell by the look on my face that I was ready to go on – for hours if necessary! – to tell them absolutely *everything* I knew about autism and communicate my son's needs.

It was the icebreaker I needed and for the first time that morning I relaxed a little bit.

'Why do you want to go back to the UK?' Juana asked me next.

That was an easy question. I explained clearly how the schools in Spain wouldn't have Sam; how I'd been met with obstacle after obstacle.

Every now and again, the judge would throw in a question to challenge me, but I always had an answer ready for him. I was very careful not to bad-mouth Jaime. I thought it would be silly to criticise him as the case was about Sam, not him. The only thing I did say was that Jaime hadn't been around much, which was completely true.

It was then Jaime's lawyer's turn to cross-examine me. She looked formidable in her stilettos, black tailored trouser suit and crisp white blouse. Her dark Spanish hair was bleached blonde and flicked out at the bottom. She was also a lot older than my lawyer, so came across as if she had a lot of experience.

I braced myself.

The woman cleared her throat and then waded in. Her MO was much more aggressive than anything I had faced so far, but I had every answer prepared. I thought it was playing out well for me.

And then, just as I was starting to think that things were going to plan, she caught me off-guard.

'What objection would you have, if any, to spending half a day with the children and for Jaime to have them for half a day?' she asked, referring to my new work schedule.

'Ah, um,' I stuttered. A wave of heat rolled up my neck. I

hadn't been expecting her to suggest joint custody. I had no answer in my arsenal prepared.

She saw the chink in my armour and went in for the kill.

'Do you have an objection to that?' she barked.

I looked at my lawyer for help; I could see her squirming. *What's the right thing to say?* I wondered. I didn't want to put a foot wrong that could jeopardise the case, so I wasn't thinking clearly. I didn't want to say the first thing that came into my head, which was: *I have a massive problem with that!* I wanted to scream it. The simple fact was, you *can't* do joint custody with a child who has autism. It went against everything I was trying to achieve – and everything I had just outlined. Sam needed predictability and security, not to be shuttling back and forth between his mum and dad every day of his life.

But the words had somehow got trapped in my throat as I dithered and stressed about how to express myself. And so, in the end, the very last thing I wanted to say came out.

'Ah, I guess not.'

'That will be all.' She smiled, smugly, as I felt my heart sink.

I couldn't bear to look at Jaime. I couldn't bear to think of Sam.

I'd blown it.

CHAPTER FIVE

Big Cats and Court Fax

I HAD MY HEAD IN MY HANDS AS JAIME TOOK TO THE STAND after me.

I was convinced that I had lost my chance to save Sam. The odds of winning had been against me in the first place, but now I'd driven the nail into the coffin by stupidly saying I'd be happy for us to share joint custody, when that couldn't have been further from the truth.

I watched as Jaime settled himself on the stand, as confident as ever. He had such presence, it was like the courtroom was the silver screen and he the charismatic matinée idol. I steeled myself to watch him give a stellar performance that would blow the judge away. Though I didn't know what Jaime was going to come out with, I thought he couldn't do much worse than the hole I'd dug for myself and would undoubtedly do better.

But, for whatever reason, though he put his case across well, it didn't seem to go his way on the day.

I felt bad for him, but I won't deny that I wasn't unhappy that it might have helped me claw back some ground. The rest of the hearing passed in a blur.

'Court adjourned.' The usher's voice sliced through the tension in the room.

It was over – for now, anyway.

I let out a huge sigh of relief; I hadn't realised how long I'd been holding my breath. I turned to Juana. 'Have we won?' I mouthed.

'You just won that all by yourself,' she whispered encouragingly, praising my efforts on the stand.

It was what I needed to hear after what I saw as my mistake regarding the joint custody question. I walked out of court feeling *slightly* more confident but only time would tell if she was right.

The boys continued to see Jaime every other weekend while we waited for the judgement to come in. I thought it would take hardly any time at all for the judge to reach a decision, but as the days and then the weeks passed, I started to feel increasingly nervous.

To make matters worse, Sam's wellbeing had gone rapidly downhill. The frequency of his meltdowns, in and out of school, had doubled. The poor thing was regularly soiling himself in class by now, his stress was so bad, which meant I was driving up and down the mountain to clean him up as the school policy was that the parents had to come and sort out their children if they had an accident.

On top of all this, I was nervous about Darren coming back. Before I knew it, October had arrived and with it the first weekend that Darren and I would be spending together after months of emailing. He'd be meeting the boys for the first time too. *What if the chemistry isn't there?* I worried. *What if the boys don't like him? What if it's the sort of relationship that works long distance but not in reality?*

But all my worries vanished as soon as Darren stepped off the plane in Málaga; I had gone to meet him alone. I'd forgotten how good-looking he was – but it was his personality that really shone. He grinned at me as he strolled through the arrivals lounge.

'Hiya.' He kissed me confidently. I had butterflies, but at the same time I was filled with this wonderful sense of things just being *right*.

That feeling set the tone for the rest of the weekend. I felt so comfortable around him, mostly because, thanks to our Messenger chats, we already knew everything there was to know about each other. We picked the boys up from my sister's on the way back from the airport and Darren was a natural with them from the moment we stepped through the door.

He unzipped his bag and pulled out two presents – one for Sam and one for Will.

'What do you say?' I prompted the boys.

'Thank youuuu,' Will screeched, shuffling to Darren's side. He was such an inquisitive child.

Sam was struggling to find the words.

'You,' he managed, repeating the last word he had heard, as he sometimes did. He was trying his best.

Darren sat on the floor with Will and encouraged Sam to come over.

'Hello, mate, come and have a look at this.' He held out the present.

Sam was like a snail cautiously coming out of his shell. He slowly lifted his gaze from the floor, curious to see what Darren was holding. He couldn't look Darren in the eye, but he wanted to get closer, that much was obvious. He gingerly made his way across the room and sat cross-legged next to his brother.

Will was having a whale of a time tearing at the wrapping paper and throwing it over his shoulder. Sam carefully dismantled his surprise, peeling each strip of Sellotape off with microscopic precision, doing his best not to spoil the paper.

As soon as Sam saw what it was, he started flapping his arms like a bird – which I now knew meant he was very excited. The gift was a model aeroplane. *How thoughtful.* I'd told Darren that Sam liked planes so it was really sweet of him to buy him one. Sam lined up the wing of the plane with his eye and made a whooshing noise as he flew it backwards and forwards.

Darren didn't even blink at Sam's unusual behaviour. Of course, he knew what to expect because I'd spent endless phone calls describing Sam, but it was more than that – he was clearly just a really kind man who was great with children.

He was keen to do something fun with the boys that weekend so I suggested the zoo in Fuengirola. The children and I hadn't done anything like that in a very long time because of the court case and because of everything that had happened. It would be a break for me just as much as it would be a fun day out for Sam and Will.

Fuengirola is the next biggest tourist destination along the Costa del Sol after Benalmádena Costa. Lots of high-rise buildings tower along the water's edge, while hundreds of holiday-makers turn lobster pink on sunloungers or shelter under thatched umbrellas. The long concrete promenade is always lined with palm trees and bars and ice-cream sellers.

It was unusually hot for October. We wound down the windows and sang nursery rhymes the whole way to the zoo; Sam didn't join in but he seemed happy enough. When we arrived, Darren was concerned the boys might get burnt in the blazing sunshine and thoughtfully smeared sun cream across their little noses.

The zoo was a ten-minute walk from the beach, right in the heart of Fuengirola. It housed over a hundred species of animal, which were all kept in enclosures where you could look at them through glass or peer at them over the walls or from viewing points. There were monkeys, tapirs, lemurs, gibbons, pygmy hippos and even Komodo dragons.

But only one animal caught Sam's attention: the Sumatran tiger.

The tiger was roaming around his lush green enclosure as we approached. I couldn't remember ever seeing Sam so alert. He was watching the tiger intently as it paced back and forth through the long grass, every now and then disappearing from view as the grass closed over his feline shape. I glanced at Darren, who had also noticed my son's fascination.

Suddenly, the grass parted and the tiger emerged only a foot from where we were standing. Just a piece of glass separated us from the ferocious carnivore.

Will hid behind my leg, but Sam was mesmerised.

The tiger slowly approached the glass and pressed his nose up against it. Sam gently placed his little hand on the glass, as if to place it on the tiger's huge nose.

My heart was in my mouth. I could have sworn there was a crack in the glass, but maybe I imagined it. In my head, I saw the glass giving way and the tiger pouncing on my boy. Part of me wanted to snatch him away to safety, but it was such a touching, tranquil moment that I forced myself to let go and savour what was unfolding in front of me: Sam had come alive.

'Darren, look,' I whispered, trying not to scare the tiger away.

'I know,' he mouthed.

And then, as quickly as the moment arrived, it disappeared, like a butterfly into the breeze.

When Sam eventually turned away from the tiger, he was smiling. This was incredibly rare: Sam did not smile very often at all. As we carried on to the next enclosure I couldn't help but think that there was something more to the encounter I'd just witnessed. Had that majestic animal unlocked something in Sam?

My thoughts were broken by Darren making hilarious chimpanzee noises as he entertained the children. I wasn't sure if I was with two kids or three! The boys loved his impressions; Will was in fits of giggles. Darren was wonderful with both the boys. He lifted them on to his shoulders in turn and ran between the enclosures, pointing out interesting things about each animal.

We had hot dogs, burgers and juice in the zoo restaurant before continuing to look at the animals, until the boys were so tired that we decided to head home to relax by the pool.

I left Darren in the shade on the veranda while I nipped into the kitchen to prepare some snacks. When I returned, Darren had Sam on one knee and Will on the other, as he read them stories. The tone of his voice was so mellow that Will was minutes away from being lulled to sleep.

I stood there, quietly observing them, soaking up the magical moment. It sounds cheesy, but the sight of Darren acting like a dad to my boys made my heart melt.

That evening, after the children had gone to bed, Darren and I sat in the wicker chairs on the veranda, our toes touching as we rested our tired feet on the coffee table. I twisted the stem of my glass between my fingers, contemplating whether to say something or just enjoy the comfortable silence. We'd said so much to each other over the past few weeks and months that I felt I'd run out of words. And, in the end, we didn't need to say anything. From then on, I was Darren's and Darren was mine. It was just the way it was.

Our wonderful weekend together came and went too quickly and, still, yet more weeks passed without a judgement. I was on tenterhooks, jumping every time the phone rang.

I started to envisage what it was going to be like if I couldn't go home to England. How on earth could I help Sam, then?

It was 7 December 2007, almost three months after we had been to court, when my lawyer Juana finally had some news for me. I was at work that day, getting ready to take a wealthy businessman out on a site visit, when the receptionist called out to me.

'Jo, phone for you!' She tapped in my extension number and transferred the call.

'Hello?' I said, my heart pounding as it did every time I received a call these days.

And, this time, it *was* Juana. I braced myself for the worst.

'Jo, I've got some good news!' she announced cheerily.

A smile spread across my face.

'You can go home!' she squealed.

Oh my God!

'I can't believe it!' I shouted in joy. I was jumping up and down and screaming in the middle of the office.

Juana told me to wait by the fax machine and, slowly, the paper stating the terms of my divorce rolled out, revealing each line of the judgement in turn. I was granted full custody of the boys. Jaime could visit the children in England for one week each month and spend half the Christmas, Easter and summer holidays with them in Spain. The rest of it – maintenance payments and so on – were just details. I didn't care about any of that. I cared about only one thing.

We were going home.

CHAPTER SIX

New Beginnings

I'D FORGOTTEN HOW BEAUTIFUL ENGLAND COULD BE IN THE spring. It had been thirteen years since I'd seen the lush green fields, the hedgerows, the daffodils and crocuses, and the blossom on the trees. Even walking through the airport had a completely different feel to it than doing the same in Spain. The arrivals lounge was covered with carpet rather than cold marble; the smells were different: the coffee, the reheated sausage rolls and pasties and the waft of newsprint as you passed WH Smith. There was a cosiness about England that Spain didn't have. There was something so inviting about coming home and being back on British soil.

As I stepped through the sliding doors of Bristol airport in April 2008 and inhaled the fresh air outside, the Spanish scents of bougainvillea vines and citrus fruits had been replaced by dewy grass and green trees. I sucked that air deep into my lungs and then released it slowly, savouring every breath.

I turned to Darren, grinning from ear to ear: 'We're home.'

As soon as the judgement had come through, I'd put my Spanish house on the market and started looking for schools in the UK – and this visit home, an adults-only affair while Jaime looked after the boys for the weekend, was to select the school that would best suit Sam. I'd decided on Devon as the location for our new home because it was a part of the country that offered great facilities for children with autism. It was also where I'd spent many a happy holiday as a child and I could just see us living contentedly amid the rolling hills.

In advance, I'd cherry-picked the schools in the area that had a specialist teaching unit for children with Asperger's and autism – what is known as a CAIRB (Communication and Interaction Resource Base). There were four such schools in the vicinity. Darren had offered to come with me while I visited each of them in turn and I was grateful to have him by my side as we picked up the hire car and started the drive to Devon.

I was determined to make the best possible choice for my son. As far as I was concerned, sending Sam to a school solely for children with special needs was never an option. The wonderful thing about CAIRBs is that, over time, the teachers introduce the autistic children into mainstream classes. I strongly believed that Sam stood a better chance of successfully integrating into society if he grew up around neurotypical children. That way, he wouldn't get a rude shock if someone was mean to him, bullied him or looked at him strangely once he was an adult, because he would have already learnt the skills to cope with it. Though I was already worrying about whether he would be bullied – what mum wouldn't? – I wouldn't always be there to protect him, so I knew I needed Sam to learn how to become resilient. Life in a special-needs school would be much more sheltered, and I was concerned that Sam wouldn't cope well when he left that secure environment.

Darren and I had a lot to get done. Timings had worked out in such a way that we had to visit all four schools in a single day – and, of course, the schools were scattered all over the county. Our schedule looked like this: Barnstaple at 9 a.m., Tiverton at 12 p.m., Ivybridge at 3 p.m. and Tavistock at 5.30 p.m. Time would be tight.

Yet despite the pressing schedule, I couldn't help but feel like a child on holiday as we swooped along the country lanes that carved through the Devonshire hillside. I stared eagerly out of the window, pointing out every landmark to Darren and recalling my beach holidays in Woolacombe, where I'd learned how to surf. It all served to cement my certainty that Devon was the place for us.

The first school was in a village on the outskirts of Barnstaple, a farming town. The school was fabulous – I was blown away by the look and feel of the modern design and architecture. It was not your typical primary: it was futuristic-looking, kind of like a spaceship with lots of 'pods' where the children sat around in circles having stories read to them.

'I want Sam to come here,' I mouthed to Darren as the headmaster led us to the CAIRB, where we watched the children painting and doodling. My heart lifted as I imagined Sam joining in with all these students, making friends – finally being looked after.

But the headmaster explained that, as much as he would like to have Sam and understood my desperate situation, we had a wait on our hands. There were only seven CAIRB places available in the entire school – and they were all taken. Even if a space was to become available, there were more than a dozen children with autism on the waiting list before Sam. I felt so deflated.

The headmaster went on to explain some of the statistics behind such a long waiting list: one in every one hundred children was being diagnosed with autism each year and boys were five times more likely to have it than girls. Worryingly for me, he added that all schools with CAIRBs faced the same challenge – they only had the funds to offer help to seven children.

'Sadly there is no fast-track system, you will be at the end of the waiting list,' he said, frowning.

And I frowned too, feeling slightly sick. I knew early intervention was the key to my son leading a normal life so I couldn't waste another second, nor hang about waiting for our names to reach the top of that very long list. I was so disappointed that this amazing school seemed out of our reach and could only hope that the other schools on our list would be able to help us. We thanked the head for his time and then it was back in the car and on to the next school.

On the way, Darren and I had an intense conversation. I'd already come so far on my quest to save Sam, but everything felt like a battle and it was hard to stay positive. What were we going to do if we couldn't find a school place for Sam?

As usual, Darren helped me see things rationally.

'It's like going to view a house that you fall in love with but finding out someone else has already put an offer in,' he reasoned. 'You have to be clinical, not emotional about these things – accept it's gone and move on to the next one.'

I was glad Darren had come along; I would have struggled alone. By now, he was very much my partner and whatever new life I was going to make for my family, he would be part of it.

We snaked our way through more country lanes, over cattle grids and through picturesque villages with medieval churches. As the countryside flew by, I regained my positive outlook and rejoiced once more in visiting this little corner of England that I would soon call home.

'Look, there's a little cafe selling cream teas!' I exclaimed as we whizzed by it.

Oh my, I thought, *it's been an eternity since I've tasted clotted cream and jam on scones.* My mouth almost watered. I couldn't wait to introduce my boys to all the treats I'd grown up on – British institutions like fish and chips and pasties. The more I saw of Devon, the more I wanted it for our new life.

Tiverton was the next location on our list. The school was also fantastic but couldn't have been more different from the one we'd just seen: it was an old Victorian building in the centre of town with a high ceiling and a grand sweeping staircase.

The experience couldn't have been further from what we'd just had either. We were shown into a reception area and asked to take a seat on miniature plastic stools that looked like they were meant for the children's classroom. How could I keep a straight face watching Darren contort his legs like a pretzel? I burst out laughing.

Suddenly, the door flew open and a man wearing a snorkel, flippers and a wetsuit charged in.

'Hello!' he announced. It was the headmaster.

He proceeded to join us on one of the tiny chairs and chatted away merrily. Darren and I glanced at each other sideways, thinking, *What the hell?*

It transpired that the school was having a charity day and the head had to wear the baking-hot wetsuit all day long. *What a great school, this is so much fun*, I thought.

He led us in his flippers to the CAIRB and, again, it was completely different to the one we had just seen. This one was quiet and quite stark. Luckily – amazingly – there was no waiting list. I'd pretty much decided that this was the school we'd go for, even as we raced across Devon to Ivybridge to make it to our next appointment on time.

Manor Primary was located in a street that had sentimental significance for me – my grandmother, who shared the same birthday as Sam, had lived on a street called Manor Way – so even though I thought Tiverton was the one, I had a warm feeling as Darren and I walked up to the school and entered it. The head of the CAIRB, Lynda Russell, met us this time. She looked exactly like her picture on the school website – in her fifties with blonde, shoulder-length hair.

Suddenly, I had a flashback to me sitting in my office in Spain, feeling desperate and at my wits' end as I tentatively investigated UK schools while I waited for my divorce judgement to come through. There was one particular email correspondence I'd had with Lynda that now came to mind. I'd opened my heart up about how much I needed to help Sam and wanted to visit her school. Her reply had conjured up a heavenly image: 'Spring is such a lovely time to come to Devon, the hedgerows are full of primroses.'

This woman, who had shown me a beacon of hope at a very dark moment in my life, was now holding out her hand for me to shake and I unexpectedly felt almost overwhelmed with gratitude.

Lynda took us down to the CAIRB. The room was bursting with colour. It was really busy, with stuff everywhere – paint pots, crayons, building blocks, even a sandpit. It was chaotic but had a joyful, happy feel to it that almost bounced off the walls. There were no children around because we'd arrived just after school had finished for the day, but I could just imagine how much they must love it.

Lynda told me that they had space for Sam at Manor Primary, but that it would be the decision of the County Council as to whether he would get a place at the CAIRB. Manor Primary also had a preschool next door, so Will, who had just turned four, would be able to start there. It seemed almost too good to be true.

There was a pub in the village, called The Old Smithy, which Darren and I decided to pop into for some much-needed food before we headed to our final appointment in Tavistock. The bittersweet smell of ale and cider, engrained in the wooden floors and on the tables from a hundred spill-ages, hit my nostrils as soon as we went inside. It was that wonderful, cosy smell that only country pubs have. A Golden Labrador, just like the one a great-aunt of mine had owned, came over and sat next to us. He rested his big soppy head on Darren's knee.

I nipped to the loo while we waited for our food to arrive and there, covering the walls, was the exact same blue-and-white flowery wallpaper that my sister had had in her bedroom in our childhood home in Essex.

I'm not the least bit superstitious but it seemed to me to be a sign – and one of many pointing to Ivybridge. The name of the street, the Labrador, the wallpaper, Lynda Russell's kind email . . .

I decided to follow my heart.

Darren looked at me strangely as I emerged from the loo. I'm not sure what expression was on my face, but I smiled at him shyly as I said, 'Don't you think we should absolutely go with Manor Primary . . . ?'

'We've still got Tavistock to go yet,' he reminded me, glancing at his watch.

But I knew I didn't need to see any more schools: something was telling me *this* was the one. As Darren and I talked it over, I found he completely agreed.

And so I held up my glass and toasted Darren. Finally, we were on the way to getting Sam the help he needed. It felt like a weight had been lifted off my shoulders. Now, our future could begin.

CHAPTER SEVEN

Slice of Heaven

THERE WERE BOXES EVERYWHERE — BUT NOT ENOUGH TIME TO fill them.

Darren worked overtime packing everything up, ready to be shipped home to England. He had two days left before he had to be back in South Korea and he didn't stop packing for twenty-four hours straight – whereas there came a point when I physically couldn't lift another thing and dropped, exhausted, into the wicker chair on the veranda. Darren, in contrast, seemed indefatigable – and still managed to find time to have fun with the boys as he worked, throwing shredded newspaper over them, much to Will's delight.

Hard as the packing was, an even greater challenge was preparing Sam for the move. Lynda Russell had been incredible – she had sent me a box full of visual aids, plus photos of the school and of all the teachers so I could piece together a story for Sam. Just as Mariángeles had taught me, I knew that if I could show Sam what was around the corner, I might hopefully reduce his anxiety about the new routine to come. It wasn't enough to show him once, but every day, throughout the day, I had to show him the cards and photos.

I would pull out the pictures as I cuddled him on the sofa. I held Sam close, not just because I loved having him near to me, but because the physical contact helped to keep him focused.

'This is your new school. This is Mr Hemelik, your new headmaster,' I said cheerfully.

No response.

'This is Mrs Sharp, she will be helping you in class.'

No response.

'Look at all our toys! We have toys outside too,' I read from the school's card, pointing to the sandpit and the climbing frames.

Finally, Sam cracked a hint of a smile.

Sam could say a few words, but not in succession. He was five years old, but his speech was equivalent to that of a two-year-old. At this point, I wasn't sure if he'd forgotten how to speak. Anything visual I could show him about our move I pulled out – such as pictures of the barn conversion we were going to rent and even pictures of the aeroplane we were going to travel on.

I prayed to God that his transition wouldn't be as bumpy as our attempts to sell the house. The sale of our Spanish home had fallen through at the eleventh hour, which meant I couldn't buy the house I'd set my heart on in Devon, and also explained why we were renting (the last thing I wanted to do for Sam, as it would eventually necessitate another move for him once we were in a position to buy). But we had no choice but to abandon the house in Spain now (I would keep trying to sell it from the UK) and depart for Devon, for Sam was due to start school the following week, in September 2008.

For our new, rented home, Darren and I had settled on a converted barn in a village called Diptford, which was half an hour away from Manor Primary by car. To my delight, when Darren came home from the oil rigs, 'home' for him would now be with us.

I kissed and hugged my partner goodbye when moving day finally arrived and told him I couldn't wait to see him in a month's time when he came back from the rig. I then stuck the 'For Sale' sign back up, closed the door, and that was it. I put Spain behind us and looked to the future.

Today was the first day of the rest of our lives.

Amazingly, the journey went fairly smoothly. Sam was calm on the plane and I managed to find the house without getting us too lost. I was lucky enough to have a crack team of relatives helping us out: my mum came over to assist, and Darren's parents and sister also kindly mucked in. We all met at the airport and drove in convoy to the barn. The boxes had arrived a day earlier, and thanks to Darren's marker-pen scribbles I could work out which ones housed the essentials. Working together, we got the beds set up and the pots and pans unpacked in time for the boys to start school the following week.

We even managed to fit in some sightseeing on the final few days before the new term began. The boys and I visited the steam railway, the otter farm and the butterfly farm. I wanted to show Sam and Will how wonderful England was and how happy we were going to be there.

I was delighted to see that Sam was responding well to his new environment. He loved the steam trains – as soon as he got home, he pulled out a drawing pad and sketched the scene from memory. His drawing had come on leaps and bounds in the past year or so, since he had first drawn that super smiley sunny face in the blue felt-tip pen. His art seemed to be some kind of outlet for him: a way to express himself, given language eluded him. Now, as I watched, Sam drew the railway signals and the diverging tracks – details other children might not have included. It was breathtakingly good; much better than most adults could have managed.

Things seemed to be getting better and better. By this time my mother had returned to Spain. I almost cried with happiness as I chatted on the phone to my mum that night, telling her how all the hard work had been worth it. She would be able to see that for herself when she moved over to the UK, though she didn't yet have a date for that. And I knew the icing on the cake would be Manor Primary; I couldn't wait to drop Sam off there the next day.

Lynda Russell had sent me a breakdown of all the different ways she would be working with Sam, and it was a far cry from anything he'd experienced so far. The CAIRB worked on the areas that children with autism struggle with, such as social interaction, attention and engagement. Lynda's teaching objectives were to develop social awareness; to develop behaviour management skills and promote behavioural improvement (such as helping Sam regulate his 'flapping'); to develop care taking (a lot of children with autism aren't aware of danger and can run into traffic blindly); to develop communication; and to develop gross and/or fine motor skills (Sam had very poor upper body strength and hand/eye coordination). Photos and video recordings were key to Lynda's teaching. For a child with autism, the use of a picture can be so much more illuminating than words.

At the start of the school day Sam would have a visual timetable so he knew what to expect. There would be symbols for everything – for books, toys, toilet, teacher, pen, sandpit, reward, reading, quiet time, car, home. Once the work or the action was completed, the symbol would be removed from the timetable: no longer something to worry about. Sam would have a work station (a type of desk that has an enclosed upper part, which makes the children feel safe and less easily distracted) so he could study on his own. The tasks the teachers set him would be repetitive and very predictable; things that Sam could do without help and not be alarmed by. He would have two baskets: he'd take the activities from the green basket and then put them in the red basket once he'd completed them. Everything was regimented and routine – just as Sam needed it to be.

Lack of empathy for others is a classic autistic trait and Sam really struggled to read other people's moods – he could never tell whether I was happy or sad. Lynda Russell wanted to tackle this head-on by teaching Sam how to read emotions and understand gestures and facial expressions. This would help him interact with others and, most importantly, make friends.

Visual aids would be used in each lesson to help pupils construct written sentences. For example, Lynda would use pictures of the nursery rhyme 'Humpty Dumpty' to help Sam expand it into a story; the aim being, as Sam progressed, that he would need fewer visual clues and just a few clearly written prompts.

Lynda also explained how those moments when I thought Sam looked 'away with the fairies' were important for his wellbeing. Children with autism need time to be alone and go into their own little world in order to reduce their anxiety levels and stop their brains becoming overloaded. As such, Sam would be given a card to use when he was in his mainstream classes. He would show it to his teaching assistant (TA) when he felt himself becoming overwhelmed and needed 'flapping' time, and he would then have permission to go back down to the CAIRB and into the quiet room to chill out. All this would teach Sam how to regulate his moods and hopefully prevent meltdowns – those moments when Sam's anxiety 'boiled over' and made him lash out, like he had done with the boy in the dining hall and with the supermarket staff when they'd tried to touch his head.

It was very much Lynda's belief that the children on the CAIRB should interact with nature to help their sensory issues. Many people on the autistic spectrum have sensory issues, which means they can be hyper- or hyposensitive to one, all or some of their senses. For that reason, there was a special garden at Manor Primary kitted out for the children with a waterfall and plants that they could touch to stimulate their senses. The school also organised regular trips to animal farms such as the Donkey Sanctuary, which offered animal therapy to the children. Riding the donkeys also helped to build their core strength; something with which, again, many autistic people struggle. Lynda's approach was a truly holistic one, which I loved.

I think Will was just as excited to see Sam start Manor Primary as I was. He bounced around his brother as I tried to get Sam dressed in his school uniform, which consisted of a white polo shirt, a green sweatshirt with a yellow school logo, grey trousers, black shoes and a matching green rucksack. He looked adorable.

'I want one!' Will tugged at Sam's bag.

'When you are a bit older, you can have a uniform too,' I reassured him, ruffling Will's blond mop.

Sam couldn't dress himself due to his poor gross motor skills. The times I had let him try, he'd ended up looking like a miniature superhero, with his pants on over his trousers! His brain couldn't process what order things should go in.

I dropped Will off first at the preschool. I gave him a

massive hug and kiss and then he spun around and confidently toddled off to meet his new classmates. I knew Will would be fine; he was a feisty little rascal.

I felt a lot more nervous handing Sam over. My heart was in my mouth as I led him down the many steps that funnelled to the school gates. It was hard to block out the bad memories of his time at school in Spain. I wondered whether Sam would be OK, or whether I had made a mistake by putting him in a mainstream school, despite the amazing facilities of the CAIRB. What if he was bullied?

But as soon as I saw Lynda's smiling face as she patiently waited for Sam at the gate, my worries evaporated. She has an indescribable aura of serenity about her and speaks in a soft, gentle voice that is almost soporific. She took Sam's little hand in hers and led him off through the arched doorway. I had a tear in my eye as I watched Sam's rucksack bob up and down. I had thought this day – the day I'd be waving him off to a school that truly understood his needs – would never come.

I was glad to have the unpacking to do to take my mind off how the boys were coping with their first day. By the end of the afternoon I was hopping from one foot to the other, desperate to get back into the car and rush to the school gates to pick them up.

Will had had a brilliant first day. He came out beaming, clutching an A4 piece of paper covered in blue and green squiggles.

'Thank you, Will, that's beautiful,' I said as he presented it to me proudly. I crouched beside him, planting a big kiss on his rosy cheek, then lifted him into my arms. We descended the steps together to meet Sam at the internal school gates.

My eyes were darting back and forth, scanning every child

who burst through the door for Sam. But, in the end, it was Will who spotted him first.

'Sam!' he screeched, wriggling in my arms.

Sam had emerged holding Lynda Russell's hand. It was such a small gesture from her, but it meant the world to me to know he was in such safe hands. As time went on, I learned that this was something the school did for the first year or so: the TAs waited for the children at the school gates in the morning and always brought them out again at the end of the school day too. The point of this was to give Sam continuity and keep his anxiety levels down, and it was clear from the off that it was working.

'Sam, have you had a good day?' I asked enthusiastically. From my research into autism, I knew to reinforce Sam's name, so that he knew he was being spoken to.

'Yes.' He nodded. *He communicated.*

My heart leapt – Sam had barely said a word to me all the times I'd picked him up from school in Spain.

Lynda gave me a quick debrief. She explained how Sam had started the morning in a mainstream class. She'd stood at the back, observing his behaviour. Within half an hour she had gauged it was too much for Sam, and had whisked him off to the CAIRB.

Lynda's aim was to integrate Sam fully into all mainstream classes eventually, but she couldn't tell me how long that would take, or if it would ever be possible.

What she did notice, though, was how much he enjoyed the CAIRB's sensory room, which had lights on the walls and the floor, and plastic towers with water bubbles. Its purpose was to stimulate the senses but in a gentle way, so the children didn't feel overloaded. Sam had loved the spaghetti lights –

LED lights set in long, 3m strips of plastic tubing; they glow and turn different colours with a dimming effect – because they were in straight lines. Lynda said he'd spent a while lying with them and clearly found them very calming.

As I gathered my sons and we headed back to our new home, I felt like everything was falling into place. Sam was sorted, Will was sorted and, just a few days later, Lynda Russell even thought of a way to integrate *me* into Devon life.

'Do you have any friends here?' she asked me one morning as I dropped Sam off.

'I don't really know anyone,' I admitted shyly.

'Right then!' she declared.

It was now my turn to be led away by Lynda Russell. She guided both Sam and me through a rabbit warren of corridors into a classroom. It was where Sam registered every morning before he was taken down to the CAIRB, but I had no idea what Lynda was planning.

'This is Sam's mum, Jo,' Lynda announced, introducing me to the teacher, Mrs Langdon.

Then she threw me in at the deep end. 'Can Jo help you out?' she asked Mrs Langdon.

'Huh?' I spluttered. I was so taken aback. 'Me? Help out here?' I looked around me at the sunny classroom.

Lynda then told me that she thought I'd be perfect for a new teaching assistant opportunity that had just come up. The school was looking for a mum to help out in the classroom, and given my language skills she also suggested that I might be able to teach the children in the mainstream school some Spanish. Lynda thought the informal role would help me to make friends and, of course, I would also be able to see Sam and check he was settling in OK.

Though I was keen, I was also concerned that my presence in Sam's classroom might affect his progress, but Lynda reassured me it would actually help to put Sam at ease, plus I'd only see him first thing, at registration. Sam would then go off to the CAIRB while I remained helping out in the mainstream class.

I mulled it over. *How can I turn down the chance to keep a closer eye on Sam after all those months of being kept in the dark in Spain?*

'When do I start?' I said, beaming at her. All the paperwork went through quickly and before long Sam and I had a new routine of our own as we both spent our days at the school.

Watching Sam in class every morning not only put him at ease, but also assuaged some of my long-held worries about his future. One of my greatest concerns had always been whether Sam would be able to live a normal life. Would he have friends? Would he be able to take care of himself if, God forbid, anything happened to me?

Seeing Sam happy in a classroom full of neurotypical children told me that he could. He didn't necessarily interact with them, but he wasn't anxious and he wasn't lashing out. It was such a relief. It gave me hope that he could one day live a full, happy life alongside others.

I always stood at the back while Mrs Langdon went through the register. With the surname Bailey, Sam was always second to have his name called.

He sat cross-legged on the floor, his arms neatly folded in his lap.

'Yes,' he responded confidently to the teacher, every morning.

And every morning, I felt a flutter of pride.

That's my boy.

My new job in the school was a mixed blessing, though, for the fact that I could keep a close eye on Sam also had its drawbacks – namely when it came to breaktime. My classroom was on the ground floor and it gave me a great view of all the goings-on in the playground. One morning, I was tidying away the toys in time for the next lesson when, out of the corner of my eye, I saw Sam standing by the fallen oak tree that dominated the far end of the playground. The children often used it as a climbing frame, but on this day my son was the only one there.

Although no longer in practice, at that time the teachers dressed the children with autism in luminous vests at breaktime. A couple of them were 'runners' – an unofficial term used to describe those children who had a tendency suddenly to take to their heels, which could be dangerous as a lot of people with the condition don't have any awareness of danger. The brightly coloured vest meant I could spot Sam a mile off, but in truth I didn't need it. He stood out a mile on his own. He was running up and down the tree, flapping his arms. Every now and then he'd stop and hold his hands in front of his face while he studied his fingers, and then he was off again, lining up his eye with the straight contours of the tree. Not one other child held his interest. Not one other child wanted to play with him.

I can't put into words how upsetting it is to look out of a window and see a playground full of other children having fun, kicking a football around and chasing after one another, and then there is one little boy, *your* boy, who is all alone, running up and down and flapping.

I felt a lump form in the back of my throat.

My only consolation was knowing that Sam wouldn't have been upset to be alone. Children with classic autism tend to seek isolation and exclusion, whereas children with Asperger's don't – many really want to make friends but don't know how to. But Sam wasn't like that.

It still broke my heart, though. So much so, I eventually thought about giving up the job. I found it too hard to watch, and not intervene – not to go and be his friend, or encourage him to join others when, really, he was happy on his own.

At this time Darren had moved to a rig just off the Egyptian coast but, of course, he was still only a phone call away, wherever he was working. He was employed by a company based in Scotland, so all I needed to do was ring Aberdeen and I'd be rerouted directly to his office. I felt so emotional whenever I told him the stories of seeing Sam alone in the playground. Darren could always hear in my voice how difficult I found it.

'Why don't you give up the job?' he said matter-of-factly one day. We agreed that it was probably best for me to give up my voluntary position at Sam's school. Darren knew that I wanted to find paid work, but as we talked he could sense my concerns about not being able to be there for Sam if I was in a full-time job. He put forward the idea of me not going to work at all.

'Well, how will I pay the bills?' I reasoned.

'I'll pay them!'

I was stunned into silence. It was the most generous thing a man had ever done for me. I was used to supporting everyone else, not the other way around. Apart from when I was on maternity leave, I'd never been without a job and I'd always paid my way. The idea of Darren supporting me went against everything I believed in: that women should be strong and independent. His generosity left me speechless.

'I don't know what to say,' I stuttered eventually.

'Say yes!' he urged.

'I don't know . . .' I started.

'You could put all your energy into helping Sam instead,' he said persuasively.

I paused to think. He had a point. Though Sam was much more settled now that he was in a school that knew how to deal with his needs, he was still struggling with the most basic life skills. Devoting my time to helping him now, while he was still young, was the best way to give him the best possible chance of living a life where he could be part of society, and not just sitting on the sidelines. That was what I wanted for him, more than anything.

I could hear Darren breathing on the line, patiently waiting for my reply.

'Thank you,' I said simply, as I accepted his incredibly generous gift.

Little did I know it, but Darren and I had just made a crucial decision. For Sam was about to need me more than he ever had before.

CHAPTER EIGHT

No Way Out

I'M NOT SURE IF IT WAS A DELAYED REACTION TO THE MOVE TO England, or the fact Sam was going to and from Spain intermittently to see his father and was disturbed by the break in his regular routine, but we hadn't been in the UK all that long before something destabilised my son – and dramatically so.

Firstly, Sam started to develop certain obsessive behaviours: actions I hadn't seen him do before, but which were all too familiar to me from my hours of reading on the internet.

He became very fussy with his food. Sam refused to eat anything that was white or even had a hint of white in it. Fish fingers and beans had previously been one of his favourite meals, but now he sat at the table staring intently at the breadcrumbed finger like it was going to leap off the plate and attack him.

'Come on, Sam, eat your dinner,' I encouraged. Sam looked in my direction, glared at the fish finger and then proceeded to surgically remove all the breadcrumbs with intense concentration. He cast aside the stripped bit of fish and munched away at the crumbs.

Just as I was working around the white phobia, Sam developed a new set of eating rituals. If certain colours touched on the plate, he refused to eat any of his dinner. He liked his food to be separated neatly, so that he could eat the items separately and identify their tastes. That way, eating his dinner was safe and predictable. But if the food was mixed up, it became something different – something disordered – and it was a change he was unable to cope with.

Knowing the reasons for his behaviour didn't help me to solve the problem, however. I had to learn which colours to put on the plate, and which to avoid. I was constantly having to think on my feet to come up with ways to get around these new problems.

The next hurdle came when Sam couldn't bear for anyone to cut his hair or toenails.

'Hurts!' He would scream and thrash his arms around, pushing me off when I tried to trim his nails. I would calm him, get into a good position and try to bring the nail scissors closed *gently*, but he'd kick off again, having an outburst of mammoth proportions. He would scream, punch, kick my shins . . . essentially, lash out in any way he could to show me the full force of his rage.

Another difficulty I faced was in not knowing what was autistic behaviour and what was 'neurotypical' – was Sam behaving the way he was because of his autism or because he was just being a typical child wanting to push the boundaries?

He had glowing reports from school; it was when he got home that was the problem. Sam was storing up his frustrations and anxiety – caused by his day not going as well as he liked; maybe it was too noisy or there'd been an unexpected change in his routine – and unleashing them all as soon as he set foot through the door.

It would have made for an easier life if I gave in to the autism, but I knew I had to be strong, to keep pushing Sam on the things he needed to do, about which there was no choice, or his behaviour would control our lives.

'If only we could build a sensory room in the house,' I said to Darren after another long and exhausting evening trying to coax Sam to eat and go to bed. Living in a rented property, though, that was out of the question. Darren came up with a bright idea, however. He suggested I buy Sam a massive beanbag that could be a 'chill cushion'. It would be a substitute sensory room – a squidgy, soft place where Sam could go to vent his frustrations.

Lynda Russell loved the idea and immediately rustled up a storybook for Sam to explain what the cushion was and when he should use it: 'This is my chill cushion. I sit on my chill cushion when I'm angry.'

It worked a treat. Because Lynda had been teaching Sam to self-regulate – for example, by showing a card to his TA in class when he needed a 'flap' – Sam could apply the same principles at home. He soon got the hang of knowing when he should take himself off to the chill cushion.

But, just as I was catching my breath, another problem presented itself.

Sam's love of aeroplanes had by now morphed into an obsession. He would spend hour upon hour drawing every model under the sun. At first we were knocked out by how brilliant they were. He was only five but he could draw in 3D – his aeroplanes looked as if they were flying off the page; it was incredible. But pretty soon the planes were all he cared about. The few words he had been speaking dried up entirely as he ceased all communication. He did this not because he had lost the little language he had, but because he was so immersed in drawing planes he chose not to speak.

Sam would sit at the table or lie on his belly on the carpet for hours, transfixed by his creations. When he wasn't drawing, Sam was in the garden gazing up at the sky for flight paths. His acute vision meant he could pick out planes that I couldn't even see.

I was on the phone to Darren one day when I heard Sam let out a roar of anger. Then came a thumping noise.

'I'm going to have to call you back,' I said hurriedly and hung up.

I rushed through to the kitchen to find Sam stabbing his drawing with his pencil.

'Sam, stop,' I pleaded.

He wouldn't listen. He thrashed at his artwork, carving it up into dozens of tiny pieces. I tried to pin his hands down but he pulled free. Sam was hellbent on obliterating every last scribble. I knew what was wrong: he had made a mistake as he was sketching. And mistakes, however minor, in Sam's mind were errors of an astronomical scale that knocked the world off its axis. Any mistake he made would cause him to become so angry and frustrated that he would have a full-scale meltdown.

I felt helpless watching him rage and destroy his work. It was one thing catching a meltdown before it started, but quite another trying to stop it in mid flow. I had no clue what to do other than ride out the storm.

It took over an hour before Sam finally calmed down. I sat at the table stroking his hair. Sam's beautiful face looked angelic and peaceful, as if nothing had happened, whereas I was left shaken and exhausted.

Sam's meltdowns continued. It got to a point where every time he made a mistake he lashed out. He spent hours drawing his planes, so by the end of the day he was sitting in a sea of shredded paper.

I should have anticipated what was coming.

Sam's anger was reaching fever pitch. And, one day, he channelled it from his pictures on to his brother.

I was making supper. Will was sitting next to Sam at the kitchen table, watching Sam draw. The boys had stopped playing together like brothers several years before, but as Will had grown up it hadn't stopped him trying. He was always ready for a game, looking to reconnect with Sam, but Sam's autism meant he preferred to do things alone. Will picked up a crayon, smiling, looking for Sam to join in. I turned my back for a moment to take the pots off the hob.

'Muuuuuuummmmmy!' Will screamed for help.

I turned around to see Sam tearing at Will's face with his hands, like it was one of his pictures.

'Sam, stop!' I restrained him, locking my arms across his body.

Will was wailing in pain. Blood was trickling down his cheek from where Sam had scraped his fingernails along his brother's soft skin. I needed to help Will, but I had to calm Sam first or he might attack him again. Sam was struggling like a fish caught in a net. I squeezed my arms harder, locking him down. Meanwhile Will was crying with pain and from the fright of having his brother lash out.

'Mummy's here.' Knowing Sam had calmed down, I rushed over to Will's side.

He was sobbing. Poor Will didn't understand – he was only four.

As I cleaned Will's cuts, Sam returned placidly to his drawing. You can imagine how difficult it was to tell him off because, just like Will, he didn't understand what he'd done. Sam obviously *needed* to draw – it was an outlet for him – and as Will had tried to distract him from that he'd lashed out at him in frustration. Nonetheless, I tried very hard to teach Sam right from wrong and to discipline him. I got out his chill-cushion storybook and reminded him again that this was where he had to go if he felt angry.

Despite my efforts, it was evident things were getting out of control. The perfect new life I'd planned for us in Devon seemed to be unravelling.

I was exhausted. Luckily, my sister and mum were due to visit that weekend. I couldn't wait for them to arrive. Sarah was bringing Tom and Dan, and I prayed that having them there would help with whatever was going on with Sam. I was pinning my hopes on us all being together as one big happy family. Darren was still stuck on the rigs, but he'd be flying over not long after.

It had been three months since I'd seen my family. The time finally came to go and collect them from the airport. Sarah abandoned the luggage trolley as soon as she saw me and came running over, her arms outstretched like wings. Any bad feeling about me leaving Spain had vanished. In fact, she had great news: she was thinking about following in my footsteps by moving to England. She had just got together with a new man – my best friend from university days, Simon – and the pair had fallen madly in love and were now making plans for the future.

I hugged my sister and my mum in turn, finding their familiar warmth comforting. 'I've missed you,' I said, meaning every word. I could empathise with how Sam must feel when he came home from school, for seeing my family made me want to release all the sadness and anxiety I'd been storing up over the past few months. I bit my lip; the last thing I wanted to do was start the weekend off by being all emotional.

Tom and Dan were over the moon to be reunited with their cousins. They chased Will around the luggage trolley, bumping into our legs as they went. Sam was smiling too. Maybe all he needed was to be reunited with his family . . .

The journey from Exeter airport was filled with making plans. My mum and sister were knocking around ideas for fun family outings, the suggestions flying back and forth in quick succession. I threw in something I'd heard about from the mums at the school gates.

'Apparently there's a miniature pig farm just around the corner from where we live,' I said excitedly.

Everyone in Devon had heard of Pennywell Pig Farm, but its fame had clearly not crossed the Channel.

'Miniature pigs?' my sister exclaimed, as if I'd said a foreign word.

I explained how they were tiny pigs that had been bred as pets. They were also known as 'teacup pigs'.

'They're all the rage, don't you know! Jonathan Ross and Charlotte Church have both bought pigs from the farm,' I added with a chuckle.

But the happy mood of the car journey was short-lived.

Minutes after stepping through the door, perhaps disturbed by finding all these people crowded into his home, Sam started running up and down the length of the living room, smacking at his eyes with his fists. It wasn't just his brother he lashed out at now: it was himself.

'Where's my plane?' he cried. *Smack. Smack. Smack.*

The noise of each punch cut right through me. I lurched into his path, trying my best to obstruct him. Sam ploughed straight into my stomach at 100mph and I grabbed at his arms to stop him in his tracks.

My mum and my sister were stunned into silence. They had both lived through Sam's regression with me in Spain, but neither of them had ever seen anything like this.

I managed to calm Sam a little, enough for him to run off and get his model aeroplane and felt-tip pens. But as soon as Tom or Dan went anywhere near him, he would lash out again.

'Leave me alone!' he yelled at his cousins, his voice rasping with anger. His world had been turned upside-down – but I could see the cousins felt the same way. Those poor boys didn't know what had hit them.

'Why don't you three go and watch some videos?' I suggested to Tom, Dan and Will, trying to contain the situation.

By now, Sam was frantically drawing at the kitchen table, clutching his model plane in one hand, trying to sketch his way out of sadness. I quietly slipped on to the seat beside him, hoping my presence would calm him a little. But there was no hope of that as I watched his frenzied scribbling. It wasn't long before his pen skidded and Sam coloured outside of the lines. He'd made a mistake . . .

'Noooooo!' he screamed.

He hurled the plane and the pen to the floor and started flicking at his eyes with his fingers.

'Sam, *please*.' My voice trembled.

But he didn't calm down. Barely two minutes later, Sam was screaming and crying because he couldn't find a grey felt-tip pen.

'Don't worry, Sam, we'll find your grey pen,' I promised. I rifled through the drawers, desperately trying to find another pack of pens.

'Jo, are you OK?' Mum had crept up behind me.

'I can't talk, Mum, I have to get these back to Sam,' I said brusquely, rushing past her, no time to talk.

I handed Sam the grey pen and, for a moment, he was calm. He started copying a plane from a sticker transfer – until he noticed the transfer had a hole in it, which meant it wasn't perfect: always a trigger to set Sam off. He whacked himself around the head with his fists. Each successive thump grew in force and anger. I straitjacketed his arms down, trying to pin his arms to his body without hurting him; trying to stop him from hurting himself. I took hold of him by his wrists and was forced to pin him into the chair.

Mum was pacing around the barn, running her hands through her short hair. 'Oh my God, oh my God,' she muttered, aghast to see Sam so distressed.

My sister, meanwhile, was trying to keep the other three boys away from Sam's violent meltdown. I was just trying to hold it together.

I wondered if I could distract Sam with some food.

'Would you like some sausages and beans for tea?' I asked brightly.

Sam looked up from his picture. His eyes were wild, as if he was possessed.

'Leave me alone!' he screamed, his little body trembling. He clenched his fists, ready to go again.

Smack! He hit himself in the face.

'Sam, no,' I murmured. He was rocking as I tried to hold his hands down.

I tried to distract him with food again. I was trying anything I could think of to calm him.

'Sam, would you like a Frosties bar?'

This time he went for it.

'Yes.' He nodded.

Relief.

I rushed to the kitchen cupboards but discovered, to my horror, that we were out of Frosties bars. I could feel my heart racing and my head started to spin. The walls suddenly felt as if they were closing in. Desperately, I tried to control my looming panic attack, inhaling deeply and blowing the breath out slowly through my tightly pursed lips. This was no time to lose it. I knew I couldn't be long: Sam was waiting.

'Sam, would you like a Rice Krispies bar?' I held out the alternative snack, praying to God he would accept it, while still trying to regulate my breathing.

'No, *Frosties*,' Sam insisted, before he burst into tears.

Mum tried to step in.

'Come on, Sam, have a Krispies bar instead,' she soothed, trying to persuade him. She didn't understand that it was almost impossible to stop the meltdown once it had started.

Sam's tears turned into thick, heavy sobs.

I scooped him up into my arms and gently rocked him back and forth, singing a lullaby and stroking his head. It was over an hour later before Sam had worn himself out enough that I could get him into bed. I curled into a ball next to him, every ounce of me drained.

'Tomorrow, we are going to Pennywell Farm,' I whispered. I could barely speak, my tongue was so heavy with exhaustion. I lay there for a long time, even after Sam had drifted off to sleep.

Then I saw a beam of light against the wall, as my mum pushed the door ajar.

'Jo, are you OK?' she asked tentatively.

'Yes,' I lied.

I was far from OK, though. I didn't know what a breakdown felt like but I didn't feel far from one. All I wanted to do as a mum was keep my children safe, but Sam's behaviour was getting dangerous – for him, for Will and for me. I'd prepared Sam for this family visit with visual aids, but it hadn't been enough. Was anything *ever* going to be enough to prevent him melting down?

My mum hovered in the doorway. She knew me well enough to know when I wasn't telling the truth. She knew I wasn't OK.

My chest was so tight inside that it felt like someone was sitting on it, crushing me. I could barely breathe. I'm not sure I would have managed to pull myself up and out of my increasing panic if it hadn't been for my mum. But she was there for me, as she always had been.

Just as I'd put Sam to bed, my mum now guided me into mine. Then she lay on the bed next to me, trying to console me, to support me.

'What am I going to do?' I asked her.

I felt as if we were reliving that moment in Spain when I'd reached breaking point and crept down to the study to ring my mum for help. I felt as desperate and as helpless now as I had been then. It seemed it didn't matter how hard I tried, every road led to a dead end.

I'd crusaded to find out what was wrong with Sam. I'd fought to save my marriage and then battled in court to win the right to get the care my child so desperately needed. I'd championed to get Sam into one of the best schools for children with autism. I'd left everything I'd known for the past seventeen years behind in order to start a new life. But it had all been for nothing. Our 'fresh start' had just been another dashed hope.

And when you lose hope, what else is there?

CHAPTER NINE

Silver Lining

MY FAMILY TAUGHT ME THE ANSWER: LOVE. I WAS LUCKY I HAD my family and Darren to pull me out of my darkest moments.

Mum told me to hang in there and when she greeted me the following morning she was still on a mission to cheer me up.

'We are going to see the little pigs at Pennywell Farm today, maybe that will perk Sam up!' she said brightly, squeezing my hand encouragingly.

I'd heard some wonderful stories about the teacup pigs and their healing powers. Being a little bit of a sceptic, I doubted a micro pig could really make that much of a difference to someone's life, let alone 'heal' them, but there was one particular story I'd heard that was hard to forget.

A mum who I'd met while working at Manor Primary had told me about a disabled boy who'd visited Pennywell Farm just days after one of the sows had given birth to a litter of eight piglets. The teenager was apparently in a really bad way: his cerebral palsy was so severe he had to have his legs strapped into the wheelchair to stop him from falling out and he needed an oxygen mask to breathe.

The boy was looking so longingly at the two-day-old piglets as they suckled their mum that the farmer had asked if he would like to hold one. His parents had been worried that their son might not have the strength in his hands to take care of the piglet but the farmer had complete faith in the teenager, plus he'd said he would be standing by if anything were to happen.

It turned out the tiny piglet was in more than capable hands. As soon as he'd been handed into the teenager's lap, he'd burrowed into the crook of his arm. His teeny eyes had grown heavy and closed as the boy had gently stroked him to sleep. The farmer had eventually had to go about his errands but when he came back an hour later the boy was still stroking the piglet. The teenager's parents had said they'd never seen their son so happy or so calm.

The story had stayed with me because some part of me had wondered whether the pigs would have the same sort of calming effect on Sam.

I was so desperate for an intervention that the memory of that story started snowballing in my head that morning. By the time we were getting ready to leave, I was pinning all my hopes on the teacup pigs.

It sounds ridiculous, I know, but I needed some kind of hope.

My sister Sarah was getting the boys in the mood by making oinking noises and singing the nursery rhyme 'This little piggy . . .'

'This little piggy is going to help Sam . . .' I sang in my head.

I told my mum and Sarah that we should meet in the supermarket car park in Totnes, a town which is a fifteen-minute drive to Pennywell, because I needed to nip into the bank on the way to the farm.

I strapped my sons into my car and set off. Will was very excited about the prospect of seeing the pigs, clapping and wriggling around in his car seat. The boys had been to the zoo and the otter farm but they had never seen a pig before, let alone a micro one! I was very curious too; I imagined adorable little things, small enough to hold in the palm of my hand. As we meandered our way through the valley, Sam gazed out of the window, lost in his own world – but at least he was calm.

It was a crisp day towards the end of November in 2008. The last of the autumn leaves that lined the road had turned into brown sludge while the hedgerows were pocketed with holes from where they were losing their foliage. We drove past an orchard where only a few remaining apples clung valiantly to the bare branches.

I still couldn't get over how different the Devon countryside was to Spain. The approach to the coastal towns of the province of Málaga had been littered with neon flashing road signs, but as we neared the town of Totnes only a simple black-and-white board showing 'Town centre this way' and 'Morrisons supermarket, right' cluttered up the roadside.

I found a space close to the entrance of Morrisons, switched off the ignition and turned around to look at the boys. Instantly, I noticed that Sam had gone from calm to seriously agitated. He was flicking his hands in front of his face. Poor Will was looking worried; he'd been on the receiving end of Sam's outbursts too often lately. Will's eyes darted between Sam and me, as if he was silently pleading for things to stay calm. Dread rolled in the pit of my stomach as I tried to contain the situation.

'Sam, Mummy just needs to go to the bank and then we will see the pigs,' I explained.

Sam exploded.

'Sam is not going to Pennywell Farm!' he yelled.

Will clasped his hands over his ears in fright.

This can't be happening – Sam needs to see the pigs, I thought frantically, but I didn't let my panic show.

'I thought you wanted to see the pigs?' I simply said, lightly, trying to mask the anxiety in my voice.

'Sam is not going to Pennywell Farm!' he shouted again.

I was particularly concerned because this was the first time I'd heard him refer to himself in the third person. I told myself to keep calm. But Sam's shouting continued as the boys and I got out of the car and walked down the street towards the bank. He clung on to every lamppost we passed, repeating that he didn't want to go.

Passers-by were now staring and whispering. I'm sure they were all thinking what a spoilt brat Sam was and how he needed to be disciplined. I felt a horrible mixture of embarrassment and anger; I was furious at the strangers in the street for making me feel like I needed to explain what was wrong with my son.

'He's got autism,' I mouthed at a woman who was pulling her son away from mine. She looked at the ground, clearly afraid to make eye contact with me.

It reminded me of a time in Spain when I'd explained to two ladies why Sam was lining his eye up with the pavement curb.

'Oh, lovely, does he sing and dance too?' they had exclaimed, thinking that I had said '*artista*', which means 'performer' in Spanish, rather than '*autista*', meaning '*autistic*'. I didn't have time to dwell on my thoughts, though, because Sam was kicking off again.

'I'm fed up of you, Mummy,' he raged.

I'd learnt two things for when Sam was losing self-control – firstly I needed to keep him safe, and secondly I shouldn't show any emotion; as hard as comments like that were to ignore. 'Don't react to the meltdown, don't give him eye contact. Only when he's calmed down should you address the problem and see what triggered the behaviour,' Lynda had told me. My son's teacher had been incredibly supportive of late. Sam's worsening behaviour was no reflection of the brilliant work she was doing at Manor Primary, it was simply all part of his condition.

'I'm fed up with you, lady!' Sam now yelled again, rudely.

I ignored him, praying the meltdown would end so I could take Sam to see the pigs. *Then everything will get better*, I promised myself, clinging to my new hope.

And then I felt a little hand sneaking into mine. Will might only have been four but he was starting to show the emotional maturity of a child much older. He had picked up the slack for his brother's lack of, or rather inability to show empathy.

'I love you, Mummy,' he now said sweetly, tugging on my hand as if he sensed how close I was to crumbling.

Somehow, we managed to make it to the bank. But as soon as we walked inside, Sam hit the deck. He threw himself on to the grey carpet, thumping his fists against the floor.

'Sam, get up,' I hissed.

I felt hot – everyone in the bank was staring at us.

'Sam, get up now,' I pleaded.

Being in situations like this was extremely difficult. I felt that if I was constantly excusing Sam's behaviour by blaming it on his autism, he would start to see autism as something negative. Still just five years old, Sam was too young to understand what autism was, but as he got older and developed more self-awareness he would have to come to terms with his condition. I didn't want to make that any harder for him than it needed to be.

Parenting when you're under duress like this is testing, to say the least. I managed to pull Sam up from the floor and he promptly burst into tears.

'I want to go home,' he sobbed.

I had to admit defeat. I called time on our bank excursion and headed back to the car park to meet Mum, Sarah and the cousins. Immediately, they could tell something was wrong. Aside from the fact that we had been gone for ages, I could have had 'stress' tattooed across my forehead and Sam's eyes were purple and puffy from crying. Mum looked apprehensive. She clung on to the car door, bracing herself for bad news.

Tom and Dan were none the wiser and rushed out to greet their cousins. They had been apart from my boys for three months so were clearly soaking up every minute they could snatch together. But Sam hung back from the reunion.

I tried one last time to salvage our pig trip.

'Sam.' I stressed his name, trying to connect. 'Tom and Dan want to go to Pennywell Farm with you.'

Sam wasn't having any of it, though. He started screaming and shouting that 'Sam is NOT going!' The other boys edged away as if he was a bomb ready to explode.

I told Mum and Sarah to take Will and go without us. But my mum protested: 'Jo, love, we are not leaving without you.'

It was a courageous effort on her part, but futile.

'Go – GO!' I waved them on.

When Sam was having a meltdown I knew the best place for him was at home because it was where he felt safe – he could go to his room, relax on his chill cushion; it was where he had his model aeroplanes and drawing stuff.

My family reluctantly climbed back into their car. Mum was shaking her head despairingly as they reversed. Will simply stared mournfully through the back window at Sam and me as they drove off.

It was an awful moment waving goodbye to my family, knowing what a wonderful time they would have at the farm – and how much Sam would have loved it if only I could have got him there.

I blamed myself for not being able to make it happen for Sam.

Sam spent the morning drawing. Watching him sat alone at the dining-room table was heartbreaking for me. I had to keep disappearing into the living room to stop myself from welling up in front of him.

Occasionally, he glanced up in my direction. He had a glassy, spaced-out look in his eyes which I hadn't seen since he'd first started to regress three and a half years ago in Spain. It was frightening. The clock in the living room ticked loudly, making me more and more aware of the hours that Sam was spending isolated at home.

Suddenly, the front door burst open and Tom, Dan and Will came running into the kitchen. They were excited, laughing and happy, full of wonderful stories about the pigs. All three of them had held the baby piglets. They were talking loudly over each other as they recounted how tiny they were; how there were black and white ones, pink ones and ginger ones. How the piglets ran up to the boys when they stood in the pen. How they had tried to eat Will's shoelaces, much like a puppy would.

Sarah and Mum were clearly affected by the magic of these micro pigs too as they were beaming from ear to ear. Mum had a list of facts ready to reel off – the miniature pigs could be house-trained just like dogs. Pigs, she enthused, are the third smartest animals after dolphins and chimpanzees, so you can even teach them tricks. Contrary to belief, pigs are extremely clean. They have a very good sense of smell. They feel emotions and know the difference between love, hate and forgiveness . . .

I looked back at Sam as my mum carried on talking. He was still alone at the table while his brother and cousins laughed and chased each other around the house. I was over-whelmed with a sadness so great I could feel a knot of pain in my stomach – not just because Sam was alone but because he didn't seem to mind his isolation. But I did. I minded very much. I wanted him to have a friend, just one friend that he could call his own.

I'd been hoping that the micro pigs would be the key to helping him find that friendship at last, but I knew all too well that once Sam had an idea in his head – such as that he didn't want to go to see the pigs – it would take a marathon effort to break those convictions. I had to resign myself to the fact that Sam would probably never meet these healing micro pigs himself.

As soon as everyone had gone to bed, I picked up the phone and called Darren, just needing to hear his voice after such a disappointing, heart-rending day.

'Sam's never going to be able to live a normal life like his brother,' I said dully. 'What more can I do?'

I was sitting on the cold hallway tiles, my back up against the wall. Though the floor chilled me, my hand that held the phone receiver felt hot and clammy from all the emotions that were pulsing through me.

For an hour and a half Darren chatted to me, gently soothing me with his calming words. I was counting down the days until we'd be together again. Darren told me brightly that tomorrow was another day and that I shouldn't give up. He reassured me that I was a good mother who was trying her best.

'Listen to me, Jo, you have to stop giving yourself a hard time,' he insisted.

Gradually, I started to believe him. Nobody could make me feel better like Darren did. With his help, I batted away the glum feelings that had been threatening to swamp me and focused on what I had to do for Sam. I had to be strong. I had to try again. I wasn't a quitter and this was one battle I was determined to win.

'Things will be better tomorrow,' Darren told me as we said goodbye.

And I knew he was right. *Tomorrow, here I come*, I thought. Nothing was going to stand in my way.

CHAPTER TEN

Pennywell Pig Farm

I WAS MORE DETERMINED THAN EVER TO GET SAM TO PENNYWELL Farm. Once I had an idea in my head I couldn't shake it, especially if there was a chance it could help my boy.

The first thing I did was call on Lynda Russell. The only way I'd be able to shift the mental block from Sam's mind was if we prepared him for his visit to see the pigs. She was more than happy to rustle up another storybook with pictures and words describing 'Sam's day out'. Lynda thought a trip to the micro pigs wouldn't just help Sam; it would also do me the world of good.

Bit by bit, I put in place the building blocks that would enable me to create a safe day trip for Sam. By the time we'd got him used to the idea of visiting the farm, a month had gone by. It was now January 2009 and Sam had just turned six.

Darren was back from the rigs at that time and found 'Operation Pig' highly amusing. Being a bit of a macho Northerner, he couldn't see the appeal in a micro pig, but humoured me anyway.

'Wouldn't you rather take the boys to Paignton Zoo?' he joked.

I explained to Darren that the miniature pigs were legendary in the area and how Will, Tom and Dan – and even my mum – had been touched by their cuteness. And, despite his teasing, Darren was keen to see what all the hype was about.

It was a freezing cold day when Sam's Day Out finally dawned, but absolutely beautiful. The sun caught the frost on the trees, turning the Devonshire valley into a sparkling white mass. We dressed the boys snugly in their hats, scarves and gloves and the four of us set off on our grand adventure.

Will was over the moon about returning to Pennywell, clapping and singing the whole way there. I think he was also happy that his older brother was coming with him this time. Pennywell wasn't far from our home – just a twenty-five-minute car journey – but I kept an eye on Sam as we drove.

'Sam, are you excited about seeing the pigs?' I asked, peering more closely into the rear-view mirror, trying to see his expression.

'Yes,' he replied flatly, gazing out of the window. But that was a very positive response from Sam, so I turned back to the road with my spirits lifted.

They were lifted too by Darren being there; I'd missed him tremendously. He had this way about him that made me feel calm, even as he helped me navigate my way through the narrow country lanes that twisted and turned their way up the hillside. Darren was a great map-reader and I felt safe in his hands.

Pennywell Farm was on the crest of a hill, overlooking the valley. The views from the top were incredible – rolling fields dusted with frost as far as the eye could see.

We all bundled out of the car. The air was fresh on our faces and made Sam sneeze.

'Come here, Sam.' I crouched down beside him, zipping his coat up, jiggling his gloves back on to his hands. Sam had lost the glassy, vacant look from his eyes that he'd had a few weeks before but he still seemed sad to me. His gaze was glued to the ground, like there was nothing worth looking up for; like the world couldn't offer him anything any more.

Darren sensed my concern and stepped in.

'Right then, let's meet these micro pigs!' He rubbed his hands together enthusiastically.

The farm building wasn't much to look at from the outside, just a large wooden barn. We followed the signs to the entrance, which was a smaller wooden hut protruding from the main building. There was a very friendly woman behind the reception desk who was armed with stickers, ready to pat them on to the boys' coats.

Will beamed as he was handed his name tag, but Sam continued to stare at the ground.

It was a shame that Sam didn't want to soak up his surroundings, as the entrance was bursting with colour. It clearly doubled up as a shop as there was micro-pig merchandise everywhere – calendars, diaries, notebooks . . . I had no idea it was such a big business. The pictures of the pigs on the calendars were to die for – just so cute. My favourite was of a black-and-white piglet dressed in tiny, pillar-box-red Wellington boots.

'Darren, look!' I almost cooed.

'Oh stop it!' Darren laughed as he herded us all towards the entrance.

I wasn't sure who was more excited about meeting the pigs now – Will or me!

The small wooden entrance hut opened out on to a massive farmyard. I felt a bit like I'd just stepped out of the wardrobe into Narnia! It looked magical with the frost dusting on the stables, pens and fields, and there were animals everywhere.

Although the micro pigs were the main attraction, there were also shire horses and donkeys, alpacas, red and fallow deer, cows, ducks, geese, lambs, hedgehogs, goats – the list went on and on. I'd had no idea that people travelled from all over the country to meet the animals, but Pennywell attracted 100,000 visitors a year.

'Poo, it stinks!' Will exclaimed, fanning his nose with his hand.

He wasn't wrong: the smell of animal droppings and straw was quite a cocktail. But there was something very comforting and nurturing about it too. We walked past the goats and then the donkeys, the latter with their heads bowed over the gate, waiting to be petted. Will waved at the shire horses and then ran to the field where the deer were kept. I signalled to him to keep going: we had no time for deer, this was Operation Pig. I was pointing out to Sam all the wonderful creatures along the way, but he wasn't interested.

'Mummy, when are we going home?' he asked instead.

He wasn't being stroppy about it this time; he was just disinterested. Sam was surrounded by beauty but he wasn't capable of engaging with it. I looked to Darren and he gave me an 'it's going to be all right' smile.

'Sam, we're just going to meet the pigs and then we'll go home.' I tried to keep him distracted from wanting to return to the house already.

We didn't need to worry about which direction to take: soon enough we came across a big sign bearing a cartoon pig that read: 'Pennywell Miniature Pigs This Way'.

My heart fluttered. I had a good feeling about this.

Will led the way and pushed open a door that took us into a small barn. The first thing that hit us wasn't the smell, but the noise! The room was filled with the sound of little squeaks and squeals. There was also loud chatter and laughter from the dozen or so children crowding around the pen at the end of the barn. I checked on Sam; I didn't want him to have a sensory overload. His arms were crossed defensively and his eyes were still fixed on the ground, but he seemed to be doing OK.

'Come on.' Will tugged on my hand, itching to see what was making all the noise.

As we edged forward, the squeals grew louder. I turned around to talk to Sam, wanting to get him excited about the pigs, but he had disappeared.

'Where's Sam?' I asked Darren.

He pointed to the bench in the corner of the barn. Sam was sitting by himself, flickering his fingers in front of his face. I glanced back at all the children laughing and having fun, and then at my boy, sitting there alone. I wasn't having it. There was no way Sam was going to miss out on this.

I marched over to where he was sitting and crouched down beside him, gently cupping my hands around his twitching fingers.

'Sam, honey, it's time to go and see the pigs.'

He raised his sad-looking eyes and instinctively all I wanted to do was to cuddle him, to protect him from everything that scared him. But I knew that I needed to keep pushing him, to make him see the world was not as scary a place as he thought. I took his hand in mine and led him across the barn to where his brother and all the other children were having fun.

Darren saw us coming and cleared a space around the pen so that Sam would be able to see in. Darren had a big grin plastered across his face as he beckoned us over.

'Oh my God!' It was my turn to squeal as I peered over the enclosure fence.

Nestled amongst the straw were seven piglets suckling, running around and clambering over their mum. They were tiny little things, 15cm in length, if that. There were black ones with white spots and white ones with black dots and tawny-coloured ones too, their tiny eyes engulfed by their long eyelashes. Some had piled on top of each other, stealing each other's warmth. One of the spotted pigs had made himself a duvet out of the straw – only his tiny nose sticking out like a snorkel gave him away.

My heart melted.

'Look, Sam!' I half expected my son to be staring at the ground, but he was mesmerised by the little pigs. His hands tightly gripped the gate, as if he wanted to prise it open there and then. His expression reminded me of his encounter with the tiger in the zoo in Spain – he had that same adoring look in his eyes.

One of the women who worked at the farm picked up on Sam's desire to be close to the babies.

'Would you like to hold them?' she asked.

'Yes, please!' Will piped up, jumping up and down on the spot. But Sam also started flapping his arms with excitement – I couldn't remember the last time I'd seen him so animated.

'Is it safe?' Darren spoke up. He was a safety officer, after all.

Under normal circumstances, the sow might have become

aggressive and protective over her offspring, but not with a Pennywell pig. The woman explained that the pigs had been specifically bred to be calm and placid – as well as tiny.

The woman, who was dressed head to toe in blue overalls with the farm logo on her chest, slowly opened the gate. My boys were like two racehorses waiting for the starting gun, so eager were they to get inside.

As soon as Will stepped into the pen, the curious pigs raced over to check him out, oinking and squeaking as they rushed around his feet.

'Arrrgh!' Will giggled as they nibbled at his shoes, tugged at his laces, their tiny teeth nipping through his trainer fabric.

But Sam only had eyes for one pig.

He was so small that I didn't spot him at first, but tucked away in the corner was the only ginger piglet of the litter. He looked sad and lonely, just like Sam had done moments earlier.

Sam cautiously waded through the straw and crouched down beside the teacup-sized animal. It was as if Sam understood what the pig was going through.

I grabbed Darren's arm, whispering to him to look; I didn't want to destroy the magic that was unfolding.

Sam scooped the piglet into his arms and buried his nose into his soft ginger fur (older pigs have coarse hair, but these tiny piglets had velvety down all over their bodies). Incredibly, the little creature reciprocated by nuzzling his snout against Sam's neck, ear and face. Sam let out a roar of laughter as the pig smothered him with affection, his hairs tickling Sam's skin.

Amongst the pig squeals and all the commotion, something truly magical was quietly happening. The connection between Sam and the little ginger pig was obvious. The pig had a calming effect on Sam like nothing I'd seen before. It was exactly like the story I'd heard of the boy in the wheelchair. With every stroke of the pig in his arms, Sam became more relaxed.

And the pig clearly appreciated all the love Sam was pouring into him. With every caress of his soft fur he let out a tiny squeak, like a cat purring with happiness.

I clasped my hands over my mouth to stop myself from squealing with joy. Could this be the solution I'd been searching for?

I turned to Darren, who seemed to know what was coming next.

'You've got to be joking!' he laughed.

'Don't you think we should buy that pig?' I asked Darren excitedly.

Sam was now lying down on the straw next to his friend – *his friend!* – and I was able to have a better look at the little piglet. He was adorable with his tiny, furless nose that wrinkled like a concertina and his smiley upturned mouth.

'If you want a pet for Sam, we could get a dog,' Darren suggested.

'I'd have a pet pig over a dog any day!' interjected a booming voice above the commotion.

It was the pig farmer, Chris Murray. He came striding over.

'How do you do?' He wiped his hand on his trousers before offering it to Darren and me to shake. He was very well-spoken, quite a dashing type of character; I suppose not quite what I had expected from a pig farmer.

'Why's a pig better than a dog?' asked Darren, with a smile.

Mr Murray rubbed his hands with glee, clearly looking forward to answering this question.

'That's easy. They are cleaner. Smarter. Easier to keep. Cheaper to keep. Don't demand so much of your time, and incredibly affectionate,' he said, lifting a black-and-white piglet up into the air. 'You can house-train them and you can even teach them to do tricks. They don't need all the vaccinations and expenses other pets have.'

Mr Murray then launched into his spiel about Pennywell Farm. He explained that 'micro pigs' and 'teacup pigs' were names that had been coined by the media. *His* pigs were officially called 'Pennywell Miniature Pigs'.

'Do you see their smiley mouth?' He pointed to the little ginger piglet's grin.

'Yes.' I nodded, still gooey-eyed.

'Well, that's the Pennywell signature. My pigs are happy pigs,' he said with great gusto. Mr Murray went on to explain a little about the history of Pennywell and the breeding process.

Twenty-five years ago, Chris Murray was making his living from selling pigs as meat. All of a sudden, the market turned on its head, as it often did in the pig world, and he was losing between £7 and £11 per pig.

' "You're going to have to get rid of them all," my wife told me.' Mr Murray waved his hands in the air – he was a very animated farmer. But he *couldn't* get rid of the pigs because he loved rearing them. He decided he was going to keep a few aside as pets.

'Something strange then happened.' He paused for effect.

Darren and I were now hanging on the farmer's every word – it was fascinating.

'I noticed when friends and family came to the farm, they were drawn to my pet pigs.'

Mr Murray described how their faces had lit up as they stroked and petted the animals – much like Sam's just had, no doubt. They all said they only wished the pigs were smaller so they could cuddle them in their arms.

'It was a Eureka moment! I thought, "Why don't I breed a pig small enough to hold in the palm of your hand?" Plus small pigs wouldn't cost so much to keep. I'd be winning on all levels.'

'Posh pigs!' Darren quipped. I dug my elbow into his ribs to shush him up.

Darren and I weren't the only ones intrigued by the pig tales – Sam was also listening intently; he wanted to know everything about his new friend.

Mr Murray next spoke about the breeding process. After a long and complicated process of trial and error involving breeding a particular sow with a particular boar, the perfect Pennywell Miniature Pig was eventually created, he explained.

'I knew how to breed pigs to make them nice and big – so I just put that knowledge into reverse! I cherry-picked the best pigs from each litter, and *voilà*!'

It had taken Mr Murray about five years to create a miniature pig he was happy with, and he admitted the task of breeding the perfect Pennywell pig was still ongoing.

'The females dictate the size of the offspring. The males think they do, but it's actually the females!' He chuckled, his eyes twinkling with mischief.

As he'd been speaking, I'd been watching Sam, seeing how besotted he was with his little piglet friend. Now Mr Murray had paused for breath, I couldn't contain myself any longer.

'Are the pigs for sale?' I blurted out, half wishing I could take back the words once I'd said them, as I wasn't quite ready to burst the bubble of excitement that was growing inside me. What if he said 'no'? What if Sam couldn't have this wonderful ginger pig that had had such an effect on him?

Mr Murray puffed up his chest in an eccentric manner.

'Now, it's funny you should ask that. The pig your son is holding is the only one of the litter that hasn't been sold.'

I was happy and sad at the same time – sad that nobody had wanted to buy the odd pig out who had stood alone in the corner, but happy because I'd be able to continue whatever magic was happening between Sam and his new friend.

I clapped my hands together enthusiastically; Darren rolled his eyes in fond exasperation.

Selling micro pigs as a business was never Mr Murray's intention, the farmer wanted to make clear.

'I originally bred them for the farm as pets, not for selling, but everyone went mad for them so I caved in a little.'

Mr Murray explained that he still didn't sell that many to the public – fifty-five in a year, if that. His main income was generated from running an open farm.

'And I'm very choosy about who I sell them to,' he said, leaning towards us and arching his eyebrow meaningfully. 'The reason being, pigs need a lot of space, *even* miniature ones. Cramped London flats will not do!'

Mr Murray needed to be assured of his piglet's happiness before he would even contemplate handing one over. He told us he hadn't even been sure whether to sell one to the TV presenter Jonathan Ross at first, who had been one of Mr Murray's very first customers.

'I didn't know who Rossy was at the time.' Mr Murray

chuckled at the memory of the awkward phone conversation. 'I asked him who was going to look after the pig. Rossy told me his wife and daughter would, that he only wanted two. I then demanded to know where he lived. When he said London, I told him it wasn't a good idea at all. "Why?" he asked me abrasively. I explained that pigs like space.

'I didn't know he was a famous presenter with a sprawling estate; I'd imagined some poky high-rise flat overlooking the railway. "Is two acres enough?" Rossy asked me, clearly amused by the whole thing.

'Although the land was reassuring, I still insisted on speaking to his wife to check the pigs would be well looked after. She was lovely and had done all her homework on pig care, so I agreed to release the pig movement forms.

'Sadly, Rossy himself had to cancel coming down at the last moment. He sent two men instead to collect the pigs. They arrived at the farm in a showbiz vehicle with blacked-out windows, wearing suits. I chuckled to myself as they trudged through the mud. It was an extraordinary sight! Not something you see every day on a farm in Devon.' Mr Murray laughed at the memory.

And that wasn't his only celebrity story. He revealed that quite a number of famous pig fans had followed in Jonathan Ross's footsteps, although he wouldn't say who they were.

'Mum's the word!' He tapped his nose discreetly. But as Charlotte Church had spoken to the press about buying a Pennywell pig he was happy to mention her . . .

'When can we . . .' I started asking the all-important question of when we could take our pig home.

But Mr Murray was on a roll; he clearly enjoyed the spotlight and his subject. He scooped up another piglet from the litter and its little trotters paddled through the air as it let out a series of tiny squeaks.

Once he had it safely cocooned in his arms, Mr Murray started stroking its tummy. The piglet's eyes slowly closed as it was soothed back to sleep.

'They love having their tummies tickled,' Mr Murray said, rubbing the minuscule pink belly with his forefinger. He explained that when a female pig is happy her hair stands on end. When the hair goes up on a boar, it means one of two things: he's happy, or you're about to be charged by an angry pig.

At this, Darren's hairs suddenly stood up on end.

'Wouldn't we be better off with a female one, then?' he asked.

But I cut in: 'No, shouldn't we have the ginger one?' That was the one Sam had befriended.

'Well,' Darren said indulgently, teasing me, 'I guess he matches your hair colour!' I flashed him a sarcastic smile as Mr Murray reassured us that all the male pet piglets were castrated so we wouldn't have to worry about hackles going up.

I was about to ask again about the timing of a piglet's homecoming but Will beat me to it: 'When can we take him home?' he yelped.

At this, Sam's ears pricked up. We all listened as Mr Murray told us we were going to have to wait a month and a half. The piglets were only two weeks old at that time and needed to grow a little more with their mum first. That was fine by me because that gave us plenty of time to prepare for his arrival.

I looked at Sam lying next to his pig and imagined our

new life with this little ginger creature. A flush of happiness rushed through me. For the first time in months I felt the dark cloud that had been hanging over our family lift.

There was something else we needed to do in that time too – clear it with our landlord.

'I'm sure he'll let us have pets,' I said confidently to Darren, 'it's only a miniature pig after all!'

But I had spoken too soon.

CHAPTER ELEVEN

Best-Behaved Piglet

OUR LANDLORD DIDN'T TAKE THE NEWS WELL.

'No, I don't allow any pets, even if they are the size of a teacup,' he said bluntly. He wouldn't even discuss it.

Uh oh. I panicked. I had never seen Sam happier than when he was with that pig. There was no way I wasn't going to bring them together.

'You are joking?' Darren chortled when I told him I thought we should move.

'I'm deadly serious,' I said, determined as ever.

He'd known me long enough by now to know that I didn't give up easily and, as we talked it over, we both agreed together that this was absolutely the best decision for Sam.

Once more, we were racing against the clock. We had just six weeks to find a new home and move all our things.

Darren was incredible: he put in hours of research from the oil rig in Egypt. We made a great team – he found the houses online and I went to the viewings. Frustratingly, my house in Spain still hadn't sold so we had to rent again.

As soon as I viewed the converted barn in the beautiful village of Ugborough, I knew it was the one. It was nestled at the bottom of a hill alongside a farmhouse and another converted barn. We would be sharing a courtyard with our neighbours but we had our own garden filled with apple trees and flowers and it even had a stream running through it.

The barn had a topsy-turvy layout – the sitting room was on the top floor and the bedrooms were spread out across the ground floor. It was just as you'd imagine a converted barn to be, with old wooden beams and sanded oak floors. It came fully furnished; some of the items, like the Persian rug by the fireplace and the plush sofa, looked quite expensive. The most important thing about our rustic new home was, of course, the fact that the landlord allowed pets. I didn't think it was necessary to specify we would be welcoming a pig just yet. A pet was a pet at the end of the day, and ours was micro!

As the time crept closer to picking up our micro pig, Darren started to ask more questions. Being a safety officer, he wanted to make sure all eventualities had been covered. His focus was on the practicalities that I probably should have thought about before I said we'd take the pig, but I was so determined to bring Sam's friend home that I hadn't even considered basic things . . . such as how much it was going to cost.

Darren rang up the farm to get some answers.

He spoke to Katie, the member of staff who had looked after us when we'd visited Pennywell and who owned a couple of micro pigs herself.

'Three-hundred-and-fifty pounds!' Darren repeated in disbelief when she told him the price.

My jaw did drop at this point. It was the price of a pedigree dog.

'I told you they were posh pigs,' he whispered to me.

But I couldn't put a value on how much the piglet was really worth after seeing the difference he had made to Sam in just a matter of minutes. Darren and I discussed it and agreed we should go through with the sale.

Darren continued to plough on with his practical questions on the phone. 'How big do they grow? How clean are they? How can you train them? How long do they live?'

Katie was clearly experienced in dealing with nervous new owners and reassured Darren that there was nothing to worry about. The miniature pigs would grow until they were two years old and reach the size of a Cocker Spaniel; they would live until about twelve to fifteen years old; they were already pretty much house-trained, as pigs instinctively make themselves a latrine; and you train them just as you would a dog, teaching them to sit, stay, roll over and so on. The best thing was you only needed to feed them pignuts – dry pellets packed full of protein, which are pigs' staple food – and these were very cheap to buy: £5 a month. Our pig wouldn't need any vaccinations. The only thing they needed us to do was sign a pig movement form: formal paperwork on pig ownership that had been introduced by the government after the foot-and-mouth crisis had broken out back in 2001.

'So there's absolutely no difference between a pig and a dog?' I shook my head in disbelief.

'No, apparently not,' Darren said, all his questions answered.

And so it was agreed. The piglet would join us in our new home. Darren and I diligently packed up the house contents we'd so carefully put in boxes less than a year before. Will was super-excited about his new home and despite the big change ahead even Sam seemed happier since his visit to Pennywell. He smiled as he watched Darren playfully pack Will away.

'All this for a pig,' Darren would tease me, as he heaved

another box into the removal van. He knew, though, that anything that might help Sam was worth the effort.

We had less than a week to go before the arrival of our pig. Whenever there was a mention of bringing the pig home, Sam's ears pricked up and he started flapping his hands with excitement. Sam's obsession with drawing had eased a little too, which was a sign that his anxiety levels were slowly dropping. I didn't want to say anything about it to him, just in case I burst the bubble. I just enjoyed those few calmer days leading up to our return to Pennywell.

I didn't really have a clue how to prepare for the arrival of a pig but Darren said we should treat him like a dog, which meant getting him a dog basket. Sam couldn't wait to help choose a basket for his new friend. In the end Darren splashed out on a cosy blue-and-white-checked padded basket. We chose a small size to fit a Jack Russell; we knew the pig would eventually outgrow it but anything bigger would swamp its tiny body. We also bought him a ceramic dog bowl – with 'dog' written around the outside – in which to serve up his pignuts, and a cuddly toy pig to play with. We even got him a harness and a lead to take him out on walks.

Sam found it difficult to make decisions but I could tell he wanted to be involved in all the preparations. I encouraged him to help me find a place in the house to put the basket. Sam took my hand and led me to the radiator in the living room. He was clearly thinking about the piglet's wellbeing, that it would need somewhere warm and snug to sleep at night.

This was such a mature thought process for my son. One remarkable change that we had noticed in Sam was that, ever since he had met our pig, he had started to show some empathy; something rarely seen in children with autism. Not only had he reached out to the loneliest pig in the litter to offer him company, but now he had thoughtfully chosen a warm place for him to sleep. It was heart-warming to watch – but it meant even more than that. Sam essentially spent most of his time in a silent world of his own; if left to his own devices, without us cajoling him to get involved in something new, he would do nothing more than draw silently or watch television. Seeing him preparing the pig's bed that evening gave me a feeling of such hope that, once the pig arrived, Sam might begin to interact and communicate; that my son would become more conscious of the glorious life that was happening around him. I was optimistic he would spend less time inside his silent world once the pig came to live with us.

I can remember the morning we left for Pennywell Farm as if it were yesterday. It was an unusually hot spring day in April 2009. The boys were excited because Grandma had flown over from Spain to meet the pig. Mum was moving to Devon in the summer but she didn't want to miss out on the big occasion so she had come over especially.

We all piled into our new Land Rover, which the boys had christened 'Lightning McQueen' (after the character in the Pixar film *Cars*). There was Mum, Darren, me and the boys, and a green cat carrier we had borrowed from the neighbours.

Sam was the most excited I'd ever seen him: he was flapping and making a squealing noise. Will couldn't stop talking about what we were going to call our new pig and we started throwing names around in the car.

Boris? Bruno? Babe?

'Porky?' Darren contributed.

It was harder than I thought to conjure up a name and we hoped it would come to us when we were reunited with him.

When we arrived, we were treated like royalty. Instead of walking through the main entrance with all the tourists, this time we had someone waiting for us, ready to show us in the side gate. Katie led us into the office and fetched all the adults cups of tea, while I signed the relevant paperwork to release the pig to us. Will stood on his tiptoes trying to see what I was up to while Sam took himself off to the corner of the room to have a flap – he could barely contain his excitement.

Katie then took us through to the barn with the pigpens. I was leading the way with our green cat carrier while Darren, my mum and the boys followed behind in an orderly line. As we drew closer to the pen, hearing the adorable soft squeaks and oinks grow ever louder, I saw something which triggered an emotion I hadn't felt for a very long time.

Jealousy.

There was a woman in a grey raincoat cuddling the ginger pig: *our* pig. She was an older lady with grey hair and seemed totally absorbed in the pigs around her. We walked over and stood by her side, watching. 'He's so beautiful,' she remarked, beaming at the pig in her arms. Her eyes were smiling with happiness.

Instantly I felt guilty for my pang of jealousy as the woman had clearly been affected by the magic of this pig in the same way Sam had.

'Yes, he's ours,' I said, with a hint of pride.

'He will make you very happy,' she said confidently, stroking his soft auburn fur. He was fast asleep in her arms and I felt bad asking to take him from her. Instead, wanting to distract myself until the lady was ready to let go of him, I turned to Katie.

'He's very well-behaved, isn't he?' I commented.

Katie explained that Pennywell pigs are bred to be quiet and well-behaved. She told me that they are so used to being handled by the public that apart from the odd squeal or oink, they barely make a sound. This made me smile, as the communal oinking from all the pigs in the one barn created a cacophony – though thankfully we were only taking the one home with us!

I nudged Darren, still on my pigs-are-great soapbox. 'Another reason pigs are better than dogs,' I exclaimed, 'they don't bark!'

'I'm sold, you don't have to keep persuading me,' he laughed.

Sam was still flapping and now making a humming noise – I think he was about to explode with elation. It was just too much for him to see his pig but not be able to hold him. The lady spotted Sam's eagerness and patted the bench seat next to her, where she was now sitting with our snoozing pig.

Almost instinctively, Sam knew he had to try and calm his flapping so as not to scare the animal. He slowly edged his way along the bench and came to rest by the woman's side. I think the piglet must have got a whiff of Sam because he lifted his tiny wrinkly nose into the air and gave it a good twitch. He then peeled open his tired eyes and fluttered his long ginger eyelashes.

It was clear that he wanted to sit on Sam's lap, as he started wriggling and digging his trotters into the lady, trying to get to my son. The woman passed him over and as soon as he made contact with Sam he was leaping up at his neck, nuzzling him, showering Sam in pig kisses. He was clearly overjoyed to be back in Sam's arms.

'He's got bigger!' Will cried, noticing.

He had grown a little – he was now more like 30cm in length, so not quite teacup size but still absolutely adorable. In dog terms, he was the size of a Chihuahua.

We all took it in turns to cuddle our new pet and started throwing names around again. Inexplicably, a word danced on to my lips. I have no idea where it came from.

'Chester?' I suggested.

Everyone looked up, including the pig.

'He likes his new name,' Will said, rubbing the piglet's tummy.

So we settled on Chester – our ginger micro pig.

Before we could leave there was one more thing we had to do. We had to meet Chester's dad. It was Pennywell policy for new owners to see where the offspring had come from so they could get an idea of how big their pig would grow. A lot of people think micro pigs stay miniature and tragically end up getting rid of them when they discover they grow to the size of a dog. Pennywell wanted to avoid 'returns' at all costs. So we'd met the mummy, now time for the dad – Pumbaa. Chris Murray, the owner of the farm, came to take us to see him.

'As in Pumbaa the warthog from *The Lion King*?' I asked Mr Murray.

'Exactly. He's king around here.' The farmer winked as he led us to another barn.

Darren stayed with the boys and Chester while Mum came with me – she didn't want to miss out on this.

As we neared the pen, a hairy-looking pig the size of a small dog came running over, grunting loudly.

'Hello, boy!' Mr Murray greeted him with a scratch behind the ears. Pumbaa had the same smiley mouth as Chester, and even though he was bigger than our pig, he was still very cute. Pumbaa was the stud of the farm. He had fathered countless piglets.

Mr Murray beckoned us into the pen. Mum was somewhat wary – she was wearing a nice pair of tailored trousers – but it was too late to back out now. Pumbaa was lapping up the attention. He rolled over on his side and waited for his master to tickle his tummy.

'Watch this, he loves the broom.' Mr Murray started sweeping the boar's belly with the bristles.

Mum and I burst out laughing; it was the most ridiculous thing I'd ever seen.

All of a sudden, Pumbaa had had enough, and rocketed to his feet. His hackles went up.

'Oooh, he's getting a bit frisky.' Mum edged away.

As she opened the pen gate, Pumbaa tried to shoot through her legs, nearly knocking my mum off her feet. Luckily, Mr Murray was there to catch her in his arms – to her great embarrassment. I was now roaring with laughter, while my mum's cheeks turned a shade of scarlet.

'I think we should get back to Sam and Will,' Mum said, blushing and straightening her jacket.

We returned to the piglet barn to find Will cuddling Chester. Sam was standing by his side, flapping with eagerness to hold him again. He would have plenty of chances to do that later. Right now, it was time to bring our new baby pig home.

Katie leaned into the pen and grabbed a handful of straw to put in the cat carrier, so that it would smell familiar to Chester. Chester didn't squeak, he didn't squeal, he didn't

make any noise as Katie lifted him inside. He was the perfect, well-behaved pig. *This is going to be so easy!* I thought.

The comforting smell of the straw, combined with the rocking motion of the car, worked a treat on Chester and he fell asleep straight away in the cat carrier on my lap. He lay on his side with his trotters stretched out in front of him, sticking through the mesh in the carrier.

'He's so sweet.' Will couldn't stop grinning.

Sam stared at his new friend for the whole car journey home. Every now and again he would lean forward, keeping a watchful eye over him.

The first thing we did when we arrived home was to carry Chester upstairs to the living room. He was now wide awake, his pink snout pushing against the grate, trying to pick out the new scents in the air. I carefully placed the cat basket on the wooden living-room floor and opened the carrier door.

Chester was far from timid about being in new surroundings and shot out like a greyhound released from a trap. The boys chased after him as he ran around the big open-plan living/dining room, sticking his nose in every nook and cranny. And then he did a wee on the floor.

'Oops!' I yelped, running for some kitchen towel. Because he was so little, it was only a tiny puddle, but I didn't want it leaving a stain on the landlord's designer floorboards.

'We will need to get him house-trained, pronto,' I said, mopping up the mess.

I spent the next hour following Chester around armed with a roll of kitchen towel. And following Chester around meant following Sam around – because they refused to leave each other's side.

If Sam sat on the sofa, Chester wanted to sit with him. If

Sam needed the bathroom, Chester insisted on following him. The pair ended up setting up camp underneath the long dining-room table – which wasn't the easiest place for me to reach if a puddle were to appear. I couldn't bring myself to get them to move from their den, though. They looked like long-lost friends who wanted to spend every last second catching up.

I remembered that horrible day when I'd looked out of the classroom window and seen my son playing alone, apart from all the other children. It was almost as if Chester knew Sam needed a friend, and that's why he wouldn't leave his side. Sam's way of thanking Chester for this unconditional love was to stroke and cuddle and smother his friend in kisses.

Their budding friendship was more than I could have dreamed of.

Being a baby, Chester soon ran out of steam and fell asleep in Sam's arms. Sam crawled out from under the table, cradling his 'baby'. He looked worried because Chester was shivering a little.

'Don't worry, we will get him a blanket,' I reassured Sam.

We wrapped Chester's tiny quivering body in a cream fleece blanket. Now he really did look like a newborn baby. We all took turns rocking him to sleep and I couldn't resist pulling out the camera when it was my mum's turn to hold him because he looked adorable with just his snout and ginger hair peeping out from the top of the blanket.

'I'm going to send a copy of that to all my friends in Spain and tell them you've had another baby,' she joked, referring to the fact that Chester had exactly the same hair colour as me.

Darren was also concerned for the piglet's welfare and decided to light a fire to keep him warm. Chester wasted no time making himself at home. As soon as the fire was roaring, he trotted over to the rug and stretched his little body out in front of the flames, belly on show, soaking up the warmth.

Sam lay himself down alongside his friend, gently stroking Chester's soft ginger fur. Every now and then Chester would let out a small grunt of happiness. As the evening wore on we all migrated to the snug, where the TV was, and left Chester by the fire in the living room. Sam cuddled into me, his face the picture of calm and contentment. I could not believe he was the same boy who had had a meltdown just a few months ago about coming to the farm in the first place. I didn't want the day to end, but sadly that time of night crept up on us.

'Time for bed,' I said to the boys, tapping my watch.

'Oh Muuuuum,' Will moaned.

We made our way back into the living room to say goodnight to our piglet – but Chester had gone.

'Oh my God, where is he?' I panicked.

But there was no need to fret. Chester had simply taken himself off to bed already. The clever little pig had worked out that the dog basket under the radiator was where he was supposed to sleep and he was already snuggled up in there, exhausted from his busy day.

Unbelievable, we thought. It seemed almost too good to be true.

We tucked Chester in by draping the cream blanket over him, so just his little snout and ears and eyes were sticking out. Sam placed the pig toy next to Chester, in case he got lonely in the night. He leant down and gave his new best friend a kiss on the nose. I felt my eyes well up with tears of happiness.

Chester being around was clearly having a positive impact on Sam. Our new pig seemed to have slotted straight in – it was as if Chester had always been one of the family.

CHAPTER TWELVE

Meet the Neighbours

CHESTER WASN'T AN EARLY RISER. IN THE MORNING WE FOUND him fast asleep in exactly the same position we'd left him in, with his nose sticking out from under the 'duvet'. We all peered into his dog basket, watching his eyes flicker and his snout twitch – he looked like he was having a good dream.

It was Sunday morning so the boys were able to spend a whole second day with their new pet before they had to be back at school. While Chester slept, Sam drew. He emptied his tub of felt-tip pens across the kitchen table, scrutinising each colour in turn as he searched for the perfect one. Every inch of me was willing him to break his obsession with aeroplanes and draw a pig this time.

I pretended to busy myself around the kitchen, casually strolling past Sam every now and again, checking the lines he'd made on the paper. My heart sank – he was drawing a plane. I guess it was too much to hope for a change overnight. I knew I could take nothing for granted when it came to Sam's autism; that I should box yesterday away as a happy memory and not expect the same contented boy to appear today.

Sam tilted his head as he lined up his eye with the wing on his model plane. He knitted his brows together with frustration.

'Grrrrrr!' he roared as he stabbed the paper with such force the tip of his pen snapped.

He was turning. I braced myself for the onslaught.

But then, out of the corner of my eye, I saw a flash of ginger. I had no idea a micro pig could move that quickly! Especially one that, just moments earlier, had been fast asleep. The next thing I knew, Chester was sitting at Sam's feet, looking up at him adoringly. He must have heard Sam's distress and wanted to help his friend. The storm cleared, just like that – Sam reached down and scooped Chester into his arms and the piglet reciprocated with a squeak and a nuzzle.

I now had a different sort of problem to worry about, though. Chester had been storing up his pee all night; it was only a matter of seconds before he would let it out.

I snatched Chester out of Sam's arms just in the nick of time.

'Oh no!' I yelped, carrying the peeing micro pig at arms' length across the living room.

'Open the doors!' I called out to Darren. It was all hands on deck.

Darren threw open the French doors which led out on to the decking that overlooked the garden. Mum was squealing in horror, Will was roaring with laughter. I placed Chester outside on the wooden slats and he was *still* going – and there I'd been thinking that, as a little pig, he would have little pees!

'We are starting toilet training today!' I announced as I got down on my hands and knees to mop up the mess he'd left all across the living room.

But Chester wasn't in the mood for learning anything. Recharged after a good night's sleep, he was full of beans and ready to play. Sam picked him up and carried him down to the lawn.

It was a beautiful spring day. The daffodils were in full bloom, craning their big yellow funnel-heads towards the light. There was a burst of colour in every corner of the garden. The place was alive with sounds – from the singing birds to the gushing water in the brook at the bottom of the garden.

Sam carefully placed Chester down on the lawn. We hadn't had a chance to mow it yet but we didn't have to worry about Chester getting lost in the long blades of grass – he stood out like a sore thumb with his ginger coat.

Sam started flapping with excitement. Unlike the children at his school, who may have thought Sam's behaviour odd, Chester saw the flapping as his cue to play a game. He started running towards the stream, his little ginger body charging through the long grass. Sam chased after him, yelping with delight. Every now and again Chester would stop and wait for Sam to catch up and then, just as he was about to be grabbed, he would take to his trotters again. Sam was squealing more than the pig.

We all stood on the wooden decking, watching the performance play out below us. Will wrapped his arms around my leg.

'Do you want to play too?' I asked Will, perceiving he might feel left out.

Yet Will seemed hesitant. He was incredibly astute for a four-year-old. He recognised that this was a big moment for Sam – he had stopped his drawing and started running – and he was also worried Sam wouldn't want him to join in. They hadn't played together for years. Will looked sad, gazing longingly at the fun that was unfolding in front of him.

But now Darren stepped in, lifting Will up on to his shoulders and carrying him down the steps into the garden. Will couldn't contain himself for a second longer: once he was down he sprang into action, chasing Sam and chasing Chester. Chester was lapping up the attention, oinking with glee as the boys bolted across the garden after him.

Sam and Will had a job keeping up with him, though. Every time the boys stopped to catch their breath, Chester would tease them, standing just out of reach. When the boys couldn't run any more, Chester was so determined for the game not to end that he started chasing them and they ended up running around and around the apple tree.

Then I heard a sound that was almost unfamiliar. I heard my older son laugh – really laugh. For so long, Sam had been so frustrated and his behaviour so dominated by negative outbursts that he barely laughed at all any more. Now, in this moment, his mind seemed to have been somehow set free as he focused solely on the fun he was having with his new friend.

It was a breakthrough moment and I hugged Darren with tears in my eyes – my sad little boy was happy! And, more than that, much more than that for me, he was finally playing with his brother, the way I had always longed for them to do; the way they'd used to do before Sam had started to regress. Sam was actually *enjoying* having Will by his side. Will dashed off to fetch the football and a match of Team Bailey versus Team Chester ensued.

'Oh, look at that!' Mum exclaimed as Chester ping-ponged back and forth between Will and Sam as they kicked the ball to each other. Chester was so quick he managed to catch up with the football and it looked as if he was dribbling it between his trotters, nudging it forward with his snout.

Sam threw his head back and chuckled with laughter again at his little football champion.

'Look, Mum!' Sam *pointed* at Chester. Sam had stopped pointing when he regressed in Spain, but the pig's football skills had somehow broken through that particular block too.

Sam's giggles were contagious and pretty soon Darren, Mum and I were all bent double watching the ridiculous spectacle of a micro pig dribbling a football.

After half an hour of football, Darren had an idea.

'Let's get the harness out,' he suggested. We'd bought it at the same time as the dog bowl, the basket and the pig toy. Just like everything else we'd purchased, it was designed for puppies. The idea was that Chester's front legs, or rather trotters, would go through the harness, it would clip together on his back and we would then attach the lead to the harness. The point of it was to enable us to take our pig for 'walkies'; once we'd got Chester au fait with the harness, the plan was to get a 'pig walking licence' (required by law) so we could take him out on strolls in public places – maybe even to the pub!

'Come on, boys, this is how you do it,' Darren said as he told them to bring Chester over. Sam carried Chester under his arm and placed him at Darren's feet. Chester gazed up inquisitively, as if to say, 'What have we got here?' Darren knelt down, puppy harness in one hand and his other hand ready to grab Chester.

But the pig had other ideas. He shimmied backwards, just far enough so that he was out of reach.

Darren shuffled forward, attempting to grab him again.

Chester shimmied back. He thought this was a very fun game to play.

Mum and I tried to stifle our giggles as Darren tried once more to get Chester into the harness – but Chester was having none of it, his cheeky grin taunting Darren.

'This is not as easy as it looks,' Darren said, trying to save face.

Will had a much better idea.

'Daddy, let Sam do it,' he said.

I couldn't see Darren's face but I knew that he would be beaming both inside and out – this was the first time that Will had referred to him as 'Daddy'. Will had also recognised that Sam had a particular bond with Chester, which is why he'd suggested that Darren hand over the harness to his brother. It was a wonderful, poignant moment that really brought us together as a family. It seemed Chester wasn't just changing Sam; he was having an effect on us all.

'Good idea,' Darren said brightly, handing over the reins to Sam.

Chester seemed to know instinctively when Sam needed him to do something. There were none of the games he'd just tried on with Darren. He patiently waited by his friend's side for further instructions.

Considering that Sam could barely dress himself, it was unlikely he'd be able to manipulate a complicated harness, but Darren helped him feel like he could do it by himself. He guided Sam through the process of how to use it and, with Sam in charge, Chester became like a floppy rag doll, happy to be bent this way and that. He clearly trusted Sam implicitly.

'Ta-da! We got there in the end!' Darren looked up proudly

at me and Mum, who were leaning over the bannister of the decking.

With Chester securely in his harness, it was showtime. But unlike the set-up at any dog or animal show, where the *owners* lead their dogs around the arena, *Chester* led the boys. Sam and Will took it in turns to do laps of the garden.

Not only did this instigate a lot of laughter but it was also a very good exercise in teaching Sam to share – something that didn't come easily to him.

Sam was very good about handing Chester over to Will when I asked him to – much better than I would ever have expected him to be, considering how he had been over the past few months. When Will had the lead, Sam would go and have a little flap to let off steam; when Sam had the lead, he giggled with happiness.

Meanwhile, Chester was lapping up the attention. He was a natural-born show pig, prancing around the garden with his snout held up high. It was quite possibly the most ridiculous thing I'd ever seen in my life. If anyone had turned up at that point, they would have thought us mad!

I started laughing.

'What's so funny, Jo?' Mum asked.

'My autistic son, a ginger micro pig, moving house so we can have a pet pig, and then putting said pig on a leash and parading him round the garden – you couldn't make it up if you tried.' I shook my head in disbelief.

'Well, I'm proud of you, love.' She took my hand in hers and gave it a gentle rub. 'You fought so hard for this and I'm proud of you for that.'

'Thanks, Mum.' I hugged her tight.

If I'd learned anything over the past few years, it was that you could never predict what was coming around the corner. You never knew what tomorrow would bring so you should enjoy what you have today.

Right now, I was having the best weekend I could wish for.

After a morning of running around the garden, both the piglet and the boys were filthy. I suppose you would normally associate pigs with mud, but not our Chester. I didn't like the idea of our precious micro pig going to bed mucky; and there was also the worry he might get our show home dirty. I suddenly remembered the paddling pool I'd brought over from Spain. If I could get the boys and Chester in it together, I'd be killing two birds with one stone.

'Mum, would you pop the kettle on for me, please?' I asked. It was Operation Clean Pig. We were going to have to make a bath in the yard, mixing hosepipe water with hot water from the kettle.

While I was rummaging around in the shed looking for the old blue pool, a thought occurred to me. *How* do *we wash a pig?* I couldn't have Chester coming out in a rash from using the wrong shampoo.

'Darren, would you mind phoning Pennywell Farm?' I shouted out to him.

Darren made the call while I set everything up. He emerged into the courtyard carrying a bottle of Johnson & Johnson baby shampoo he'd found in the bathroom.

'That's OK, is it?' I queried, reading the back for the ingredients.

Darren recounted his conversation with Katie at the farm. Pig skin is similar to human skin so we could use our cosmetics on Chester. Katie had also made Darren aware that, because of Chester being ginger, he would be prone to getting sunburnt in summer, but we could use our regular sunscreen on his pink skin to protect him.

'I thought it best to pick out a gentle shampoo, though.' He smiled sheepishly. He really was macho on the outside but a big softie underneath.

Finally the paddling pool was full of warm water and we were ready to go. We didn't fill it very deep as Chester was so small – we didn't want there to be any danger of him drowning in it. Mum had helped Sam get dressed into his swimmers and he raced Will to the paddling pool. It was so warm outside it could have been a summer's day.

'Now, listen, don't splash too much as you don't want Chester to be frightened or get water in his lungs.' I gave the boys a stern warning.

'Yes, Mum!' Will said, groaning a little as he loved to splash at bath time.

I then went to collect our pig, but Chester was two steps ahead of me. He was already under my feet, waiting to be lowered in. I thought Chester would hate the water but he loved it. He waded around, happy as a pig in mud – as they say.

Just as Chester had looked out for Sam earlier when he'd got upset about his plane drawing, Sam now repaid the love, looking out for his friend in return. He had taken my warning to heart and was being very protective of his piglet, making sure no splashes went over Chester's head.

'Hold out your hands,' I told the boys. I squeezed a blob of shampoo into both their palms.

They then got to work building up a huge frothy lather all over Chester's thick ginger fur. They worked the soap through one trotter and then the other. Chester merrily allowed himself to be moved this way and that as Will and Sam scrubbed all the mud away. He looked like a tiny white fluffy cloud by the end with just his brown eyes, pink ears and nose poking out from the foam. It was such a wonderful sight – the boys and their pig playing in the paddling pool in the courtyard, which was walled in by the old stone farm buildings.

The neighbours – we had two sets, one on either side of us – must have wondered what on earth was going on by this point. I'd met both couples on a number of occasions since we'd moved in, and the laughter now drew them out; or rather the sight of a pig did. The first couple to come and say hello were Neil and Brenda, who had chickens in their garden and a trampoline, which my boys had been eyeing up ever since we moved in.

'Oh, is that a pig?' Brenda exclaimed. I'm surprised she could tell what Chester was as he was so unrecognisable covered in soapsuds.

Chester looked up at the strangers with his smiley face.

'Oh, he's so cute! Look, Neil, he's a teacup pig!' She clapped her hands with joy.

Her husband, Neil, didn't seem quite so taken by our new addition to the family. He just stood there in silence, staring at Chester, with a slightly displeased expression on his face.

'I don't think he's very impressed,' I said, once he'd gone back inside.

'Oh, don't mind him.' Brenda waved off her husband's concerns.

Darren found the whole thing amusing, as if he had foreseen the situation. I'd had no idea a small pig could cause offence, but maybe Neil was worried Chester would eat their chicken feed. I should have explained how, so far, our pig had been nothing short of the most perfectly behaved pet.

Next to check out the commotion were Henry and Liz, who owned the main farmhouse. They had been very welcoming and had suggested we pop round for supper one evening. Liz had big cheeks that were rosy as apples, always flushed red from the country air.

She too seemed a little doubtful about Chester. She brushed her brown fringe from her eyes as she gave Chester the once-over.

'We used to keep pigs,' she said, hinting there was a lot more to her story.

'Oh, aren't they just wonderful?' I said breezily, blissfully unaware.

'Hmm. I wonder when he will start turfing over the garden.' She looked at Henry, knowingly.

Turfing over the garden? The thought hadn't occurred to me. I still saw Chester as behaving like a dog rather than a pig.

'Really, he won't do that? Surely not?' I blurted out.

Henry raised his eyebrows. 'Good luck,' he said with a wry chuckle.

But I didn't think we needed luck. Our pig was the best-behaved pig ever; the neighbours may have had bad experiences but we had a micro pig and they were different – posh pigs have manners!

It was time to wash off the soap and dry Chester before he caught a chill. Sam took such care as he rubbed the pig down. I was half expecting Chester to shake himself out like a dog, but instead he pressed his wet fur against our legs.

'Thank you, Chester.' I patted down the damp patch on my jeans.

The boys were so worn out from all the excitement that they bedded down in the snug to watch Sunday night television. Chester was sandwiched between them on the green Habitat sofa that I'd shipped back over from Spain.

Meanwhile I sat with a cup of tea at the dining-room table with Mum and Darren. I had a few things on my mind – first and foremost, a worry that our pig could be taken from us.

'What if the neighbours put a bad word in about Chester to the landlord?' I fretted, taking another slurp of the hot brew. The landlord had told us we could have cats and dogs and because Chester was the *equivalent* of a dog, I hadn't thought twice about it since we'd signed the lease. The neighbours' reaction was now making me worry. I couldn't bear the thought of the landlord taking Chester away from Sam.

As usual, Darren calmed me down with a well-timed joke.

'We can always move again,' he said wryly.

Mum nearly sprayed her mouthful of tea everywhere.

Darren may have been joking, but right then I would have done anything to keep Sam and Chester together.

And Sam would do anything to keep Chester by his side, so it transpired.

I tucked the boys into bed at 7 p.m. Chester was two steps ahead again – he had already taken himself off to his dog basket underneath the radiator.

Mum also decided on an early night and I got to have Darren to myself for the evening. We cuddled on the sofa in the snug. He wrapped his arm around me and I pressed my face into his big chest. Every time he came home, we grew closer and closer, and it was getting harder and harder for me to say goodbye to him each time he had to return to the rigs. I'd become well aware of how Darren's calming influence was such a positive force in our lives, and was so happy being with him.

There was only one thing that could make the moment more perfect; I crept off to the kitchen to fetch a bar of chocolate.

'Oh my God,' I suddenly shrieked, as I passed Chester's basket by the radiator.

It was empty. Where was Chester?

I checked every corner of the room, panicking he might have escaped somewhere or got stuck in something. I looked under the chairs, under the sofa, beneath the coffee table, behind the curtains ... I even searched the kitchen cupboards. He was so tiny he could have squeezed in anywhere.

Then it suddenly dawned on me where he might be. I dusted off my knees and made a beeline for Sam's bedroom.

I tiptoed down the stairs and quietly pushed open the door. There was a mound of duvet and sticking out from it were two heads on the pillow – Sam and Chester. My boy had his arm folded over his micro pig.

I caught Sam blinking – he was pretending to be asleep.

'Sam, no!' I told him firmly. 'Chester is not allowed in the bedrooms.'

It was hard to keep a straight face, though; they looked so adorable together. But Chester wasn't yet toilet-trained so some rules simply had to stay in place.

'You can play with him tomorrow.' I prised the piglet from his arms. 'And it's time for *you* to go to your own bed,' I said to Chester as I held him up to my face.

He twitched his pink nose and blinked a few times too – the picture of innocence.

Is he putting on a performance just like Sam? I caught myself thinking. Then I shook the thought away. *He's just a piglet. How could he be that cunning?*

CHAPTER THIRTEEN

Squealing with Laughter

DRIP, DRIP, DRIP.

Something was splashing on to our duvet. And not just dripping – pouring.

'Darren.' I shook him awake, pointing to a stream of liquid that was cascading from the ceiling on to our bed below.

'What time is it?' He rubbed his bleary eyes.

It was 6 a.m. and it took Darren several minutes to come round and absorb what was happening. Because our house was inverted, i.e. the bedrooms were on the ground floor, the first thing we thought was that there must be a burst pipe or a leaking radiator. But then another thought occurred to us. We looked at each other and screamed in unison: '*Chester!*'

I'd never seen Darren move so quickly. He threw back the sodden duvet and raced up the staircase. Then all I heard was a string of expletives. Chester had let out such an enormous pee that it had leaked through the floor of the snug into our bedroom below.

'Oh my God, it's pig wee.' I jumped out of bed hurriedly, quickly grabbing some towels and placing them on the bed underneath the leak.

Our screaming had woken the boys. They stumbled into our bedroom in their PJs, rubbing the sleep from their eyes.

'Mummy, what's wrong?' Will asked.

'Chester's weeing on the bed, stay back!'

'Yuck!' Will yelled.

Sam was more concerned about Chester's wellbeing and scrambled up the stairs to check on him.

I was feeling quite put out, I will admit. He'd ruined our nice clean white sheets, not to mention the ceiling paintwork. I told the boys that there would be no more playing with Chester until we'd house-trained him and we would start as soon as I had picked them up from school later that day.

I was reluctant to go upstairs – if the mess in our room was anything to go by, then heaven only knew what the study looked like. Luckily it only had floorboards in it so we didn't have a soaked carpet to contend with, but nonetheless I braced myself for the worst.

As I climbed the stairs, I found the family outside on the decking, circled around our micro pig. Chester was sitting on his haunches, staring up at them and grinning innocently, as if to say, 'Me? What did I do wrong?'

It was hard to be cross with Chester when he looked so cute. Plus it wasn't his fault; it was ours for not starting house-training earlier. Also, he was only a 'puppy' so accidents were to be expected.

'Right, boys, time to get ready for school.' It was easy to while away the hours with Chester – he was such a distraction – but Monday morning meant school, even if there was now a pig in the house.

While Darren cleaned up the mess in the snug, I followed Sam to his bedroom to help him put on his school uniform. Even though Sam's gross motor skills weren't likely to improve any time soon, I always talked him through what order I was dressing him in, in the hope that one day he might get the hang of it himself. Routine was critical for his wellbeing.

'So next we put your shoes on,' I instructed, wiggling his black lace-ups on to his feet while he sat on the bed. It was very hard to keep Sam's attention. He was either obsessively into something or couldn't concentrate at all. All he cared about at this particular moment was getting back to Chester, so I had a real job on my hands to get him dressed.

This particular day at school was set to be a big day for Sam, as it was his first day back since taking ownership of Chester and he would be able to share his Chester stories with the children at the CAIRB – with the help of Lynda Russell. Lynda had established a system of communication called a 'home link diary'. This was simply a ruled exercise book we both wrote in that Sam carried back and forth in his book bag. In it, Lynda would describe what Sam had been up to during the day at school and what his behaviour had been like, and I would report back on how Sam had behaved at home. It was quite an old-fashioned system when you think about it, but very effective. It filled in the blanks for me and for her and, more importantly, provided continuity for Sam. The home link diary would enable Lynda to prompt Sam to discuss Chester at school and allow her to start conversations with Sam and the other children about the pig.

It also gave me ideas of what I could say to Sam in the evenings. For example, if Sam had spent the morning in the sensory garden I could ask him about the water features he had played with. If Sam became obsessive with his drawing at home, the diary was a way of helping me break his thoughts with conversation. I didn't need these tools at the moment, though – I had Chester. I wondered if Lynda would notice any change in Sam's behaviour, as I had even in the short time the micro pig had been one of the family.

I struggled to get Sam into the car that day – he didn't want to leave Chester. He stood by his pig's side like a body-guard, arms crossed in protest.

'Sam, get in the car now.' I pointed to the silver Land Rover.

'Sam does not want to go,' he snapped. His body was rigid with tension, his eyes glistening with tears. I prayed that a meltdown wouldn't follow.

'Sam, if you are a good boy and go to school now, you can help train Chester tonight.' I reminded him of what a special treat lay ahead.

He looked down at Chester, his bottom lip quivering with sadness.

'Chester needs you to be a good boy and go to school.' I tried to use his friend's needs to persuade him.

Sam tilted his head as he digested the deal.

'All right,' he sighed, a little huffily, but nonetheless in agreement with my request.

That had been a little easier than usual.

I'd told Lynda Russell we were getting a pet pig, so that wasn't news as such, but Sam's transformation over the week-end was. At the school gates I excitedly shared with her Sam's progress in just a few days, in particular the story of my boy giggling and laughing as he played with the pig. It was such a contrast to the frightened, anxious little boy who had started at Manor Primary. I told Lynda how my son was filled with joy to be with Chester.

Lynda was clearly moved as she heard about Sam's experiences over the weekend. Parents were coming and going around us as they dropped their children off and there we were, excitedly exclaiming about Sam's achievements in the midst of the morning rush.

'Bye, sweetie,' I said eventually, kissing Sam on his forehead. As I walked away, I hoped the weekend's positivity would permeate through to Sam's daily routine at school too.

In the meantime, I had a lot to keep myself busy with – mostly working out which techniques I could use to train Chester. Darren had grown up with dogs so had a few ideas of his own. He wanted to make sure his approach married up with the micro-pig skills handbook, though, so he gave Pennywell Farm another call.

Katie teased us for being back in touch – the second time in twenty-four hours. She then revealed a tip I would never have thought of – toilet training using grapes. Apparently micro pigs can't get enough of the sweet fruit so if you want to bribe them into performing – just hold out a grape or two!

Darren and I headed into Totnes to do a supermarket shop. I couldn't help but chuckle to myself as I watched Darren rummaging through the fruit and veg – here was a tough man who regularly dealt with fires breaking out on oil rigs, now deciding whether to buy white or red grapes for our miniature pig. We settled for a punnet of white. Now we had everything we needed for Chester's toilet-training session later that day.

When the time came to collect the boys from school, I couldn't wait to tell them what we had in store. I was also eager to find out if Sam had mentioned Chester in class. Sadly, that was a little too much to wish for. It reminded me that there was still so much to learn about his condition.

The confusing thing about autism was that although I was

learning how to read Sam's behaviour, I could never predict it. His mind was a law unto itself. The smallest thing that might go unnoticed by you or I could trigger a strong reaction in Sam. Something as minor as sitting in a different seat than usual could upset him for the rest of the day.

Nothing had upset Sam at school – but nothing much had changed either. Lynda reported that Sam had spent a while soothing himself with the spaghetti lights in the sensory room and then spent a lot of time drawing.

'He did start drawing something new, though,' she said.

My heart leapt – *Chester?*

'Ben 10.'

I sighed. Ben Tennyson was a cartoon character – a ten-year-old boy who discovers a magical device that can turn him into ten different alien heroes, each with its own unique abilities. At least he'd moved on from planes. Maybe Chester *had* affected him in some way.

Lynda had told all the children in the CAIRB about Chester, though, and they had shown such interest. Although Sam shunned the spotlight and hated anyone looking directly at him, Lynda had caught him smiling as she spoke – a 'that's my pig' moment.

'Chester's missed you very much today,' I said to Sam as we made our way home.

Sam was lost in his own world, staring out of the car window and ignoring me. I knew better than to allow his lack of communication to upset me, though. His behaviour was like the weather: some days it was sunny, other days it was rainy and every now and then you got turbulent storms. We just had to take each day as it came.

And on this day, Chester was waiting by the front door for

Sam when we got home. As soon as we pushed open the big green front door, our pet pig mauled us with the exuberant happiness of his greeting.

'Oh, look, he's wagging his tail!' I squealed in delight. Penny-well hadn't told us about that quirk – he really was like a dog. It was all that was needed to snap Sam out of his daydream and bring him back to us.

He crouched down to Chester's height and opened his arms as wide as he could stretch them, embracing his friend. Chester butted his snout against Sam's face – they had clearly missed each other.

As touching as the reunion was, I knew I couldn't let them spend all evening catching up: there was a plan we needed to execute.

'Right, boys!' I clapped my hands, getting everyone's attention. Darren was already standing behind me, armed with the punnet of grapes. 'Every time Chester starts weeing,' I instructed, 'we have to take him outside and give him a grape.' The aim was that Chester would soon come to associate going to the loo outside with food, and be so desiring of said food that he would eventually always go to the loo outside. The boys nodded: everyone knew what they had to do.

Half an hour later, the boys were playing with Chester on the rug and there was still no sign of him needing a 'comfort break'. We couldn't get him to stop peeing earlier – but now the thing wouldn't wee. Darren was sitting on the sofa, tapping his foot impatiently. I was analysing every move and squeak Chester made for signs of him needing to go.

Of course, we had lift-off the moment my back was turned.

'Now!' Darren shouted to the boys.

Sam picked the weeing piglet up and scrambled across to

the decking. Darren was hot on his heels with the grapes. As soon as Chester had finished his business, Darren gave Sam the nod.

'Sam, give Chester a grape,' he instructed.

Sam held out the green oval fruit on the palm of his hand. You didn't need to tell Chester twice; he had hoovered it up before we had time to blink.

'Good boy,' I praised our piglet. His pink nose was twitching furiously as he sniffed the air to see if there was more where that came from.

And that's how we house-trained our micro pig.

Sam loved every second of the exercise. He always took comfort from routine and the predictability of knowing grape and praise came after weeing put him at ease, which in turn made Chester happy. Amazingly, Chester was house-trained within just a few weeks.

Sam even got the hang of saying 'Good boy, Chester,' which was great progress as he still really struggled with his language. His sentences were usually only a few words long, at best, and they would not necessarily be in the right order or grammatically correct.

Darren felt happier leaving us for the rigs knowing Chester wouldn't be damaging the landlord's floorboards any more. It was harder than usual kissing him goodbye because life seemed so incredibly positive at present. I wanted him to share in all that.

I promised I'd keep him updated on all the latest pig news as I waved him off at Exeter airport. He was heading for Rio de Janeiro this time. He pretended that he wasn't that bothered about a progress report – but I could tell he secretly couldn't wait to find out what Chester had been up to next. I wondered if he was going to tell all the lads on the rig that he'd got a mini pig rather than a dog as a pet!

Chester was such a clever little thing; in fact I'd under-estimated quite how smart he was. Sam and Will were play-ing with him in the garden one day not long after Darren had left when Will noticed some suspicious behaviour.

'Mum!' he yelled out.

I peered over the balcony of the wooden decking.

'When Chester goes to wee, he doesn't really wee!' Will pointed at the pig, just as Sam was feeding Chester another grape.

What does he mean? Is Chester holding in his wee? I went to investigate.

I didn't have to wait long to find out what Will meant. After only about five minutes, Chester squatted on the grass – only nothing came out. Nevertheless, he then raced over to Sam for his reward. The cheeky devil! Chester was pretending to go to the toilet so he could get extra grapes.

I watched him do it again. It was hysterical. Our pig had hoodwinked us!

'Sam, honey, don't feed him any more grapes or he'll get a sore tummy,' I told my son. Goodness knows how many extra grapes Chester had scrounged in the last week or so. *I thought we'd got through an awful lot*, I thought to myself as I examined the near-empty punnet.

There was nothing I could do about it, other than make the boys aware of Chester's fake weeing and tell them they should reward him only when he did the real deal. I hadn't anticipated we would have such a genius on our hands!

It wasn't all bad, though . . . it made Sam giggle. And

Chester's brains and love of grapes also meant we were able to teach him much more than simply how to wee outside. The boys took it upon themselves to teach Chester how to sit, stay and roll over, using the same reward system. It was their idea to have these tricks ready as a surprise for Darren when he came back from Rio.

Of course, I gave them a helping hand, but only at the beginning.

'Sit, Chester.' I pushed his tiny bum to the grass. He sat on his haunches, gazing up at me, Sam and Will through his long ginger eyelashes.

'Good boy.' I ruffled his mop of hair, just as you would a dog, and then fed him a grape. With one inhalation the fruit had disappeared from my hand and all that was left was a little trail of slime.

Once the boys got the idea, they took it in turns to teach him tricks. I limited them to half a punnet of grapes per session as I didn't want Chester getting an upset tummy; apart from the fact that I would have hated to see him suffer, I'd just started to enjoy not clearing up after him!

So first came the sitting and then they taught him to stay – and then Sam accidentally taught Chester to moonwalk.

Sam was holding a grape above Chester's head and as he took a step backwards, he moved the grape down Chester's back towards his tail. Instead of the pig turning his body around to reach the grape, Chester decided to reverse himself in a wriggling motion, taking a sliding step backwards as he tried to keep the grape in line with his nose.

'Mummy!' Sam screamed with delight.

I watched in awe as Sam repeated the motion. Sam took one step back holding the grape at Chester's eye level and then the micro pig put himself in reverse, sliding his trotters in a slick Michael Jackson-esque moonwalk.

It was just too much. If only I'd had my camcorder! In fact I often wished I had a camcorder on Chester all the time as he was doing so many funny things.

'Darren will love this!' I enthused, praising Sam for invoking the King of Pop's famous moves.

Every day with our pet pig brought a new surprise. Some were better than others, though. After three weeks, Chester started to show his true colours. When you think of a pig, you imagine oinking, grunting, squealing and squeaking noises. You don't think 'non-stop ear-splitting squeal that is so loud the entire village can hear it'.

Our discovery was made one evening as I lifted Chester up to bring him from the garden into the living room (our upside-down barn meant he couldn't climb the decking stairs by himself). As his trotters left the ground, he started yelling – a high-pitched squeal which sounded like a screaming firework – and carried on and on until I'd put him down.

'What is wrong with you?' I said to the piglet. I thought maybe he was unwell at first. Perhaps he had eaten too many grapes and his tummy had hurt when I'd touched it.

Oh no: it turned out that it was Chester's new party trick. From that moment on, whenever anyone tried to pick him up, including Sam, he squealed in excitement. The second he felt your hands under his tummy he started and he would go on, and on, until you put him down. It was almost as if once he had settled into our house – once he knew he had us wrapped around his trotters – he started pushing the boundaries.

If Chester was tired he wouldn't squeal – then he was happy to jump on the sofa and lie on us. But if he was awake,

Chester wanted to walk around the house and garden undisturbed. Anything we did to get in the way of that would set him off squealing like a noisy firework. I suppose it was a bit like Sam and his drawing – Chester was so into what he was doing he didn't want anyone to distract him. Of course, the boys found it hysterical, and would pick Chester up just to hear him squeal.

I was also worried what the neighbours thought. I didn't want them to be upset with Chester, and the last thing I needed was the landlord knocking on the door.

'What am I going to do?' I turned as always to Darren for advice.

There was a funny sound on the line as I waited for his words of wisdom: he was trying to stifle his laughter on the other end of the phone.

'It's not funny!' I said, smiling despite myself.

Darren reminded me that our landlord lived up north – he'd originally bought our barn as a holiday home for himself before renting it out – and with a bit of luck he wouldn't find the time to come down and pay us a visit. I'd been very careful about cleaning up after Chester so I didn't need to worry about damage to the property; it was just the noise that was hard to contain. *I'll just have to find ways around picking the pig up*, I decided. I reassured myself that at least we were living in an isolated place, so we only had two sets of neighbours, which lessened the collateral damage.

Or so I thought.

The following week, Darren arrived back home (he was working one month on, one month off the rig) and took us to the local pub in Ugborough for Sunday lunch. Ugborough was a picturesque tourist spot thanks to its square in the heart of the village. It also had a huge old church, which dated back to 1112, and a post office. The Ship Inn was a beautiful old white building at the top of the hill; the pub and the post office were, of course, the hubs of the village gossip.

It was a warm spring day so we decided to have our food in the beer garden. As usual when we were out, Chester was locked in the living room. We had barricaded the stairs to the bedrooms with a bookshelf so he wouldn't tumble down.

Darren and I had been to The Ship a number of times since I'd moved to Devon so we knew the barman, Paul, well enough for him to let us in on the village gossip. He was a young chap with a cheeky dimpled grin and dark-brown hair. He came outside to take our order. We'd told him about Chester when we first got our pet pig and he now told us what everyone had been gossiping about.

'People in the pub have been asking if there is a pig in the village,' he smirked, giving us a knowing look.

My mouth dropped open. I looked at Darren in horror. Surely Chester's squeals couldn't be heard all the way up the hill? But they had been.

'Everyone's been saying they can hear a pig squealing!'

Will started sniggering, Sam's eyes were wide as saucers at the mention of Chester and Darren was chuckling under his breath – but I didn't find it all quite so funny. It was easier for Darren as he wasn't there most of the time and didn't have to deal with any upset locals.

'It's not funny,' I insisted.

'It is kind of funny.' He couldn't hold it in any longer and burst out laughing, as did Paul, Sam and Will. So we were now famous in the village for having a screaming micro pig; I guess there are worse things to be known for.

161

Perhaps Sam picked up on the suggestion that people might have been complaining about Chester, for he suddenly seemed to be overcome with pride and protectiveness as he leapt up from the picnic bench, almost knocking over the salt and pepper pots.

'Chester!' he shouted.

Paul realised what he was getting at.

'Your pig is called Chester, is he?' he asked in his thick Devonshire accent.

Sam nodded with his hands on his hips, as he wordlessly defended his pig.

'Well, I'll make sure everyone knows.' He gave Sam a friendly wink.

I beamed at my boy: I was incredibly proud of my son for finding the confidence to stand up for his friend. Six months ago he'd been having a meltdown about going to Pennywell Farm – he'd come so far!

Darren helped me to see the good in the situation and by the end of the Sunday roast we were giggling about how famous our pig was and how far the word would spread about him. I joked that Chester would become so famous the BBC would want to film him.

Meanwhile Sam was, of course, thinking about Chester and what he could do for him – I caught him smuggling a Yorkshire pudding from the pub in a napkin.

'Got you!' I surprised Sam with a big cuddle. He smiled sheepishly as he tucked his treat for Chester into his lap. It was heart-warming to see Sam thinking about another creature's wellbeing and it reinforced how much being with Chester was helping him. I reminded myself to tell Lynda all about it at school on Monday.

But even though Sam was showing happiness and love for Chester at home, he was yet to express anything similar in the classroom. His mind had somehow compartmentalised the two settings and never the twain shall meet. Nonetheless, Lynda Russell and the CAIRB teaching assistants often relayed all the funny pig stories I'd documented in the home link diary to the other children, bringing Chester to life in the classroom in the hope that all the children, including Sam, would engage with him.

There was one little boy in Sam's class who had particularly enjoyed hearing the stories about Chester. It came to light that he and Sam shared a passion for Ben 10. One day, when this particular little boy was having a bad day, Sam picked up on his mood and went out of his way to cheer him up. Sam drew some Ben 10 characters, which Lynda then helped him to cut out so that they could stick them on the boy's work station. It was a small gesture, but it made a difference, and I was delighted when Lynda told me about what Sam had done.

Lynda took a breath as she prepared to tell me something else incredibly important: 'I've never seen any other child on the CAIRB look after another one in such a way before.'

Tears welled in my eyes as I looked down at my son. Sam had had a lot to deal with himself but he'd still found room in his heart to love others.

There was no doubt in my mind that that was thanks to Chester.

CHAPTER FOURTEEN

Cheese and Swine Party

THAT SUMMER OF 2009 WAS A GLORIOUS ONE. NOT ONLY WAS Sam doing brilliantly, but the brighter weather was good for us all. Chester especially enjoyed being outdoors a lot, running about the garden with Will and Sam as one sunny day followed another. Sam often fed his pet pig ice pops to keep him cool; the orange-flavoured ones were Chester's favourite!

One weekend in June, I arranged a little get-together in our garden for family, friends and neighbours. With the move to England having been such a rush and then the regularity of Sam's meltdowns when he'd started at Manor Primary, I had never had the chance to have a house-warming party. Better late than never!

My mum, my sister and her boyfriend Simon would be coming over and I couldn't wait for Sam and Will to be re-united with their cousins Tom and Dan – it had been a bit of a disaster the last time they'd met and I was hoping this visit would go a lot more smoothly. Best of all, however, Darren was home from the rigs.

Chester was at the door waiting to greet us when I brought Darren home from the airport. Our pig's snout lifted in the air, twitching wildly as he remembered from the scent of him who Darren was. Pigs have terrible eyesight; they are led by their noses instead. I glanced at Darren to see he was smiling. That was one of the great things about Chester – one look at his smiley little ginger face always put a smile on your own.

And then Darren said something a little disturbing.

'Hasn't he grown!' he exclaimed.

Chester was five months old and had more than doubled in size since we'd first seen him. Of course, he was always going to get bigger, to the size of a Cocker Spaniel in fact, but Darren noticed that there was a big difference in Chester's size since he had last been at home. Naturally the change was much more evident to Darren as he'd not seen Chester for a while, whereas I saw him every day.

'He wasn't going to stay a baby forever,' I reminded Darren.

Darren furrowed his brow and, for a moment, he had the same look in his eye that Neil, our neighbour, had first given Chester when he'd seen him waddling around the paddling pool. It was an 'I'm not sure about this pig' expression.

'Leave my pig alone,' I joked, making my way to the kitchen to prepare us some lunch. But Darren had sown a seed of doubt. Was Chester growing faster than should be expected?

The day of the party dawned bright and beautiful. I welcomed my sister with open arms, glad to be reunited. Sarah and her boys hadn't met Chester yet and I wondered what they would make of our ginger micro pig. Her reaction was really to be expected.

'Oh, he's adorable!' Sarah hooted, picking him up in her arms before I had a chance to explain . . .

Chester squealed, of course. Loudly! Dan and Tom clamped their hands over their ears while Sam and Will chuckled. The squealing wasn't ideal, but it had become manageable. Chester just liked to make sure everyone knew he was around.

I had to admit, occasional squeals aside, Chester had been the perfect pet since we'd got him three months before. I couldn't wait to show him off to all the party guests, especially to the friends we had made in the village. Part of me was relishing the opportunity to squash any gossip that might have been circulating about his vocal acrobatics. I knew that, as soon as they clapped eyes on our angelic pig, they would never be able to say a bad word against him again.

Famous last words.

I'd spent a lot of time planning the party as we were hosting around twenty-five people. I'd even hired some caterers to lay on a spread of food, borrowed a gazebo from someone in the village and paid a magician to come and keep the children entertained. Sam and Will helped me set up the table and chairs in the garden. I covered our long wooden dining table in a white cloth and bunched all the champagne flutes together at one end: it was going to be a real celebration.

I really wanted everyone to have fun – it was my way of thanking all my loved ones for supporting me through all the difficult times of the past few years. It was also an anniversary of sorts, for it was almost exactly two years since Darren had come into our lives and I wanted to celebrate him. I had an awful lot to thank him for. He'd walked into the role of 'dad' without a second thought about Sam's condition. He'd offered to help us financially. He'd pulled me out of the deep depression I'd been slipping into when we'd first met and he did it all with a smile on his face, a can-do attitude and that kind, caring manner that I had grown to love.

It was such a special occasion that I'd bought the boys matching crisp white shirts and beige chinos with matching waistcoats for them to wear at the party. It was the first time I'd really made a thing of getting them dressed up and I felt like the proudest mum in the world as I got them ready.

But then Sam had a bit of a wobble. Even though I'd prepped him for the party with a storybook, he didn't like the idea of so many people being in his house. Sam has always struggled to look people in the eye or be in the spotlight. People on the autistic spectrum experience the world more intensely than others, so they often try to lessen the intensity of their surroundings by seeking less contact with people, less sensory stimulation, or by hiding somewhere that is safe and familiar. The idea of people invading his home, all of them with eyes that Sam wanted to avoid, was too much.

It's not for nothing that people say 'eyes are the window to the soul'. The human brain is wired to find eyes stimulating. Which means that some autistic brains find eye contact too much – a double dose of intensity. Trying to make sense of words and read facial expressions at the same time is extremely difficult for people on the spectrum. By not looking at someone's face, Sam reduces the task to just having to understand and process the language. But sometimes even that is too much – just as it was at this moment, as I tried to reassure him before the guests arrived.

Despite my pleas, I couldn't get him to move from his bed. Sam was huddled in a ball with his knees tucked tightly into his chest, flickering his fingers in front of his eyes as he stared into space.

'Sam, honey!' I sat next to him, softly rubbing his knee.

Will scurried into the bedroom, took one look at us and then scurried out, sensing that Sam was at tipping point.

'Leave. Me. Alone!' Sam pronounced every word with force.

Finding Sam a school that specialised in autism hadn't stopped me from wanting to learn more about the condition. I wasn't researching on the internet with the ferocity that I'd had when we were in Spain but I still wanted to learn. Only recently I'd read an article about 'vestibular and proprioceptive input' – how I could calm Sam when he was having a sensory overload or a meltdown by rocking him, hugging him, and even applying deep pressure with part of my body weight on him if he was really out of control. So that's what I did: I threw my arms around my boy, and hugged him.

At first Sam resisted, his body rigid like a board. As I gently rocked him and kissed his head, he relaxed in my arms.

'It's OK, you don't have to do anything you don't want to do.' I reassured him that he could hide away in his room if that made him feel safe. Then we both heard a very familiar sound – it was the noise of little trotters; but they were scrambling down the stairs . . . Chester had just worked out how to get from the living room to the bedrooms below.

He poked his ginger head around the door.

'Chester!' Sam's whole face lit up.

The pig rammed his body through the opening in the doorway and charged for the bed.

'Not on the . . .'

'Bed', I was about to say, but Sam had already scooped Chester into his arms. Strangely, he didn't squeal this time. It was as if he knew Sam really needed a hug.

At that moment, Will burst into the room, as giggles from Sam could mean only one thing – there was a pig present. He did a running jump on to the bed and then there were three of us huddled together with a miniature pig.

Then I heard a stampede from above as Tom and Dan made their way downstairs: they also wanted in on the fun. That was my cue to leave; the guests were arriving in just over an hour and I still had so much to do. I went to put the finishing touches on the table.

The caterers had delivered an impressive feast. There was smoked salmon, roast chicken drumsticks, coronation chicken in thick creamy spiced mayonnaise, sausages and every salad you could imagine, from rice to leafy greens scattered with pomegranates.

I couldn't have wished for a more dreamy summer's day in the Devonshire countryside. Our garden was now an explosion of colour with daisies sprinkled across the lush green lawn, pink blossom in the apple tree and honeysuckle climbing up the grey stone wall.

One by one, the guests started arriving. Our lawn filled up with laughter and happiness as friends and family chatted away merrily. The children were playing, threading their way through the grown-ups.

I'm not sure if it was Chester who gave Sam the courage to face the crowd, but my son eventually emerged with Chester by his side. There was a chorus of 'ahhhhhhs' as everyone clapped eyes on our cute micro pig.

Unlike Sam, Chester adored every second of being in the limelight. He scooted between each person, lifting his snout in the air as he waited to be petted. I was quite happy to leave Chester to his own devices; he was such a well-behaved pig I knew I had nothing to worry about.

'Hello!' Our neighbours Henry and Liz popped by to

join in the fun. Chester ran up to them to say 'hello' as they must have had a familiar scent. Henry raised his eyebrows, apparently not softened by the friendly greeting, but Liz was delighted by the attention.

The next to arrive was the magician. He set up shop in front of the atrium (which connected the downstairs hallway to the spare bedroom). The children gathered around and sat cross-legged on the grass, gazing up at the magician, who was wearing a bright green shirt and spotted bow tie.

I grabbed a bottle of bubbly and went in search of anyone who needed topping up. Spotting Darren chatting to my mum up on the decking, I went to join them.

'What do you think?' I asked them, wondering how they felt the party was going, but I could see they hadn't heard me: they were absorbed by what the magician was doing. I peered over the decking bannister to catch him making a wallet go up in flames. The children all screamed with surprise. Sam was sitting at the back of the group, transfixed by the magician's hands.

From the decking, I had a bird's-eye view of everything that was going on in the garden. I could see the children, people milling around, chatting and topping up their plates from the buffet, and Chester . . .

. . . who was hoovering up the food from my sister's plate while her back was turned. It was as if I was watching the whole thing in slow motion: Sarah put her hand behind her back, feeling for her plate, only to encounter Chester instead. She let out a scream and Chester bolted, knocking her wine glass over in the process.

'That pig!' she shrieked.

Everyone stopped what they were doing to see what the

fuss was about. As soon as they realised Chester was at the centre of it, they laughed and pointed.

'Isn't he adorable!' I heard someone say.

The noise of the party revved up again and I carried on chatting to Mum and Darren. Every now and again I peered over the bannister to check on the boys.

Then I did a double take. I couldn't believe it – Chester was gobbling up the food from another plate that had been left on the grass. As soon as he had cleared up there, he was on to the next one, and the next one. He was minesweeping the lawn. He wasn't going unnoticed, though: one by one guests were letting out shrieks of surprise and disgust.

I needed to contain the situation – and quickly.

I ran down the stairs, arms open, ready to snatch the little hooligan. I didn't care if he was going to squeal when I picked him up; that was better than him slobbering over everyone's food.

Chester saw me coming. He darted this way and then that way, charging through people's legs. I followed him as best I could. Everyone was laughing but I found it far from funny, though with hindsight it must have looked hilarious, like a Benny Hill sketch starring a micro pig.

It was Sam who came to the rescue. Chester was just about to make another run for it when Sam caught him in the nick of time.

'Sam, keep hold of him!' I cried, so pleased my son had stepped in.

Chester was wriggling like a fish caught in a net, his snout covered in mayonnaise. I bundled the naughty piglet under my arm and headed for the downstairs French doors. Chester, naturally, screamed in protest, wanting to be put down to continue his snackfest. And we had a little shadow: Sam was hot on my heels, wanting to make sure Chester was OK.

I needed to keep Chester somewhere tucked away, as people were coming and going through the living room. I decided to put him in the downstairs bathroom.

'Sam, will you get Chester's basket for me?' I asked my little shadow. That way, our pet would at least be comfortable while he waited on his own.

Sam came back with his arms full, carrying the basket and Chester's favourite toy pig. It was sweet that Sam was thinking about Chester's wellbeing, I thought. But I didn't trust our pig not to find his own amusements. I removed everything he might be able to chew on, such as the loo roll and the plastic bin.

'Stay!' I wagged my finger at Chester.

He sat back on his haunches and stared up at Sam and me forlornly. I felt a little pang of guilt as I closed the door on him. I hated the idea of keeping him away from the fun, but I felt I didn't have any other option.

'Let's go, Sam.' I took my son's hand in mine and gently pulled him away, as he was reluctant to leave Chester's side. I promised him we would check up on the pig very soon.

About forty-five minutes passed before I headed back to the bathroom to see how Chester was getting on. I thought he would probably have gone to sleep in his basket on the terracotta tiled floor.

But Chester wasn't asleep. Oh no: he was sat in the middle of the bathroom floor with what looked like a cape of wallpaper strips trailing down his furry back. They looked like super-long dreadlocks.

I couldn't believe it. He had used his little razor-sharp

teeth to grip the paper just above the skirting board, pull it up above his head, rip it off the wall and then toss it over his head. He'd stripped the entire wall between the basin and the loo of its expensive burgundy-and-cream wallpaper.

'Chester!' I exclaimed at the top of my voice.

Who, me? He looked up, grinning.

It was a ridiculous sight. If I hadn't been so cross I would have found it funny.

'What's wrong?' Darren arrived, out of breath, as he'd run from the other side of the garden on hearing me cry out.

'*That's* what's wrong!' I said, pointing to our naughty piglet.

Sam had also heard the commotion – his ears were always tuned into anything involving Chester. Sam, Darren and I were all now peering down at Chester, who was grinning merrily from ear to ear.

'He's done this to get his own back!' I would have used much stronger words if Sam hadn't been there. 'He didn't like being locked up so he took his revenge on the wallpaper. How on earth are we going to fix this?'

Obviously my prime concern right at that moment was the landlord. Darren was as steady and reassuring as ever. He directed me to collect all the wallpaper strips from Chester's back and promised me he would do a DIY job on the bathroom later. If Darren was cross, he was hiding it well – he had the patience of a saint.

Sam, on the other hand, found the whole thing hilarious. His whole body was shaking with laughter.

'Take that pig outside, right now,' I ordered. Everyone had finished eating so it was safe to set him loose in the garden again. A lot safer than keeping him in the bathroom, anyway; goodness only knew what he would destroy next.

'Chester, Chester!' Sam patted his leg to get Chester's attention and his pig followed him outside like an obedient dog.

I emerged into the sunshine to a lot of bewildered faces. Everyone had heard my scream and wondered what on earth had happened.

'Chester has pulled our wallpaper off the downstairs bathroom wall,' I announced to my audience. There was a chorus of gasps and stifled sniggers and then a surge of friends and family stepped forward, wanting to inspect the damage for themselves.

My mum had a few things to say on the matter: 'Do you remember what they told us at Pennywell?' she said. I shook my head, not knowing what she meant specifically. 'Mr Murray said you had to give the pig a tap on the nose when they are being naughty,' she continued. 'Nothing too hard, mind, just a gentle smack.'

The science behind this was that pigs' noses are super-sensitive – thus them using their snouts to guide them rather than their eyes. *Chester was definitely led by his nose at our garden party* . . . I thought now.

To be honest, I'd forgotten about the nose tapping. I mused on my mum's words. If there was to be another occasion when Chester needed disciplining, I thought perhaps I would try it, but I was very confident that was a big if. Chester had been so well-behaved up until now I was convinced the wallpaper disaster was a one-off.

We had a very full house that night: all our bedrooms and floors were taken up by sleeping family and friends. Chester was as good as gold, though; if he wasn't dozing on someone's knees or across his favourite green sofa, he was lying flat out on the Persian rug – his belly on full display. Both

Sam and Chester were exhausted and, come bedtime, I found them lying together under the dining-room table in their little 'den', with Sam's arm protectively wrapped over his pig. It was easy to forget the drama of the day when they looked so at peace together now.

Breakfast the next morning was a little chaotic, with many mouths to feed and lots of clearing up to do. Chester was waiting by the door that opened on to the decking so he could go out for a wee.

'Off you go.' I pushed it ajar. Chester scooted between my legs, across the decking and down the wooden stairs (a former obstacle which he had also now mastered). I had so much to do that I completely forgot about him until Sam raised the alarm.

'Where's Chester?' Sam's brow was furrowed with concern.

Mum, who was busy washing the dishes, told Sam not to worry and to come and keep her company. But Sam couldn't bear the thought of Chester being out of his sight for too long and went on the hunt for his pig. Will, Tom and Dan followed his lead as they smelled the start of an adventure.

Two minutes later, I heard peals of laughter coming from the decking. I glanced across to see all four boys were bent double. As I carried a tower of plates and bowls to the kitchen, I popped my head out of the door to find out what was so funny.

'Mummy, look at what Chester is doing.' Will pointed across the stream to Neil and Brenda's garden.

Far off in the distance, next to the chicken houses, was an orange speck. I narrowed my eyes to get a better focus. It was definitely Chester, with his head down . . .

'Oh my God!' I practically threw the plates on to the ground. Chester was eating our neighbours' chicken feed.

I ran down the stairs as fast as my legs would carry me, across the bridge and up the sloping hill that led to the chicken coops. The whole time I was glancing back at Neil and Brenda's converted barn, hoping they wouldn't catch me. They were rightfully proud of their garden – I didn't think they would appreciate me being in it, let alone a greedy pig. I also felt bad about having to go and fetch my pig from their property.

This will be over in a minute, I thought, as I headed towards Chester and the chickens. But the cheeky thing was ahead of me. He saw me coming and started packing as much food into his mouth as he could manage. I could hear him snorting and oinking as he stuffed his cheeks full of chicken feed. He kept checking over his shoulder to see how close I was getting as he gobbled up some more.

'Come here, you!' I went to grab him, but he shot off in the other direction, towards the neighbours' trampoline. Chester was so clever that he had worked out that I wouldn't be able to catch him if he hid under the trampoline, right in the centre where I couldn't reach him.

'You little . . .' I muttered under my breath as Chester frantically tried to get everything he'd stuffed into his cheeks down his neck before I got to him. I had to get down on my hands and knees and crawl underneath the trampoline to reach him.

'Chester!' I hissed at him, trying not to alert the neighbours, as I dropped to my belly and squirmed my way across the lawn. Chester was licking his chops, taunting me. I swiped my left arm, and then my right, missing him by a matter of inches each time as he dodged this way and that. I caterpillared my way forward a bit more and then decided that there was only one thing for it – I was going to have to ambush him.

I lay completely still for as long as it took for Chester to remember he had a mouthful of food in his chops that still needed devouring. As soon as he was distracted, I lunged.

'Got yer!' I said, fastening my grip around his wriggling ginger body. Of course, the minute I touched him, Chester started screaming. I might as well have set off a car alarm. I realised I had to get him out before the neighbours saw us. Somehow, I managed to reverse out from under the trampoline, bum in the air and Chester under my arm. I then made a run for it, down the garden and across the stream with Chester squealing the whole way. I felt like the character from the nursery rhyme 'Tom the Piper's Son', stealing the pig from the market.

By the time I was safely back in our garden, all my family had gathered on the decking to watch what was going on. They were holding their stomachs because they were laughing so much. Sam was almost crying with joy and it suddenly dawned on me that the naughtier Chester was, the happier Sam became.

Of course, that put me in a catch-22. Did I curb Chester's behaviour to keep my sanity – or did I let Chester get away with murder for the sake of Sam's happiness?

I had a feeling that I didn't have much choice in the matter . . .

And so that became the weekend we waved goodbye to our angelic micro pig.

CHAPTER FIFTEEN

Teacher's Pet

ONCE CHESTER HAD GOT A TASTE FOR THE 'GOOD STUFF', IT was impossible to wean him off. I lost count of the number of times I had to fetch him from the neighbours' garden. Sometimes it would be several times a day. I would cringe to myself as I took the well-trodden (and trottered) path across the bridge, through the apple trees, past the roaming ducks and to the chicken houses.

Of course, Neil and Brenda would sometimes be in their garden when Chester escaped.

'I'm so sorry,' I would say as I darted this way and that, trying to catch our naughty pig. 'Chester, will you come *here*,' I would hiss. I could always feel my cheeks burning with embarrassment. Neil would grumble that Chester was eating all his chicken feed while Brenda tried to help me catch the little devil.

The problem was, I had to leave the back door open so Chester could go outside when he needed the loo. Even though I always kept our gate shut, Chester was like Harry Houdini – he could still flatten his full belly and squeeze underneath it. The whole thing was becoming very stressful.

There was only one thing for it: I was going to have to do a bit of DIY in order to secure the gate and stop Chester from getting out. Darren had just returned to Rio, so I was going to have to work this one out for myself. Before picking up the boys from school one day, I took a detour into town to the DIY superstore. I grabbed a trolley, went through the turnstile and then stared blankly at the dozens of aisles selling everything from hammers and nails to lighting fixtures. I wondered where on earth to start.

I'd never had to do anything like this before. Darren was a master at turning his hand to practical things like this. I'd never imagined I would need to escape-proof the garden when we'd bought Chester. I scanned the shelves searching for wire mesh, cable ties, and anything else I could think of to stop him from getting out. I left the checkout with my arms full but with a lighter conscience – at least I was doing my bit to stop Chester leaving our garden.

I told the boys what my plan of attack was as we were driving home. Sam had stopped staring out of the window and was now listening intently – anything that involved Chester caught his attention.

'You can help me if you like,' I said, peering in the rear-view mirror to check on their enthusiasm. Will started clapping his hands in response.

It was 4 p.m. on a Monday afternoon when we started work on the fencing. I needed to block off the whole bottom part of the gate so that there would be no chance of Chester squeezing under any more. I locked Harry Houdini in the living room – I could do without his input on this one. I'd carefully selected a white plastic grating with holes so small a rabbit couldn't fit through. Will was going to hand me the cable ties and Sam was going to hold the fence in place while I measured up.

I knew Sam wanted to be involved in anything to do with

Chester but, because his gross motor skills were so poor, he struggled with his task.

'Arrrrrrrrgh!' Sam yelled, frustrated at himself every time he lost his grip on the fence.

'Sam, it's OK.' I tried to reassure him.

It fell on deaf ears, though. Just as Sam needed to get his drawings just so, he couldn't rest until the fence was perfectly horizontal. He tilted his head and lined his eye up with the wood.

'Won't work!' He started smacking his face, punishing himself for his body failing him.

I was quicker off the mark this time than when he'd hurt himself before and I knew what to do. I threw my arms around Sam, pinning his hands by his side. It was one of the few moments of late when I wished I hadn't locked Chester in the house as he always had such a calming effect on Sam.

'Shh, it's OK.' I rocked him gently, using my presence and my tight hug to soothe him. Will hung his head; he couldn't bear to see his brother hurt himself. A lot of children would have run a mile when they sensed trouble, especially when they had been on the receiving end of Sam's rage, as Will himself had. Now, though, he wrapped his arms around his brother's back, mirroring my movements, so we had Sam locked down in a family hug.

It was just the medicine Sam needed to help him calm down. He stopped fighting us and allowed his brother and me to take care of him. It wasn't just Sam's mood that had darkened, though: so had the sky. It looked like a storm was brewing. But I'd started so I was going to finish – it wasn't in my nature to give up. I wanted to put an end to all the dramas I was having with the neighbours.

I led the boys inside, threw on my raincoat and then went back out. I pulled out Darren's tape measure and got to work on cutting the plastic grating to size.

A loud thunderclap rolled overhead.

Next, I needed to attach the grating to the existing gate with the cable ties. It had to be rock solid so Chester couldn't barge past it.

The rain started pelting down. I ignored it. It was running down my cheeks and dribbling off my nose but I determinedly hammered the corners into place. As I staggered to my feet, what felt like hours later, I felt a huge sense of satisfaction. I looked up at the living-room window – and there were two pairs of eyes blinking down at me. The boys had been watching my heroic efforts in the rain. I did a little victory dance and then made a run for it. I was drenched through but at least I could rest tonight knowing I had put the matter to bed.

For one whole week we had our perfect pig back. Chester didn't put a trotter wrong and there were no more grumbles from the neighbours. Then, one day, just as I was on the phone to Darren, excitedly telling him about how my DIY skills had put an end to all the mischief, I spotted something out of the corner of my eye.

'Hang on a minute!' I exclaimed, bringing the portable phone with me across the living room. In the corner of the room was a bookcase, full of my favourite reads. I'd brought them over from Spain and each book had enormous sentimental significance. I was now staring down at three of my cherished novels, all of which had been chewed: they had the mark of Chester all over them.

'That pig!' I screeched in outrage. Poor Darren probably had to hold the phone away from his ear.

'What's happened?' He tried to get an answer out of me but I was too busy examining the leftovers. Chester had taken a nibble from the spines and chunks from the covers. My poor books!

I told Darren the pig was in the doghouse again. Darren was chuckling away, able to see the funny side of it as always. He then launched into a series of nostalgic stories about how, when he was growing up in Yorkshire, his pet puppy Charlie had eaten the legs off his mum and dad's kitchen table before destroying the chairs too. Darren clearly thought Chester was just behaving like a naughty pup and would grow out of it, but I struggled to share his optimism. I had a bad feeling about our 'dog pig' and felt that this was more than just a phase.

I was right. The chewing incidents became more frequent, and more severe. Every morning I'd wake up to find that something else had been reduced to remnants. He tore his dog basket to shreds – there was not one thread of fabric intact by the time he'd finished with it, just stuffing and fluff everywhere. He used his snout like a lever to turn over his dog bowl; I lost count of the number of times I had to scoop all the pignuts from the floor. He snuck down into my bedroom and pulled out everything from the wastepaper bin so my carpet was littered with shredded paper. It was one thing after another. I'd turn my back for a second and he would destroy something else. It was like having a small child on my hands.

And Chester's destructive behaviour was not limited to the house – one of his favourite pastimes was to pull the clean washing from the line, drop it on to the grass and roll around on it. One day, he got hold of my mum's best white lacy nightie during one of these washing 'games' ... and somehow managed to get it wrapped around his head. He then spent half an hour charging around the garden like some kind of pig bride, as the boys howled with laughter from the upstairs window – not just at the sight of Chester, but also at their grandma, who was shrieking in horror.

And, of course, the more he vandalised, the harder Sam laughed. Yet my stress levels were increasing by the day. I was terrified Chester would turn his attention to the landlord's furniture – then we really would have a problem.

My mum had a theory on the matter. She said Chester was merely at a loose end. 'He's a clever thing; he gets bored easily so he starts chewing.'

If that was true, how was I supposed to deal with it? I could hardly throw him a bone to distract him – he wasn't that much like a dog.

I turned to Google to ask it how you kept a micro pig entertained. I was shocked to see how many horror stories were out there about misbehaving pigs. This didn't bode well. One website said: 'Pigs are social animals who enjoy interaction with their owners. Providing toys for your pig to play with will help keep her occupied indoors. Pigs tend to cajole their way into getting what they want, so keep this in mind when setting boundaries with your pet. Much like dogs, pigs follow a pack hierarchy, so it's important to establish yourself as the leader.'

I needed to set more boundaries. I had to show Chester who was boss.

'No, Chester!' I wagged my finger at him when he had turned over his bowl of food for the umpteenth time that day. He looked up at me, grinning, without the slightest trace of guilt. He then raced off across the living room and dived on to the sofa. The phrase 'pig-headed' was created for a reason, I began to realise – because pigs are extremely stubborn. If Chester wanted to do something, then there was nothing we could do to stop him.

I was now having second thoughts about saying yes to Lynda Russell's idea of bringing the CAIRB children to meet Chester. I could just imagine him misbehaving and the whole morning being thrown into chaos.

I warned Lynda that Chester had turned into a hooligan. Of course, she found the whole thing hilarious too. She felt for me but said that Chester must be doing something right as she'd seen a transformation in Sam over the past few weeks.

Lynda revealed how Sam had finally started to talk about Chester with the other children. He was speaking about his pet with pride. 'My pig': he would tap his chest whenever Lynda mentioned our micro pig in class. Chester had given Sam a surge of confidence, which in turn had helped his vocabulary. He could now string six or seven words together in succession, which was a vast improvement on when he had first joined Manor Primary.

'That's why I suggested we take the children to see Chester,' she explained.

For Chester was not only helping Sam come out of his shell, he was uniting all the children in the CAIRB – Chester was the glue holding everyone together, it seemed.

The children were due to arrive at our house mid-morning, partway through the summer term, which gave me just enough time to whip up a lemon drizzle cake after I'd dropped the boys off at school first thing. It also gave me a

Above: This gorgeous photo was taken on the day we took Chester home from Pennywell. Sam chose the spot by the radiator for Chester's basket himself.

Right: Chester basking in the warmth of our open fire.

Below: Mum and Chester: 'I'm going to send a copy of this to all my friends in Spain and tell them you've had a new baby!'

Left: Taken during the weeks when Chester was the perfect pet pig. A very warm and happy spring day in 2009 spent drawing in the garden.

Right: After the boys had gone to bed, Chester would sit on the sofa with Mum, as if butter wouldn't melt! He was still a perfectly behaved pig at this point (most of the time!) but beginning to show some signs of growth.

Below: My nephews, Tom and Dan, with Chester sitting beautifully in return for a grape. Chester might look the image of the perfect piggy here but this photo was taken the day after he stripped the wallpaper off the bathroom wall and gobbled food from everyone's plates at the housewarming party. Who would have thought it?

A trip to Pennywell Farm (after we had purchased Chester) to get to know some of the other animals. Sam and Will cuddle some guinea pigs and feed the sheep and goats.

Left: Snow in Devon! Sam and Will's first real taste of snow since we had left Spain and their first ever snowman! Even after the snow had melted, their hardy snowman stood there defiantly for days.

Right: Chester in the garden of our rental house, taking a stroll in his new bandana. He is about a year old in this photo. If you look closely, you can already see some of the many potholes he has created.

Left: Easter Sunday. The boys take a break from their Easter Egg hunt to say hello to Chester.

Below: Christmas at Keeper's Cottage. When this photo was taken, Chester had already taken a tour around the house and Sam was busy enticing him back down towards his pen.

Above: Chester makes another bid for freedom. Much to the boys' delight we found him waiting on the patio when we returned from the school run and he got a huge hug from William.

Above: Armed with a jug of pignuts to entice Chester back into his pen. Time for a quick cuddle first though!

Above: It's not often you find Darren inside the pen with Chester. Here I catch him sitting on Chester's new pig ark, having just treated him to some weeds from his beloved vegetable patch.

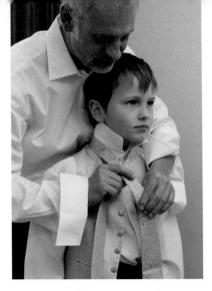

Above left: Chester smiles at us from atop our wedding cake in December 2011.

Above right: Darren helps Sam get ready for his important role of walking his mum down the aisle.

Below left: Enjoying a quick cuddle with Sam at the wedding breakfast and feeling so proud of him. This was prior to the meltdown he had at our wedding.

Below right: Our first photo taken as a family following our wedding. For a long time afterwards, the boys referred to this photo, which is in a frame in our living-room, as 'the day we all got married'.

A family holiday – and our belated honeymoon – to beautiful Mauritius in August 2014.

Above: Taken on a day trip to the Ile aux Cerfs.

Right: This photo was taken by Will. Darren and me enjoying a few honeymoon cocktails (mocktails for the boys!) down by the waterside, Port Louis, Mauritius.

Below: It took us over a week to prepare Sam for this dive but he did it! Not only did he learn how to communicate underwater, he was also brave enough to jump off a boat backwards into the ocean. He talked about this for days afterwards. He was so proud of himself and his beaming face and 'OK' sign says it all! Just incredible.

Above: Life has come full circle, with Sam now volunteering to work with the pigs and all the other animals at Pennywell Farm. I am so proud of Sam and so grateful to the team at Pennywell for all their support.

Below: Here, Sam is enjoying giving Chester a good brush in summer 2016. The traffic cone, television aerial and stepladders to the right of the picture are makeshift barriers to prevent Chester escaping his pen and charging on up to the cottage.

chance to give Chester a little spruce up; I couldn't have him looking grubby for Sam's big day. I managed to bribe Chester to sit still for a few minutes with some pignuts, while I used a dog brush to groom his thick ginger hair.

'Now, you be a good pig today,' I warned him.

Chester gave me his usual cheeky grin and then scuttled off into the garden.

I didn't realise how anxious I was for Sam until the cars belonging to Lynda and the TAs pulled into our courtyard. My stomach clenched. Sam was going to be showing off Chester and I worried how he would react to being in the spotlight. Was he ready for this?

'Hello!' I greeted the children as they were helped out of the cars. All seven from the CAIRB had made it – six boys and one little girl called Mya. The first thing that struck me was how much support there was for these children. Three teaching assistants had come along – that was almost one TA per two children. It couldn't have been more different from how Sam had been looked after in Spain. It filled me with joy to see so much love and attention being poured into helping them.

Sam was leader of the pack – he flapped his arms with excitement as he led the children towards our garden. They looked adorable as they followed in an orderly line. The protective mother in me wanted to make a fuss over Sam and check he was OK, but I reminded myself that this was Sam's time to shine. Just as I couldn't intervene in the playground when I'd watched him flap alone by the tree, it wasn't my place to interfere now.

I needn't have worried, though, because Chester was there to look after him. The ginger pig was waiting at the gate for his best friend, wagging his tail and oinking with happiness. I was terrified that, as soon as I opened the gate, Chester would run off into the neighbours' garden. He must have been missing his chicken feed, after all! I was shifting from one foot to the other, getting ready to pounce at the first sign of trouble.

But Chester didn't show the slightest interest in escaping: he was loving the attention far too much. As all the children crowded around to pet him, Chester stood perfectly still, posing like a show pony. I had to hand it to him: Chester was a great performer – which was just as well, as I'd bought a couple of punnets of grapes so that Sam could show the others all the tricks he'd taught Chester to do.

'He's gorgeous!' Lynda Russell cooed over our micro pig.

She wouldn't be saying that if she'd seen him last night, pulling all the contents of my bin over the floor again, I thought. That was the thing with Chester, though – he looked like butter wouldn't melt in his mouth, so it was hard to stay cross at him for long.

I was about to ask Sam if he wanted to show the other children how to make Chester sit, but he beat me to it. Without any prompting, without any encouragement, Sam took a handful of grapes and called Chester over.

Lynda and the teaching assistants rounded up the rest of the children and got them to form a semicircle. All eyes were on Sam and Chester.

My heart was in my mouth: I knew Sam must have been feeling the intensity of everyone's eyes on him. I was very anxious that he would hate being the centre of attention and then not be able to cope. I was worried that he might lash out at himself.

I was waiting for the bomb to explode.

But it never happened and instead Sam rose to the occasion.

'Sit, Chester!' Sam held out a grape. Just like a dog, Chester sat for his master.

Sam took five paces backwards and held out another grape. 'Here, Chester.' He beckoned his friend over. Chester wagged his tail and obediently did what was asked of him.

My heart just swelled with happiness. There was my boy, who used to hate being the centre of attention, with enough confidence to feel able to show his peers what Chester could do. I felt so incredibly proud of him. Sam had transformed from a lonely, sad child who could barely say a single word to a self-assured boy giving orders, pointing and directing.

And he wasn't the only one who had been transformed. Chester had gone from naughty to well-behaved overnight. It was almost as if Chester knew Sam needed his help. He wasn't going to let his best friend down on such an important day. It also suddenly dawned on me that Sam was using Chester as a means to communicate to the other children. Chester had given him the confidence to help him find his words – a way to untangle his sentences. It was incredible.

I'd originally bought Chester because I thought he would lift Sam's spirits. Never in my wildest dreams did I think he would help him speak and make friends.

When I say 'friends', I'm using the word loosely, as Sam wasn't playing and kicking around a ball with the other children like Will would have done with his classmates, but he *was* interacting with them, and wanting to show Chester off, which meant he cared about what they thought.

He was also allowing the other children to have a go at teaching Chester tricks, which I know would have been very hard for him because Chester was his pig and Sam found sharing difficult. My son had learnt how to take turns with his brother, but only just, so this was a huge leap forward in his development.

Being very in tune with the children's needs, Lynda Russell knew when it was time to take a break and gathered the boys and Mya together for food. I'd laid a little spread out on the white patio table: there was the lemon cake, sandwiches, orange juice and lemonade.

It was a wonderful moment, as the children sat together like one big family. Lynda Russell pulled out her camera and started snapping away. She revealed that she would be making a picture book of the day for the children to remember it by.

Meanwhile, Chester rummaged under all their feet, hopeful for any leftovers. It was reassuring to see he hadn't *completely* changed. He oinked away as he threaded his body through the dangling legs. Every now and again you'd hear a yelp as his coarse hair tickled their skin. His 'poor starving me' routine worked a treat, though, as one of the boys threw him a corner of his cake.

Chester hoovered it up from the grass and there wasn't a crumb left after he was done suctioning it into his mouth. He lifted his snout, checking to see if there was any more where that came from.

I'm not sure if Mya was shy because she was the only girl of the group or for some other reason, but she was much more withdrawn than the other children. She hid her face behind her long brown hair; a few strands dangled in front of her eyes, concealing her cute, button-like features. Her expression reminded me of Sam when he was drawing his planes – total concentration as she carefully dissected the cake, scooping out the icing and leaving the sponge to one side. Mya was a tiny little thing, much smaller than all the others. She had a vulnerability that made you want to wrap her up in your arms and protect her from the world.

I wasn't the only one to pick up on this.

I'd noticed that Sam couldn't stop checking on Mya to see if she was OK. He would glance across, look away, and then check on her once more. It was very sweet. Just as he had sensed his classmate's unhappiness not long ago, Sam instinctively knew Mya could do with some cheering up.

Sam put his food down and got up from his chair. I watched in awe as he gingerly made his way over to Mya's side.

I would never have predicted what Sam did next.

First, he called Chester to his side. Incredibly, the pig stopped everything he was doing, namely looking for scraps, to be with Sam.

He then took Mya's little hand in his and led her to the apple tree, with Chester acting as their escort. Watching the three of them walking in a row across the lawn was the most adorable sight.

Just as Sam had once used his drawings to cheer up the boy in his class, he now wanted his pig to bring a smile to Mya's face. Sam went about this the only way he knew how – by performing tricks.

'Sit, Chester,' he said.

Once again, Chester didn't put a trotter wrong. He did everything Sam asked of him, ignoring the delicious smell of cakes and treats that must have been wafting across the garden.

And it was when Chester moonwalked that Mya finally let out a bubble of giggles.

Mission accomplished! Although he would never say it, I could tell Sam was incredibly happy and relieved that he had made Mya's day. Lynda snuck up behind me with the camera to show me the pictures she'd taken. She'd made sure to capture the magical moment for their storybook.

'I told you Sam showed the most empathy for others,' Lynda said proudly, as if he was one of her own. I guess when you put that much love and care into helping children, you can't help but get involved. I didn't know how Lynda did it; her passion and commitment were extraordinary.

It was time for the children to say goodbye to Chester and return to the CAIRB. Sam insisted on chaperoning Mya to the waiting cars. As they walked back across the sun-dappled lawn, he put his arm around her – it was Sam's way of showing Mya he cared. I couldn't have wished for a more perfect day. I needn't have spent all that energy worrying about Sam, he'd more than coped – in fact, he'd shone.

The beautiful weather lasted into the evening. My plan was to bath the boys and then sit with a drink on the decking and watch the sun go down. Chester's good behaviour was also going the distance. Even though the doors to the garden were wide open, he was far more interested in seeing what Sam was up to. The pair had spent the best part of the time since he'd come back from school camped underneath the dining-room table.

'Will, Sam, bath time!' I called up the stairs. I'd filled the tub half full with water and bubbles. I heard the familiar sound of the boys' feet thumping down the stairs, followed by the slightly lighter noise of Chester's trotters.

'No, he's not allowed in the bath with you!' I announced before they had a chance to ask. I had to draw the line somewhere.

Chester looked longingly at Sam and Will as they plunged into the soapy suds. He really had mastered that wistful look. I guess he was probably remembering back to that day when they had all got in the paddling pool together; pigs have excellent memories.

'Right, who wants their hair washed first?' I asked, turning my back on the pig and noisily squeezing a blob of shampoo on to my palm. As I massaged it into my sons' hair, I noted how their locks, which had started off blond, were now turning dark brown: their Spanish roots were coming through. It was a reminder they were growing up: Sam would turn seven that coming winter while Will would be five at the end of the summer.

As I staggered to my feet to reach for the shower head to rinse them off, what did I see out of the corner of my eye? A flash of ginger running past the bathroom window! I craned my neck to follow where Chester was heading.

'Oh, you little . . .' I muttered under my breath.

Chester was using his nose to lever a hole in the fence I'd painstakingly built.

'Don't move!' I told the boys and then dropped everything I was doing to catch Chester in time.

He saw me coming. He was looking over his shoulder, oinking, scooping the fence up a bit more with his nose, and then looking back again to check how close I was getting to him.

'Come here, Chester!' I called. He'd been so obedient with

Sam earlier – surely our well-behaved pig was going to listen to me?

But Chester had other ideas. He flattened his body and wriggled through the opening he'd gouged out. No prizes for guessing where he was heading! Off he went, across the bridge, through the gate, past the ducks and the apple trees to Neil and Brenda's chickens.

Now it was my turn to check over my shoulder as I darted across my neighbours' garden, praying they wouldn't see me. There had been so much bad feeling over the chicken feed, another disagreement was the last thing I needed.

Chester and I played our usual game of cat and mouse – which entailed Chester stuffing his face and then running off just when I got close to grabbing him. Miraculously, the chase ended by one of the henhouses instead of the trampoline this time. He screamed in protest as I carried him home. *I need to get back to the boys*, I thought, *I don't have time for this!* Goodness knows how much he stole that time but Chester was still munching through the food when I locked him inside the house.

'I'm very angry at you, Chester!' I said, sharing my feelings.

He looked back at me innocently, munching away.

I rushed back down to the boys. I was now a hot, sweaty mess, with perspiration running from my brow.

I pushed open the bathroom door and was hit by a tidal wave of soapy suds. There was water *everywhere*. The boys had been play fighting while I was chasing after Chester, having a whale of a time, and had completely flooded the bathroom floor.

They both stared back at me, blinking, like butter wouldn't melt in their mouths.

I waved goodbye to my relaxing evening as I traipsed back up the stairs to fetch the mop and bucket.

But such naughty behaviour from my three charges wasn't the only problem I had to deal with. We soon had a new challenge on our hands – Chester just wouldn't stop growing.

CHAPTER SIXTEEN

Porker

PENNYWELL FARM HAD SAID THAT OUR MICRO PIG WOULD only reach the size of a Cocker Spaniel. What's more, they had good reason to think that such proportions would be accurate – Mr Murray had shown me what Chester's dad and mum looked like.

But the farm's assertions were sounding more like fiction by the day as by the end of August 2009 Chester was looking more like a Saint Bernard than a Spaniel! He was easily five times the size he'd been when we'd brought him home in the spring. In fact, it would be fair to say that he was now looking more like a regular-sized pig than a miniature pig.

It was my mum who was the first to say something. She had finally made the move over from Spain and was living at our house; the original plan had been for her to find a place of her own, but she had really struggled to find anywhere decent. As Darren and I didn't want her to delay the move any longer, we'd suggested she take our guest bedroom until something suitable for her came on the market. And, of course, it would be easier for her to research houses while actually living in Devon. It was a treat for the boys to have Grandma living with us and naturally I was delighted to have Mum close by again. In turn, Mum was over the moon to be living with the boys and me, but I also think Chester had a *lot* to do with it – she loved that pig to bits. Yet, as she pointed out to me one day, he was hardly the cute little thing we'd picked up from the farm any more.

'Jo, love, I think there's something not right here,' she said as she looked at Chester, who was lying outstretched on the sofa having a siesta. I scratched my head as she spoke, wondering how he'd gone from taking up a quarter to three-quarters of the sofa. He'd had some serious growth spurts in July and August and was now about a metre long.

'I'm sure he won't get any bigger than this,' I said, in an attempt to reassure both my mum and myself.

But my mum wasn't the only person to notice Chester's increasing size; the neighbours had a thing or two to say about it too.

'BIG PIG,' commented Henry, who lived in the main farmhouse, signalling with his arms outstretched as he walked past our garden one morning. I let out a nervous chuckle.

The boys didn't mind in the slightest, though – a bigger pig meant there was more of him to hug. It wasn't as if he behaved any differently for being larger. He still wanted to follow Sam everywhere, tried to jump on the boys' beds at night, leapt on to the sofa, lay by the fire and hid under the dining-room table with Sam. Chester acted as if he thought he was still miniature, which would have been endearing – if it weren't for the fact that it led to a whole new set of problems.

'Big pig' thinking he was micro meant the slow decline of my favourite Habitat sofa – the bottom collapsed under his weight so it dipped like a hammock. If we all wanted to watch TV in the snug, one of us would have to sit on the floor cushions, as Chester needed the whole sofa to himself. Sometimes, though, it did work out well for us as he would lie on the floor at our feet and then we would use his big belly as a footrest (we'd tickle his huge tummy with back scratchers too). Chester just loved any attention, in whatever form. A favourite trick of his was to back up to me while I was hanging out the washing and rub his rump against my calves, as though I was a tree trunk and he was having a good scratch. He did it to Sam too, using the top bit of Sam's wellies, which were made of a slightly harder rubber and gave Chester immense pleasure. He'd scratch and scratch until the pressure of his bottom made Sam topple over, at which point my son would roar with laughter and encourage Chester to do it again!

Our pig's growth spurt also meant that any mischief he made tended to cause greater damage – he now had the strength to turn over more than just the dog bowl. I'll never forget the day I walked into the living room to find two of the landlord's beautifully upholstered leather chairs knocked over on their sides, and Chester sniffing the freshly unearthed section of rug for crumbs.

'Chester!' I said in my most stern voice, truly cross with him. But Chester didn't seem to register the tone of my voice – he was just happy to see me and started grunting and wagging his tail.

'Outside, *now*!' I pointed to the door.

He looked at the garden, and then back at me, clearly weighing up his options. He wasn't going to throw away his chance of finding food, however, so he turned a blind eye to my evident displeasure and carried on smelling the rug for anything he could find. *That pig* . . .

But it was extremely hard to stay angry at Chester: one look at his happy face made you forget whatever bad day you were having.

Lynda Russell had also been affected by Chester's smile. It

had been the missing piece in a puzzle she had wanted to solve to help Sam.

One of Lynda's initial objectives had been to teach Sam how to read emotions. Although Sam was now showing clear signs of having empathy, he was still struggling with reading whether someone was happy or sad. Lynda had come up with a brilliant idea to help him with this particular challenge – to use Chester's face to illustrate to Sam what happy looked like: the starting point of a photo book she put together for him featuring several different facial expressions such as sad, scared, surprised, angry and tired. The first picture was of Chester, with his big smiley face, and written underneath was the word 'happy'. It made me happy just opening the book and seeing a gorgeous picture of our grinning not-so-micro pig. It may have been a little unconventional, but it worked. Because Sam loved Chester, he remembered what his smile meant, and whenever I started laughing, he'd shout, 'Mummy, you're happy!' – which, to be honest, wasn't that often once Chester started to turn the furniture over ... 'Angry and exasperated' face was a more common look by then.

Things quickly came to a head. Chester had grown so big that he couldn't get up on to the decking, or lumber up and down the internal stairs any more. His body was too large for his trotters, so by two-thirds of the way up the stairs, his centre of gravity would shift and he'd roll backwards. It was the same if he was going downstairs – towards the bottom, his weight would take over and he would roly-poly down the last few steps. It was heartbreaking to watch – he was so desperate to follow Sam that he would keep trying, and tumbling, and trying again. He was both stubborn and clever, so not only could he not be persuaded to give up but he also tried every trick in the book to make it up those stairs. He even tried a run-up towards them. He would give the impression of just nonchalantly wandering about downstairs when, suddenly, he would turn sharply and belt down the corridor, grunting as he ran. The sound of his trotters hitting the terracotta tiles echoed through the house as he charged at the stairs with such velocity that the hall curtains flapped with the turbulence as he ran by.

'Come on, Chester!' The boys would be shouting and jumping up and down on the landing, cheering him over the finish line.

There is one time in particular that I remember when he tried this technique. He hurtled down his 'runway' and pounded up the stairs, going for gold. For a moment, I thought he was going to make it.

But he came crashing down with a thud and, without properly thinking things through, I threw myself between Chester's backside and the bottom steps as he fell.

Smack!

I felt his full weight as I cushioned Chester's landing. If his larger appearance hadn't been a wake-up call for me, feeling the difference in his weight certainly was. It didn't hurt, but I was well and truly squashed.

Even as I was dusting myself off and sweeping my messed-up hair from my eyes, Chester was preparing to launch himself again. His determination to beat the laws of gravity knew no bounds and he charged again and, once again, was thwarted. It was very sad to watch and I couldn't let this go on a second longer; it wasn't fair on Chester or the boys to see him suffer so.

The only thing I had to hand that was big enough to block the stairs was a mirror from one of the downstairs bedrooms. I quickly put it in place. Part of me also thought that seeing his reflection might keep Chester amused while I worked out a more long-term solution – that's how ridiculous things had got. Thankfully, it worked and we had no more instances of the pig who flew.

Mum was deeply concerned for Chester's wellbeing now he could no longer get upstairs. So much so, she suggested that he sleep outside her bedroom. It did seem like the perfect solution. Mum's guest room was on ground level with the other bedrooms, but it was attached to the main barn by a square atrium, off which was the front door, which led on to the patio. This atrium, adjacent to Mum's room, was where Chester would sleep. It meant Chester could be on the ground floor and get in and out of the house easily whenever he needed to go to the loo, plus he would have my mum for company.

That night, the boys helped me move his toys and his dog basket (we were on to his third dog basket now, as he'd chewed through the first two . . .) and Mum fussed over her new neighbour, scratching behind his ears and rubbing his belly.

Chester seemed happy in his new home. Even though he wasn't next to Sam's room (and we shut the atrium off from the rest of the main house by using the big mirror that had previously blocked Chester's route upstairs), he was a lot closer to the family than he had been when he'd slept on the floor above us. Pigs have a keen sense of smell so he probably got a reassuring whiff of his best friend as he lay in his basket at night.

'Are you sure you're all right with him being out here?' I double-checked with Mum before I took myself off to bed that night. After all, she hadn't been here to witness the majority of his naughty antics.

'Me? I'm fine. He's a sweetheart, what's going to go wrong?' Mum said, smiling confidently. We both looked over at Chester, who was sitting in his basket, grinning, his typically innocent expression plastered all over his face.

Mum was right – there was nothing Chester could get under, or over, or into. It was just him, the dog basket and a corridor with glass walls. Of course, he *could* chew his basket to shreds, but I'd already assumed that we would probably have to buy half a dozen more anyway. It was a small price to pay for the happiness and life-changing magic he brought for Sam.

'Night, Mum.' I gave her a kiss.

'Night, love. Night, Chester,' she said, shuffling to her room in her dressing gown and slippers. Chester padded around in his basket, just like a dog would, before settling down and bedding himself in for the night.

The house quietened. But, for some reason, I couldn't get to sleep.

It suddenly dawned on me why. I couldn't sleep because I was worrying about whether Chester would be able to sleep in his new 'bedroom'. Would it be too cold down there? Or, conversely, would the sunlight be too bright when it poured through the glass in the morning?

Yes: I was fussing over a pig.

But I think I knew why. Ever since Chester had come into our lives, the cloud of depression that had been hanging over my head had slowly lifted. He had injected happiness, laughter and light into our whole family. I felt a happier person having Chester around. He also stressed me out a lot, true, but the good far outweighed the bad. I promised myself that I would make an extra fuss of Chester in the morning to make sure he really knew how much he was loved by all of us.

I really had grown soft.

The first thing I did when the alarm went off in the morning, even before making breakfast for the boys, was to check on Chester. I peered over the mirror apprehensively, expecting to see shredded dog basket everywhere and an overturned dog bowl. I couldn't quite believe it – the hall was immaculate. Chester was patiently waiting by the front door to be let out on to the lawn.

Mum, however, was nowhere to be seen and she was normally an early riser. She didn't appear until 10 a.m., after I'd come back from the school run. As I made us a pot of tea I had a bit of a heart-to-heart with her about her move from Spain, wanting to be sure she was happy given she had left her life there behind. My sister was making plans to move over to the UK soon, to Wiltshire, with her sons and her boyfriend Simon, but Mum would be missing them in the interim, not to mention all her Spanish friends. Then there was the climate: England wasn't a patch on the balmy heat of the Mediterranean.

'I'm fine, dear,' she said, stifling a yawn.

'Are you sure?' I asked, sensing she was a bit tired. Maybe all the moving had worn her out.

'Stop fussing.' She waved away my worries and took another slurp of her tea.

Mum changed the subject to Darren and me. She wanted

to know how things were going and, most importantly, if I was happy.

'I'm *really* happy,' I confessed with a shy smile, rolling the warm mug between my palms. Everything had always seemed such a struggle in the past, but with Darren it was all so easy. For the first time in my life I had a man who loved me, and my boys, unconditionally.

The time in Spain now seemed like a distant memory. The only time I was reminded of it was when Jaime called to speak to the boys. There was talk of Will and Sam having a holiday with him and I was glad their relationship was continuing, but my ex-husband was no longer a major part of my life.

'I'm proud of you, love,' Mum said. Every now and again she liked to remind me of all that I had achieved. If it hadn't been for my perseverance, I knew Sam wouldn't be the happy-go-lucky boy he was now turning into.

'And if you don't mind, I might just have to take myself off to bed again,' she said, rising from her chair.

I glanced at my watch. It was 11 a.m. – this wasn't like Mum.

I shook off my concern that morning but I couldn't help noticing Mum was equally tired the next day. By the end of the week, when Darren was due to arrive home from the rig, Mum had noticeable dark rings under her eyes and she was disappearing for naps throughout the day. She kept insisting nothing was wrong but I was really worried about her health. This wasn't like her at all; she was usually so full of beans.

I confided my worries to Darren on the car journey home from the airport. Darren agreed it didn't sound like my mum and said we should push for her to see the doctor.

'It's been a big adjustment for her moving to England, it's probably got something to do with that,' he said, trying to reassure me.

The problem was, I couldn't get the thought of something being wrong with Mum out of my mind and by the time we arrived home I was even more worried about her.

I switched off the ignition and Darren turned to me. He cupped his hand over mine, the way he used to do when I lived in Spain and he could see I was struggling.

'Try not to overthink things,' he said softly. I was glad Darren was home. He kept me grounded and stopped me from getting too worked up about things.

'I know ...' I started, but Darren's attention had shifted elsewhere. His mouth dropped open and the colour slowly drained from his face.

'Bloody hell!' he gasped.

'What's wrong now?' I panicked.

He pointed across the yard, to where Sam and Will were hanging off the garden gate, waiting to greet Daddy, and Chester was oinking at their feet.

'Chester's not a micro pig any more!' He looked at me in horror.

'Ah, yes, *that*.' I grimaced.

Darren said I should give Pennywell Farm a call and find out if it was normal for their micro pigs to grow so large. Chester was now well over a metre long and 55cm tall. Darren reminded me that Chester was only seven months old, so there was a question over how much bigger he was going to get.

I shrugged. 'It's not like we can do anything about it.'

Part of me just wanted to ignore the issue of Chester's size.

Large or small, he was the reason Sam was a happier boy. I had no plans to ring Pennywell (and in fact we never did). I was much more concerned about getting inside the barn and checking on Mum.

As we made our way up the wooden stairs, Darren was still firing questions at me. He was concerned about the practicalities of how we were going to cope if Chester grew any bigger.

'How much are you feeding him?' he joked, dropping his heavy travel bags on to the living-room floor.

Just then, we heard a loud chortle coming from the direction of the kitchen; Mum was flicking through the morning's paper while dunking some biscuits into her tea. We hurried into the kitchen to greet her, and I brought her into the ongoing conversation about our pig.

'Darren is worrying about how we are going to look after Chester if he gets any bigger,' I told Mum, 'but he's been extremely well-behaved since we moved him to the atrium, hasn't he? He sleeps throughout the night and doesn't cause any fuss.'

Mum started coughing.

'Mum, are you all right?' I asked for the umpteenth time.

'Yes, I'm fine,' she said.

Darren sensed my growing unease as I watched my mother slide her eyes away from mine awkwardly, as though she wasn't quite telling us the whole truth. He stepped in to help, revealing to my mum that I'd been really worried about her recently. He asked her again if anything was wrong.

She took a deep breath, and slowly let it out.

'Mum?'

The tension was unbearable.

'I didn't want to make a fuss,' she began.

My heart dropped through my stomach. This was the moment she would reveal she had some terrible illness.

'What, Mum? You can tell us.'

'I haven't been getting much sleep because . . .'

Darren and I were now hanging on her every word.

'Because Chester has been keeping me up.'

'*Chester?!*' we both exclaimed.

That was the last thing I'd been expecting her to say.

'He keeps banging on my door at night wanting attention, and I just don't know how to say "no" to him.'

It transpired that Chester had been butting his nose against her bedroom door every half an hour or so and the best way she knew to silence him was by throwing down some pignuts. The problem was, once he had eaten them, he would come back for more.

'This is ridiculous; I can't have you losing sleep because of Chester,' I said.

'You could always move him outside. He is a pig, after all,' Darren suggested.

Mum and I both looked at him as if he had gone mad. It had never crossed our minds to send Chester out into the cold. He might have grown, but he was still very much like a dog in our eyes. More importantly, how would Sam cope if we moved Chester? Would it cause a setback in his development if he didn't have his pig in the house all the time?

'I won't have it.' Mum shook her head vehemently.

'But I can't have you losing sleep,' I reasoned with her.

Mum and I then entered into an intense conversation about Chester, with Mum insisting we give the pig a while longer to settle into his new environment. She was convinced the door-knocking was a settling-in problem and that he would grow out of it soon.

Darren shook his head in disbelief as he listened to us talk it over.

'You'd think that pig was a person,' he remarked wryly.

But Chester *was* like a person. He was one of the family.

CHAPTER SEVENTEEN

Pig-Headed

THE NIGHT SKY EXPLODED WITH ANOTHER RAINBOW OF COLOUR.

It was Guy Fawkes Night and we had the best seats in the house. Every year, the village of Ugborough put on a fireworks display for the locals in the farmer's field behind our garden. Thanks to our decking area, all we needed to do was step outside our door to watch the show. There was a huge bonfire and we could see everyone's faces lit up by the roaring flames. There were fireworks of all kinds shooting up into the clear starry night.

It was an old-fashioned, small-scale community celebration where families could bring their own box of fireworks for the organisers to let off and people stuck foil-wrapped potatoes into the burning embers of the fire to roast them. It reminded me of when I'd been a kid growing up in England.

When we'd lived in Spain, we'd never celebrated 5 November, so the boys had never seen anything like it before (Mum had taken Will to a public display the year before, but Sam hadn't wanted to go). Sam was wearing earplugs to protect his sensitive hearing but he was loving the colours which were stimulating his senses in a positive way, just like the spaghetti lights did at school.

I pulled out a packet of sparklers – the evening wouldn't be complete if we didn't use them to write our names in the air. And, after we had finished writing our names, Sam was determined not to leave Chester out of our game. I helped Sam along by encouraging Will, Mum and Darren all to write Chester's name at the same time. I counted us down: 'Three, two, one – CHESTER!'

We all swirled our sparklers in the air to spell out our pet pig's name.

As another rocket screamed through the air it occurred to me that I'd better check on Chester again. We'd locked him inside the atrium to protect him from the noise of the display and I'd given him a bowl brimming with food to help distract him. I'd also left the lights on so he wouldn't feel abandoned while we all had fun upstairs.

I popped my head around the door.

'Are you OK, Chesty?'

Chester was more than OK. He was sitting, like a dog would, with his head lifted high, ears pricked up, watching the fireworks. He barely noticed me come in. He'd also eaten every last pignut from his bowl so the noise clearly hadn't put him off his food.

I left him to it and took a detour past the kitchen to fetch another round of hot drinks to keep everyone warm. When I emerged on to the decking with a tray full of goodies, I noticed something strange. To access the field in which the fireworks were held, the villagers had to walk down a pathway alongside our house. Usually it just meant a steady trickle of people going by, but those walking past had stopped stock still. Half the village wasn't watching the fireworks, but peering over the wall into our garden.

There was a group of about twelve adults and children laughing and pointing. I wondered what everyone was looking at. Then I realised that because I'd left the lights on in the atrium, Chester would have been lit up for everyone to see! Due to the location of the path anyone passing would have got a fantastic view of our not-so-micro pig, sitting proudly right inside our house in his snug dog basket. Never mind the fireworks, Chester now seemed to be the main attraction.

Knowing full well that Chester was no stranger to showing off, I needed to see this for myself.

'Wait, Mummy!' Sam said, chasing after me as I ran down the decking stairs to the atrium. He didn't want to miss out on Chester fun.

'And me, Mummy!' Will ran after Sam, his bobble hat bouncing up and down in front of his eyes as he ran to keep up with us.

And there was Chester, lapping up the attention, a big grin plastered all over his face, sitting in exactly the same position as when I'd left him.

'So *you're* the ones who have the famous pig!' an older gentleman in a flat cap said from over the wall.

I was suddenly filled with pride and realised how Sam must have felt when he showed Chester off to his classmates.

'Yes, that's our pig!'

If only his model behaviour had lasted all night. Unfortunately, someone had left the door to the cupboard that housed the boiler open – and Chester seized the opportunity to get inside and have a nibble. In the morning I got up to find he'd had a go at the insulation – there were clumps of glass fibre everywhere.

This time, he hadn't just destroyed another bit of our landlord's property, but he'd also endangered himself. Insulation can be harmful to touch, let alone swallow. It was the final straw. We had to resign ourselves to the fact that Chester was now too big to be in the house. He was causing serious damage to it, he couldn't get up and down the stairs any more and he was still waking my mum up in the night. She needed a good night's sleep and we all needed our sanity back.

It wasn't an easy decision to make and I was anxious about how Sam would react to the idea of being separated from his best friend. Geographically, a move to the garden wasn't a big one, but mentally it could cause a huge setback in Sam's development.

Chester's happiness meant everything to him. That's why he spent hours stroking him, caring for him, washing him, and making sure he had plenty of pignuts. If Chester was moved outside, Sam wouldn't be able to keep such a close eye on him. Would he lie awake at night worrying about his pig? Would *I* stay up at night fretting about Chester? I knew I had on countless occasions already.

I couldn't bear the thought of Chester spending nights alone in the cold. I could therefore see only one solution – we would have to buy Chester a house of his own.

'Not a real one,' I explained to Darren. 'One of those Wendy houses you can buy from the garden centre.'

Darren was looking at me as if I'd lost my marbles. I didn't see what the big deal was – it made perfect sense. A home from home. We could put it on the patio just outside the front door and make a little fence to keep him in.

My job now was to prepare Sam for the news. I thought if I drew up a storybook, along the lines of 'This is Chester's new home and this is Chester happy in his new home', he might be OK with it.

I called on Lynda Russell for help. She understood more than anyone the importance of getting this right. She'd seen for herself that Chester had become Sam's way of communicating with the world. She put together a story for me using a close-up of Chester's smiley face to show how 'happy' he was to be living in the garden.

I chose a quiet moment one evening before dinner to break the news. Mum took Will off downstairs so I could have some time alone with Sam.

'Sam, come here and sit next to Mummy.' I patted the sofa cushion.

I could hear the anxiety in my own voice when I spoke. My stomach was all knotted, my body braced for a meltdown from Sam.

Sam was clutching a Ben 10 figurine in his left hand. It was a soother for him because it fitted nicely into the palm of his hand and had a lovely smooth texture: for Sam, it was like holding on to a security blanket.

I was glad he had it to hold, because I had no idea how this conversation was going to go.

I turned the first page of the book and Sam and I were looking at the big smiley close-up of Chester's face.

'Chester is happy because he is moving into his own house . . .' the story began.

Sam tilted his head, as if he was examining the information. He lightly brushed his fingers across the picture of Chester's face as if he was actually stroking his friend's fur.

I looked at him, tentatively. He seemed fine. I turned the page.

Lynda had gone to town on designing Chester's house; it even had a chimney with smoke bellowing out and a white picket fence.

Sam's eyes lit up.

'Sam, you can help Chester move into his new home.' I tapped the picture with my forefinger. The thought of helping Chester be happy was just what Sam needed to hear. He started flapping his arms with excitement. A wave of relief flooded through me. It could so easily have gone the other way.

I was certain that all the work Lynda had been doing on facial expressions had helped. Connecting Chester's smiley face with him being happy in his new home had in turn brought a smile to Sam's face.

Now all we needed to do was to find our pig a house – just like the one in the picture!

'Darren,' I called out lightly, 'fancy a trip to the garden centre . . .?'

We had some house-hunting to do.

Darren and I thought it best to get the house-buying bit over quickly so that the boys could get on with helping us to move Chester in. Darren was fully on board with the idea; I think he was secretly quite relieved to be moving Chester out of the main house. While Mum looked after the children, the two of us jumped into the Land Rover and headed off to the nearest shopping centre.

We were both pretty taken aback at the prices of the Wendy houses; some of them reached into the thousands of pounds. It was quite fun checking them all out, though, and there were so many to choose from. There were some that looked like something out of *Little House on the Prairie*, mini castles, ski lodges . . . some were even stretched out over two floors with slides coming out of the top window.

There was one particular house that caught our eye, however. It was made out of pine and had the sweetest windows – they were plastic with a green frame and had green petals painted around them. The house also had a smart front door with a green letterbox. It happened to be the cheapest one we saw, although it was still a lot of money at £180.

Although we'd chosen the house, we weren't quite done. I was worried Chester would be cold at night – he was used to the warmth of central heating, after all.

'Do you think we should fit the house with a carpet?' I asked Darren, beckoning him over to the flooring aisle.

Darren stopped in his tracks.

'You are joking?'

But, of course, I wasn't . . .

We spent a good twenty minutes flicking through the fabric book, and eventually settled on a blue carpet with a rubber underlay. I imagined laying Chester's basket on top of the carpet, and giving him an extra rug to keep him warm – he'd be as snug as a bug.

Having chosen the carpet, Darren was keen to get going – he had a Wendy house to put together before dark, after all! Luckily Darren loves anything to do with building or fixing things – it's his forte. He also loves to include the boys in these kinds of projects. So, as soon as we got home, Darren spread all the different parts of the Wendy house out across the patio and called on Will and Sam to lend a hand. Will was his right-hand man, handing him bolts, nails and screwdrivers on demand. Darren was very sensitive to Sam's limitations, so he didn't push him too hard, just let him join in when he felt like it. Sam could barely contain his happiness as Chester's house was built; he stood over his brother and Darren, the energy radiating out of him, and would then disappear for a flap to let off steam.

Meanwhile Chester was keeping a watchful eye on the

developments from his base in the atrium. Part of me wondered whether he was eyeing up the house as perfect material to destroy with his razor-sharp teeth. Then I dismissed that idea. Surely even Chester wasn't that strong?

As night fell, it was time to introduce Chester to his new home. Sam was keen to do the honours so we all stood back to give him centre stage. He opened up the front door and called Chester over. Sam was the only one in the family who didn't need to bribe the pig with food – his best friend would have followed him to the ends of the earth just to remain by his side.

'Here, Chester.' Sam disappeared into the luxuriously carpeted Wendy house. He sat on the floor cross-legged and waited for his friend to join him.

Chester scurried across the patio and dashed through the front door. Whenever pigs see a door or a hole in something, they will invariably try to get through as they're such inquisitive creatures. This now worked to our advantage as Chester eagerly explored his new setting. We all took up our various vantage points to watch him at it: Will observed him from the door while Mum, Darren and I peered through the Perspex windows.

After having a good sniff, Chester climbed into his dog basket bed, which we'd already moved into the house, and then let out a huge grunt as he rolled on to his side. *We're going to have to buy him a bigger bed soon*, I thought, seeing Chester's trotters poking out of each end. Sam unfolded the cream fleece blanket that had been Chester's since he was a piglet and tucked it around his enormous belly. He might not have been micro any more, but Chester looked just as adorable as the day we'd brought him home, with his ginger face peeping out from under the blanket.

Sam leaned forward and gave him a kiss on the snout.

'I love you, Chester,' he whispered, loud enough for us all to hear.

Sam closed the front door behind him and then stood on his tiptoes to take one final look through the window. I didn't want to hurry Sam, as I knew how important it was for him to know Chester was going to be OK, but the November chill was biting and I didn't want the boys to catch a cold. I blew on my hands to keep warm and my hot breath billowed through the cold evening air.

'Night night, Chester,' Will and Sam chorused together.

Chester didn't make a sound, which meant he was already nodding off to sleep. That was our cue to leave. We all tip-toed back into the house and closed the door.

Later that night, when I was snuggling under the duvet with Darren, I reflected on the day's events.

'That went more smoothly than I expected,' I said brightly, pulling the blanket up to my ears. Although our barn was beautiful, it was quite drafty and it was nice to have Darren's warm chest close by to snuggle into. It was a cold night out there – and that got me thinking. 'I hope Chester will be warm enough,' I said: one last worry before my eyes grew too heavy to keep open. I drifted into a deep, peaceful sleep.

The next morning, I woke up feeling fresh as a daisy. As the light teased its way through the gap in the curtains, I had a strange flashback.

'Did you hear a banging noise in the night?' I croaked to Darren in my just-woken-up voice.

'No,' Darren groaned, rolling over to catch some extra lie-in time.

I must have dreamt it, I thought.

Then I sat bolt upright. *Bang! Bang! Bang!* I wasn't dreaming *that*! It sounded like someone was battering down our door.

'Darren, can you hear that?'

We both jumped out of bed and grabbed the nearest clothes to hand. I threw on some jeans and one of Darren's big knitted jumpers. It drowned my body but I didn't have time to care.

Bang! Bang! Bang!

This time the thumping was followed by: 'Oink! Oink! Oink!'

Chester.

Sam, closely followed by Will, came running into our bedroom.

'Chester is trying to break into the house, Mummy,' Will announced calmly.

He wasn't exaggerating. We all piled into the atrium just as Chester was taking another run-up to the door.

Bang! He rammed his snout against the wooden doorframe.

'Darren, stop him!' I cried out, worried for Chester's safety as much as the house's foundations.

Darren flung the front door wide open. Chester charged towards us ... and covered us in pig kisses. He had just wanted to be with his family when he woke up, the poor thing.

For a moment, we were so swept up in this affectionate reunion that we didn't notice what had happened outside ...

We couldn't see the patio tiles for all the debris. Chester had pulled out every log from under the decking stairs – strips of bark were strewn everywhere. He'd chewed his carpet to shreds and chomped through the windows and the letterbox of his Wendy house. Bite-sized pieces of green wood and scratched pine were strewn as far as the eye could see. And as for the garden – the little devil had left potholes across the lawn where he had turned up the grass with his snout.

'That pig!' Darren shouted, surveying the damage. 'I'll have him!'

Sam clamped his hands over his ears, Will put his hands over his eyes, I let out a nervous giggle and I think that Darren was probably making a mental tally of the cost of all the damage.

'At least the house is still standing,' I joked, trying to make light of the situation.

The boys found it all hilarious, of course. Sam and Will were howling with laughter.

Chester knew exactly what he had done and hung back, just that little bit out of Darren's reach. This had clearly been his way of telling us he didn't take kindly to being moved outside.

And poor Darren had to stomp off to get his tools again. It was just as well he liked DIY . . .

Moving Chester back into the house was simply not an option. Darren was going to have to patch up the damage and we were going to have to pray that Chester would soon tire of these antics.

Luckily we had bought an extra roll of carpet, and Darren was able to hammer the Perspex windows back into place, but Chester was going to have to make do without his letterbox.

The following night, Chester didn't even wait until we'd gone to bed to let us know that he wanted to be let in. The banging on the atrium door started at dinnertime, and went on, and on, into the night.

I felt stressed about it on so many levels – worrying about the damage he was causing, about whether the noise was upsetting our neighbours, but, mostly, I felt so very guilty for sending Chester out into the cold.

Every knock he made on the door was a reminder of how desperately he wanted to be with his family. I'd never foreseen this happening – we bought Chester to be a house pet, a 'pig dog', but what other choice did we now have?

No one understood what it was like to be 'different' more than Sam. He knew it wasn't Chester's fault he'd grown too big. Sam couldn't bear to see his friend suffer so he went out of his way to look after him and to make sure Chester knew he was still loved.

Every time Chester banged at the door, Sam went downstairs to check on him. He brought him more food, topped up his water, and despite my protests about the cold, he insisted on keeping Chester company in the Wendy house.

You could tell Chester was overjoyed to have Sam by his side. As Sam lay next to his best friend, softly stroking his belly, the pig sighed little grunts of appreciation, just like a cat purring with contentment. Only when Sam was convinced Chester was happily tucked up for the night would he come indoors.

And so began Groundhog Day. Every night, Sam tucked Chester into bed and every morning we woke up to something resembling a war zone in our garden. By mid December Chester had shredded everything in the Wendy house that he could possibly get his teeth into. It was a miracle the thing was still standing.

But worse than that was the state of our lawn. Chester just loved to turf up the grass with his snout. We tried countless ways to keep him contained to the Wendy house, so that he didn't ruin the lawn, but all to no avail. Getting desperate, we even rigged up a makeshift electric fence to keep him off what remained of the grass. But Chester would simply take a running charge at the DIY fence, smash through it without a moment's hesitation, and continue turfing over the garden, completely unaffected by the fence's supposed shocks. Mum and I would leave pignut trails to entice him off the grass, or try to shoo him off using brooms, but nothing worked. He'd just sit on his haunches, like a dog, smiling at us. Mum and I would eventually give up and retire to the house, leaving Chester to continue happily with his digging.

So every day I, or Darren if he was there, would patch up the damage as best we could. In the end, there was not one blade of grass left on our 'lawn'. And Chester's escapades weren't just limited to our garden – now he'd realised he could get out and about, he started taking himself off on little trips. We weren't even aware he'd gone, but while we thought he was snoozing in the Wendy house, he was actually having a good old nose around the village square, rooting through the bins and saying hello to all the villagers. He always came home of his own volition, and usually the first we knew of it was when a friendly villager made a joke about it to us! Despite doing everything in our power to keep Chester within our property, it seemed nothing stood in the way of our very determined pig!

Although Chester was acting like an absolute hooligan, his nightly desecration of the Wendy house was the vandalism I felt most badly about – simply because I couldn't stand the thought of him not being comfortable at night. By this time, however, I was fast running out of options for flooring in his house, for we had now been through countless strips of carpet.

A chance encounter with a woman in the village who always had her ear to the ground changed everything. You could often find her down the pub having a good chinwag with the locals.

One day, we happened to be standing next to each other in the queue for the post office. She asked me how our pig was. She told me that Chester wasn't just known in our village any more; apparently word had spread across the entire valley.

'You're joking?' I nearly choked on the news.

'Oh no, he's well famous, he'll be on TV before you know it,' she teased.

'Chester?! Nah, don't be silly.' I waved away her idea as being far-fetched, although a little part of me glowed with the idea of Chester being famous.

I suddenly felt an overwhelming urge to confide in her about our recent pig dramas. She was one of those great listeners who had a kind, friendly face that made you want to spill out your life story to her.

'Chester keeps tearing the carpet in his Wendy house to shreds and I'm running out of options,' I confided as I shared with her my problem about what I should use to keep him warm at night, given he shredded absolutely everything I'd tried.

For a moment, the woman was speechless. She looked puzzled, as if I had been speaking another language.

'Sorry,' she laughed, 'I was just trying to get my head

around what you were saying. Are you telling me you've been buying carpet for a pig?'

Suddenly, I felt a little silly.

'Yeees . . .'

She half laughed, half coughed into her fist.

'What about laying some straw down in there?' she said matter-of-factly. 'He's a pig, not a dog!'

Her words sank in. *Of course!* It was just that I'd never looked at Chester in that way before. Pennywell Farm had likened him to a pet pooch so everything we had ever bought him had been designed to fit a dog. We'd taught Chester to behave like a dog – to sit, stay, roll over. In my eyes, Chester *was* a dog.

It took this woman, on that cold December morning in the post-office queue, to open my eyes. Chester was a *pig* – and it was time for us to finally start treating him like one.

CHAPTER EIGHTEEN

The Pig Move

AS IT HAPPENED, WE WERE ABLE TO PUT OUR PLAN INTO action almost right away – and not just by adding straw to Chester's Wendy house (which, as the woman in the village had predicted, he adored). No – we had bigger plans to put in place. My house in Spain had finally been sold, which was wonderful news as it had been on the market for nearly two years. Finally Darren and I were able to purchase a long-term family home and we had found the perfect property to buy: an old farmhouse nestled amongst the rolling hills with enough room for our human family *and* Chester!

But with the move confirmed the pressure was now on to get everything sorted in our rented house in time for the sale to go through. We had to patch up the converted barn so we could get our deposit back . . . and I had a terrible feeling it was going to cost an awful lot.

Darren sat at the dining-room table, trying to figure out the sums. One hand clutched his head while the other tightly gripped his biro. It didn't take a genius to tell he was stressed.

I tiptoed past Darren, trying to peek over his shoulder at the total he'd come to. I took a big gulp as I saw the final sum. *Three thousand pounds!*

There was the damage to the boiler; the ceiling that Chester had left a wee mark on; the wallpaper he'd peeled off the bathroom wall and tossed over his shoulder; the gate he had bent out of shape (countless times); the damage to the lawn ... What had once been a beautiful, lush green garden filled with daisies and daffodils now looked more like a quagmire. The garden would need to be completely returfed, which would be a big expense, but the main cost would be replacing both the front door – Chester had split the wood from months of repeated banging – and the French doors to Mum's bedroom, which now had mud a foot high across them from where Chester had spent a great deal of time pressing his snout up against the glass, trying to sneak a peek of Mum in her bedroom.

There was also the small problem of where Chester was going to live while we fixed everything – we'd probably have to fork out another few hundred pounds to rehome him temporarily.

'Whoever said getting a pig would be cheaper than a dog was lying!' stated Darren bluntly. You have to choose your moments in life, and now really wasn't the time to reason with Darren about how much good Chester had done ...

'Cup of tea?' I said instead: a peace offering.

Darren looked at me through weary eyes and sighed deeply. It seemed his love/hate relationship with our pig was as complicated as ever, but no matter how he felt about Chester, he was still prepared to work incredibly hard to make things right. I really felt for Darren – he had to be back on the rig in a few days but the need to restore the property was pressing, which meant he would have to spend his last hours with us working instead of relaxing and spending quality time with me and the boys.

'I'll think I'll start with the patio doors,' he said glumly. 'Just keep that pig away from me!' he growled as he disappeared to fetch his toolbox.

That was a job for Will and Sam – they would have to keep Chester entertained for the interim. Mum wouldn't be able to distract him with pignuts as by this time she had quite wisely moved to a house down the road in Ivybridge. She'd finally had enough of Chester banging on the door day and night.

I have to hand it to Darren: he worked nonstop to get the barn straightened up. Just as he'd done when he'd packed up the house in Spain with me, he was like a whirlwind, whizzing from one job to the next.

The French doors took some work. Darren was on his hands and knees, filling the cracks, sanding, painting and restoring the wood to its original mahogany brown. Luckily I'd saved all the strips of wallpaper from the bathroom, so it just took a careful eye to line up the stripes and glue it all back into place.

I kept handing Darren cups of tea with biscuits while the boys played football with Chester in the mud. That night we used a padlock to keep Chester inside his house – we couldn't have him banging on the doors and undoing all the hours of work Darren had put in.

I'm certain Chester knew he had stepped over the line, as for those two days he was the perfect example of a well-behaved pig. Either that or he had wisely worked out he needed to give Darren a wide berth! Whatever Chester's motivation, it had a positive impact, as Darren was slightly less cross with our pig by the time I dropped him off at the airport. He even showed a hint of concern about where I was going to keep Chester while we returfed the lawn. At that time, I didn't have the answer.

With Darren back on the rigs, it was over to me to get the rest of the house sorted. I didn't have much time as our scheduled move was only a few weeks away now. I turned to our local paper for help, spotting an ad for a freelance gardener at the back. *He'll do*, I thought.

'So what have we got here?' He leaned on the gate, practised eyes raking across the remnants of our former lawn as he shook his head at its poor condition.

Richard was the man's name; he was in his mid-thirties. He wore jeans, boots, a fleece with his catchy logo stitched across the back and a blue woolly hat that had been battered by the weather.

I explained the Chester story and he gave me the same look the woman had in the post-office queue – one of disbelief.

He quoted me a price. I wasn't used to negotiating, that was Darren's forte, but it sounded reasonable to me, so I just agreed the price as I needed it done a.s.a.p. Then Richard came up with a brilliant idea that saved the day.

'I've got a field about fifteen minutes from here if you want to keep your pig there while I get this done,' he offered.

'How much?'

Richard and I came to a happy agreement. Chester would only need to be there for a couple of weeks, while we fixed up the house and moved. A field sounded suitably pig-friendly and I knew how important it was to reassure Sam that Chester would be safe in his temporary home.

I also needed to work out how to move Chester. It wasn't going to be easy – in just a year he'd grown from a micro to a full-size pig, weighing in at 15 stone. But Richard was able to solve that problem too.

'We'll put him in the back of my van.' Richard pointed to his white Transit parked in our yard.

I had a bad feeling about that: driving down the twisting country lanes with a loose pig in the back of a van could be rather dangerous, especially as Chester would struggle to keep his balance. But I didn't have any alternatives so I agreed we should try it the following day.

That evening, I did my best to explain to Sam why Chester needed to move temporarily. Darren and I had laid the foundations for the big house move by showing Sam pictures of our new house, and telling him what his bedroom would look like and how we had chosen his room for him because it would overlook Chester's new home. We had already designed the latter: an escape-proof pen for a pig, not a dog. Naturally, Chester had played a key part in us deciding which house to go for.

Will joined us on Sam's bed as I drew pictures of Richard's field, telling Sam that Chester would be staying there until it was time for us all to be reunited in the new house. I'd done my research – the field in question was a circular one high up on the hillside overlooking Ugborough Beacon. There were only half a dozen such fields dotted around Dartmoor. Richard's was one of the few remaining that hadn't yet been excavated by archaeologists.

'And we are going to put Chester's Wendy house here.' I drew a big X to mark the spot. I wouldn't have dreamt of moving Chester without his house – he needed somewhere snug to hide at night when we wouldn't be there.

Sam's eyes suddenly turned big and watery.

'What about the foxes?' He whimpered at the thought of a wild animal attacking his best friend.

The Pig Move

Sam's acute hearing meant he could pick up on all the nocturnal sounds that you or I would miss. There had been many mornings when Sam had come into my bedroom and described all the different animals 'talking' at the bottom of our garden. The noises the foxes had made must have worried Sam.

'No, honey, the foxes won't get to Chester because he'll be safe in his Wendy house.' I put my arms around the boys and pulled them close for a cuddle, planting a dozen kisses on both their foreheads. 'We will check on Chester every day on the way home from school,' I promised them.

Sam took the reassurance well; much better than he would have done a year previously. There had been so many wonderful changes in my boy. Not only was his vocabulary really coming along – now he'd just turned seven he was stringing more words together in succession – but he had also recently been integrated into three mainstream classes outside of the CAIRB: art, PE and music.

But while Sam took the news well, his fears for Chester had affected me more than I'd realised. That evening I had a bad night's sleep dreaming about the foxes and pondering how we were going to move Chester safely.

The next morning, Richard reassured me that it would be a piece of cake.

'We just need to get him up the ramp and into here,' he said as he opened up the double doors at the back of his van. You could tell by looking inside that he was a gardener – it was plastered with mud and dirt. But there also wasn't that much room for a full-size pig; I wondered if he had any idea just how big Chester was. I didn't say anything about it just yet. I thought I would leave that surprise for when I opened the gate.

'Chester! Here, boy!' I shouted out his name. Chesty shot across the mud as fast as a bullet. He was so excited to have attention that he lifted himself up on to his hind legs, using the gate for leverage.

'Bloody hell!' Richard spluttered, taking a step back.

I guess to an outsider Chester could look quite intimidating – to me, though, no matter how large he got, he would always just be our little micro pig.

'He's harmless,' I said protectively. 'Just a little stubborn at times.'

I could tell Chester was being protective of me too as he gave Richard a good old sniff. I have to admit, it warmed my heart to see him behave in that way – just as we had all grown to love Chester, he'd grown to love all of us.

Even Darren at times too, I was sure.

We decided to tie a rope around Chester's neck and lead him up the ramp and into the back of Richard's van. Chester didn't mind the rope, in fact he wagged his tail at that part, but as soon as Richard started tugging, Chester literally dug his trotters in. He would not budge. He was squealing and oinking and telling us in no uncertain terms to leave him where he was. I couldn't even persuade him with pignuts.

Then I had an idea. 'What about sticking a sack over his head, like they do with horses to get them in a box?' I suggested.

To try that, we needed to lock Chester in his Wendy house first so he wouldn't run off anywhere while we sorted out the sack. That part I could do without too much trouble. While Richard located a handy sack, I escorted Chester to his house and then carefully threaded the rope that was still around his neck through the window, so I could hold him in place from the outside – now it was my turn to dig my heels in. The plan was for Richard to open the front door of Chester's house and put the sack over his head, while I held Chester steady.

Richard was braced like a rugby player about to dive into a tackle as we counted down: 'Three, two, one!'

But the second Richard opened the door, Chester charged out, almost knocking the gardener face down into the mud as he went. Chester knew what we were trying to do and he didn't want any part in it.

The rope burned through my hands and trailed off behind Chester into the mud. *Oh, Chester*, I thought. If only he knew we were doing this for his own good, to take him somewhere safe while we returfed the lawn.

By now, two hours had passed. I was so stuck for ideas that I even turned to Facebook for help.

'How does one get a 15-stone pig into the back of a Ford Transit van?' I posted on my page.

I should have expected the sort of answers I received, such as, 'Open the door for him.'

Great advice. As the hours crept past and Richard and I gave up on the idea of leading our recalcitrant pig into the van, I could see no alternative but to ring the vet. It pained me to say the words: 'Could you please sedate my pig?'

The vet asked where I wanted to take him. I explained about the field being fifteen minutes away. But the vet told me he was unable to help; I think because it was such a short journey and Chester would need another dose of drugs to wake him up when we got to the field, the sedation was too dangerous. I can't recall the exact details now but the short answer was, 'No.'

It was at moments like this that I wished there wasn't a

time zone and thousands of miles between Darren and me because I knew he would have been able to calm me down and think of a solution. Luckily, the vet came up trumps.

'I do have another idea,' he told me on the phone.

He said he knew a local pig farmer who was retired but might be able to come up with a solution for transporting Chester. It gave me a glimmer of hope.

It turned out that the farmer lived very close to our barn. He had handled pigs for twenty years before he switched to lambing. He drove into our yard in his big red tractor the very next day, shortly after I'd picked the boys up from school. He took one look at Chester and wasn't the least bit fazed by his size or bolshiness.

'This is easy,' he said, unpacking a stack of wood better known in farming language as 'pig boards'. He slotted them together, building a walkway directly from Chester's Wendy house into the rectangular metal container hooked on the back of his tractor. The walkway was like a giant rat run. I sprinkled a trail of pignuts along it just in case Chester needed some encouragement.

Sam and Will helped me count down this time.

'Three, two, one . . .'

I opened the Wendy house door and once more Chester shot out. He ran all the way into the metal box, which had a door you could open, close and lock shut. The whole thing was over in minutes.

'Oh, thank God.' I breathed a sigh of relief as the farmer locked Chester in. I'd thought we were never going to be able to transport him. I felt like doing a victory dance – but we still had to get Chester and his Wendy house to the field safely.

I'll never forget the sight of Chester's half-chewed Wendy

house being spiked on to the front of the tractor (the farmer used the two huge spikes normally used for picking up hay bales to scoop up Chester's house), while Chester sat in the metal box attached to the back, his cheeky orange face peeping over the top. Sam was insistent that we drive behind the tractor so we could keep a watchful eye on Chester. I gave the farmer directions to the field and off we all went.

How ridiculous we must have looked, driving in convoy up and down the country lanes with a battered Wendy house wobbling along on the front of the tractor, straw flying from the holes where its windows used to be, and a big ginger pig suspended in a metal box at the back. Chester looked the picture of happiness, though. He was sitting on his haunches, grinning from ear to ear, the wind sweeping through the ginger tufts of fur on the top of his head. His head was in fact the only bit of him we could see, just poking over the side of the box: his big, ginger head and his smiley face.

I looked in the rear-view mirror and saw that Sam was laughing, real belly laughs, at the ridiculousness of his pig. Sam's happiness was contagious, and pretty soon all three of us were in fits of laughter.

At the top of the hill Richard was waiting to let us into his field. The Wendy house was lowered to the ground and put into position. The sight of Chester's battered house plonked in the middle of a huge circular field that overlooked half of Devon was so incongruous I couldn't help but laugh.

'Aren't you a lucky pig, Chesty!' I exclaimed as the farmer let our happy-go-lucky pig out of the metal box.

I expected Chester to run around as soon as he was out, relishing the fact he had a whole field of grass he could turf up; the field was covered in the stuff, some of it waist-high.

But no: he casually strolled around, sniffing the air, and then headed into his house for a snooze. The boys followed him into the Wendy house to check he was tucked up in bed, and gave him a kiss goodnight.

'How much do I owe you?' I asked the farmer who had saved our bacon.

He was such a lovely man that at first he said we owed him nothing, and even after much cajoling by me said just something to cover his petrol costs.

I handed him five times that amount, as I really wouldn't have known what to do if he hadn't come to the rescue.

'Bye, Chester!' We all waved from the gate.

It felt strange driving off and leaving him there. I hoped he would be OK all alone in that huge field and that no harm would come to him. I couldn't explain why, but I just had this niggling feeling that something awful was about to happen.

CHAPTER NINETEEN

Poorly Pig

AN EAR-PIERCING SCREAM CUT RIGHT THROUGH ME. I DIDN'T have to see Chester to know he was in trouble.

'Hang on, I'm coming!' I shouted as I bounded out of the Land Rover towards the field. He'd only been in his new home for a few days but it seemed we had already hit a crisis. Luckily I'd just dropped the boys off at school before coming to check on Chester, so they weren't around to hear his cries.

As I ran full pelt into the field I saw what the trouble was at once. Chester's mouth was hooked on some barbed wire. The poor thing had somehow managed to get it trapped between his bottom front two teeth. He was screaming and wriggling, caught on the fence, desperately trying to set himself free.

I didn't know how long he'd been suffering for – possibly all night. I didn't know if the barbs had cut through his tongue. I didn't know what to do.

I tried pulling the wire free – but Chester was so agitated that he fought back. Every time I tugged, he pulled backwards, the wire becoming even more embedded between his teeth with every movement he made. It was simply awful to see him so distressed.

'Come on, Chester.' I tried to get him to move forward to loosen the wire, as his backwards motion was pulling it taut, but he was tugging too much in the opposite direction and all the time the wire was slicing deeper. I didn't have anything to hand with which I could cut him free. I had no choice but to get behind Chester and push his rump forward to create some slack.

I squatted into a scrum position and bulldozed with all my might. Chester screamed, trampling further backwards, knocking me to the ground. I felt helpless, the two of us all alone in the field, and me unable to cut him free.

But I couldn't give up. I had to save Chester.

I tried pushing him again, and again, and forty minutes later I was still pushing. Every muscle in my body was burning under his 15-stone weight.

'Come on, Chester!' I shouted for the umpteenth time.

Suddenly, he lurched forward and I grabbed the loosening wire. I tugged, he pulled, and somehow, between us, it became dislodged from his mouth. I fell backwards into the grass, exhausted.

I looked over at Chester – to see him bouncing in the air: he was literally jumping for joy. He rushed over to me and smothered my face in pig kisses. His oinking was deeper and more breathless than usual, like he couldn't thank me enough for helping him.

I lay like a starfish in the middle of the huge field, staring up at Chester's big orange face. I gently stroked the fur on his cheeks, telling him how happy I was that he was OK.

The whole incident really shook me up, though. It was the first time I'd had a real scare about Chester. It made me realise how vulnerable our enormous pig actually was and that I would have to keep a closer eye on him. It made me realise just how much I loved him.

'What if something happens to him again and I'm not there?' I asked Darren when I called him later that day.

'He'll be fine; he's as tough as anything.'

Rational as ever, Darren reminded me that Chester would only be in the field for one or two weeks. We would soon have him back under our watchful eyes again and everything would be fine.

Unfortunately, things didn't go quite according to plan.

A few days later, we found out that there were some problems with the sale of my house in Spain. The paperwork needed to be redone – and it would take time. Chester was going to have to remain where he was for months rather than weeks.

This news meant that I wasn't now just anxious about Chester, but about Sam too. How was I going to break this news to him? A couple of months didn't seem like a lot in the grand scheme of things, but it could tip the balance in terms of Sam's progress. I had told him that he and Chester would only be apart for a few weeks. How would he cope not only with the change of plan, but with not having Chester around all the time?

Darren gave me another pep talk. He told me Chester was happy because he had a big field to roam around in and Sam would rise up to the challenge rather than melt down. And Darren was right. Sam more than coped with the long-distance relationship – he actually flourished with the additional responsibilities that Chester's new location brought. For he was determined to carry on caring for his pig.

Sam took great pride in lifting the straw bales over the fence; he delighted in carting the bags of pignuts and buckets of water through the field to Chester's house. All this physical work had a positive effect on Sam's strength, too – every time he heaved, lifted, carried and climbed, he was working out his upper body and arm muscles, helping him build strength in those particular areas.

Lynda Russell was quick to remark on the changes. She noted how much more energy Sam had at school. Typically, he would have been slumped in his chair by the end of the day because he was so tired from holding himself up. But in just a few weeks Sam had gone from lethargic to full of beans.

His caretaking responsibilities had also given him another surge of confidence. He was talking even more about Chester at school, proudly telling the other children on the CAIRB about Chester's new home and how he had to look after him.

As the spring days changed into the summer of 2010, I now looked forward to our early-morning rises. Not only were our pre-school visits to Chester precious bonding time with the boys for me, but it was also a magical time in the countryside. Chester's field was an oasis of calm away from the rest of the world. The musical chatter of the birds, the dew on the cobwebs, the smell of the wild flowers and grass – it was divine. On a clear day you could see for miles below.

In those moments, it felt like we were the only people on the planet: me, Sam, Will and, of course, Chester.

Every morning without fail, Chester would belt towards the gate to greet us. His tail would be wagging and his nose twitching as he got a whiff of Sam's bag of pignuts.

'We'll bring him some apples on the way back from school,' I told the boys one morning as I leant on the gate, breathing in the fresh country air. Sam flapped with excitement at the thought of treating Chester.

We all climbed back into the Land Rover, and I dropped the boys off at school as usual. I had a lot to get on with that morning: I had to speak to my lawyer in Spain about finalising the deal on the house, I had to organise a removal van to move our things from the rented barn to our new house, plus there were still some outstanding bits of damage to fix in the barn.

The day was going really well until Richard, the gardener who'd returfed our lawn and owned the field that Chester was staying in, called me partway through the afternoon.

'There's something not right with your pig,' he announced.

'What do you mean?' Chester had seemed fine that morning.

Richard, who lived only a few hundred metres from the field, said he'd just stuck his head over the gate and seen Chester lying motionless in his Wendy house.

'He was probably just snoozing,' I said. Our pig did that a lot, so I dismissed Richard's worry at first.

'No, Jo, he couldn't get up, something is wrong with him,' he said gravely.

I fell silent. I could hear Richard breathing on the other end of the line, waiting for me to say something. But I didn't know what to say. I imagined Chester lying helplessly in his home. Maybe a fox had attacked him and left him for dead? Had he somehow hurt himself? My mind was conjuring up all sorts of dreadful images. I suddenly felt sick with anxiety.

'I'm on my way.' I hung up and raced to the car.

I didn't want to take the boys to see Chester without finding out what was wrong with him first, but I didn't have any choice. They needed collecting from school. I picked the boys up and then headed straight to the field. I forced myself to take some deep breaths, as I didn't want to alarm Will and Sam.

'Mummy, did you get apples for Chester?' was the first thing Will asked as we drove, a little faster than usual, towards Chester's field.

Damn. In my panic I'd forgotten to swing past the shop to pick them up. I looked in the rear-view mirror – Sam looked upset at the news he wouldn't be able to treat his friend, as had been timetabled in his ordered day.

'We'll feed him apples and carrots next time, I promise,' I said, in an attempt to salvage the situation. Thankfully, it worked. I checked again in the mirror and Sam was now smiling at the thought of bringing Chester extra treats.

I weighed up in my mind whether I should warn the boys about Chester. Sam couldn't handle surprises at the best of times, let alone the news that his best friend might not be well. I decided that I had to bite the bullet.

'Listen to me, Sam and Will, Chester might not be feeling very well, so we need to check if he's OK,' I said carefully.

As I spoke, I was glancing in the rear-view mirror, waiting for Sam to explode. But he didn't. In fact, Sam stayed perfectly calm. As we pulled off the lane and on to the grassy verge by the field, Sam grabbed the bag of pignuts, ready to carry out his usual duties. If I hadn't been so worried about what state we'd find Chester in I would have praised Sam for how well he'd taken the news. My boy was learning how to deal with stressful situations.

Will and Sam raced ahead of me to the gate. Sam's face dropped.

'Where's Chester?' he asked. He looked so disappointed that his pig was not there to greet him as usual, especially as he had a bag full of food for him.

'Chester!' he called out, his voice echoing across the valley.

We all waited by the gate for Chester to show his smiley face.

'Here, Chester!' Sam shouted again.

Nothing. I felt very uneasy.

'Chester!' we all called out together, our voices breaking the peaceful country silence.

Still nothing in response.

I felt a shudder run down my spine. Richard was right: something was seriously wrong. It was so unlike Chester not to greet us.

We all climbed over the fence and waded through the long grass and nettles towards Chester's Wendy house. As we drew closer we could see his back trotters poking out through the door. Then we heard a noise – it was loud, rasping breathing, like an old man's dying breaths.

Something was terribly wrong.

Sam squeezed inside the Wendy house while Will and I peered through the windows. Chester was lying on his side, groaning with pain. Every small breath seemed like a gigantic struggle. Tears started to collect in Sam's eyes as he lay on the straw beside his friend and started to stroke his belly gently.

'It's going to be OK,' I said to the boys. I was lying to myself as much as them. I couldn't bear the thought that there could be something seriously wrong with Chester. Will and I squeezed inside the Wendy house too and we all huddled around our pig on our hands and knees in the straw, as if we were crowding around a hospital bed.

'Chester, what's wrong?' I asked our pig. Silly, really, as he couldn't answer, but at that moment I felt like I was addressing a person – he was one of the family, after all.

He grunted.

'Oh, Chester!' We were all stroking his belly now.

He gave another heaving grunt. I had no idea what was

wrong with him; I just knew I needed to get help immediately. I reached for my mobile phone. Thank goodness I had mobile reception at the top of the hill.

I didn't know if I needed a vet who specialised in farm animals or if one who dealt with cats and dogs would do; pigs in general don't need veterinary care so I'd never had to call one to attend to Chester before. I phoned the local practice and prayed that, if they couldn't help, then they would at least be able to point me in the right direction. The receptionist said she would send a vet up right away.

'Can I have your address?' she asked.

I looked around at the big open expanse before me and wondered how I could describe where I was. Somehow I managed to cobble together a description of lanes, crossroads and features along the way.

'How long do you think they will be?' I asked, anxiously looking back at Chester.

It was going to be about an hour before they could get anyone to me. We were going to have to sit tight and hope that Chester's condition didn't deteriorate. The minutes dragged by. Sam didn't leave Chester's side once; he kept stroking his tummy, doing his best to ease his friend's pain. Despite being in terrible agony, Chester clearly appreciated being soothed by Sam. With every gentle stroke and soft murmur Sam made, Chester grunted back his appreciation. It was a beautiful thing to watch.

I don't know how the vet managed to find us but he suddenly appeared at the gate carrying a bulging leather bag full of equipment. He looked like a typical country vet in his corduroy trousers and checked shirt as he threaded his way through the grass and flowers towards us.

We all held our breath as he examined Chester. Sam watched the vet's facial expressions carefully, searching for an answer, perhaps mentally flicking through Lynda's 'emotions' book as he tried to decipher what the vet's frowns meant. The vet checked Chester's tummy, gently pressing on different areas. Our poorly pig let out a groan of pain as he felt the vet's fingers push on one particular area. The vet looked worried and turned to us for help.

'We've got to get him on his feet,' he said, without any explanation as to what was wrong yet.

'Come on, boys.' I rallied Sam and Will to help.

Chester's belly was so long we all managed to fit our arms underneath him. I took the front, the vet held Chester underneath his back legs, and the boys hooked their arms underneath the fattest part of his belly.

'One, two, three!' We hoisted him on to his trotters. Chester squealed in pain, poor thing. We managed to get him standing for a few moments before he fell back on to the straw, groaning.

'This isn't good, is it?' I asked nervously, half of me not wanting to know the answer. The vet rooted around in his leather bag and pulled out a needle and a vial of clear liquid.

'Just going to give him some painkillers,' he explained. I held Sam and Will's hands as he stuck the needle into Chester's neck. A trickle of blood ran down his dusty skin and on to the straw. The sight of his blood suddenly compounded the seriousness of the situation.

The vet flashed me a look as if to confirm how serious it really was. I gestured for him not to mention anything in front of the boys and to follow me out of the Wendy house so we could talk outside. The vet dusted the straw from his knees and clambered out into the sunshine. My heart was thudding in my chest as I waited for him to deliver the verdict.

'He has an obstruction,' the vet whispered.

'What? How could that be?'

'He's eaten something he shouldn't have and it's blocked his intestines.'

'But all we've been feeding him is pignuts,' I said, confused by this news.

I started to worry that we had put him in a field with some poisonous plant or flower, but the vet reassured me that the blockage wasn't caused by something he'd eaten in the wild. It would have been caused by him eating something processed, like bread.

I was thrown. I just couldn't think how that would have happened. I didn't have time to think about it further, though. I needed to find out what I could do to help Chester. 'So, how do we get rid of the blockage?'

The vet went very quiet and shook his head.

'If we can get him walking, we might be able to get the blockage to shift. But it's by no means certain. And,' he hesitated, clearly not wanting to go on. I gestured to him to do so and he jutted out his chin as he continued bluntly. 'Blockages can be fatal for pigs. I can give him some painkillers but I don't think he will last the night.'

My mouth fell open, but no words would come.

As I absorbed the enormity of what was happening I glanced back at the Wendy house, at my boys stroking Chester. Chester wasn't just a pet. He was like a person. He was one of us.

I started to panic. I couldn't imagine how Sam would take

this news. 'Oh my God, how am I going to tell my son, who has autism, that his pig is going to die?' I blurted out to the vet.

'How can you tell *any* child their pet is about to die?' he countered.

His words made me realise that I was always going out of my way to protect the more vulnerable of my children. He was right, though: Chester was just as much Will's pig as Sam's. If Chester died, we would *all* be grief-stricken.

It was at that moment that I decided we were *not* going to let Chester die. I was determined to save our pig. The vet had said if we could get him walking there was a chance we could shift the blockage. Walking it was!

I started marching back towards the Wendy house with the same determination that took me over whenever I had a battle to fight. I'd battled to protect my son and give him the best possible life, and now I was going to fight to save Chester.

'Come on, boys, we've got to get Chester on to his feet,' I directed. We all leapt into action.

It must have looked like the most absurd sight, the four of us with our arms around this giant pig as we tried to heave him up. I think we were grunting and groaning under the weight just as much as Chester was groaning from the pain! But it was worth all the effort: Chester eventually got to his feet and staggered out of the Wendy house with all the grace of someone who has had a little too much to drink.

I knew if there was something Chester couldn't resist it was chasing the boys, so I turned to my children and told them to run. Sam bolted across the field with his brother in tow. And Chester immediately started to follow them. He only managed a few steps before he collapsed – but at least we'd got him moving. And then, in a sign of just how poorly he was, even the draw of playing with his Sam wasn't enough and he staggered back into his home and lay down on the straw, grunting.

But I wasn't done yet.

'Again, again!' I beckoned the boys back to the Wendy house.

The vet commended my determination. He could see I wasn't going to give up on Chester so he handed me a huge syringe and a bottle of liquid paraffin, explaining there was only a small chance it could help, but it was worth me trying it.

'Inject a shot of this down his throat twice a day and feed him anything that might get his bowels moving, like fruit,' he said. 'I can't make any promises. I hope it helps.'

I thanked him for everything he had done and then returned to Chester's side. The boys and I sat next to our poorly pig for as long as we could, getting him up on his feet as much as he could manage. Too soon, it grew too late for the children to stay with him any longer. The boys gave him a kiss on his furry face and told Chester how much they loved him.

He grunted back. It was his way of saying thank you.

The drive home seemed to take much longer than usual. The boys were trying to be brave but I caught their tears in the rear-view mirror.

'We've got to make him better. We have to do everything we can,' I said. I was trying to sound authoritative but my voice was quivering with sadness as I spoke.

I knew the family would want to know about Chester's illness. It was too early to call Darren with the time difference between us, but I phoned my mum as soon as we got home. She was devastated to hear the news about Chester. Even though he had driven her up the wall with his banging on her door, she still loved him to bits, as did we all. She came straight round to the barn to comfort Will and Sam and to cook up some apple sauce for Chester.

'This should help get him moving,' she said, stirring the big pot of peeled apples and water on the stove.

Poor Sam and Will couldn't stop crying that evening. I didn't know how to console them, other than by promising we would do everything in our power to make Chester well again. After cooking the apples, Mum helped me put the boys to bed but Sam didn't want to be alone. He was glued to my side. Wherever I went, he followed. I tried tucking him into bed but a few minutes later I heard a tap at my bedroom door.

'Mummy, I can't sleep,' he said, clutching his Ben 10 figurine in his hand.

I knew Sam was at his most distressed when he wanted to climb into my bed.

'Come here.' I patted the duvet.

I wrapped my arms around Sam and smothered him in little kisses, just as Chester would have done if he was well. I did what every mum does and promised my child everything was going to be OK.

'Chester will be fine,' I whispered, stroking his hair.

Sam eventually nodded off to sleep but I lay awake for much of the night. I couldn't sleep with Chester's – and Sam's – fate hanging in the balance. What would happen if we lost our pig? He was a lifeline for Sam; without him, how would my boy cope? He'd come so far, I couldn't bear to see him regress all over again. I wasn't sure if *I* could go through it all again. Eventually, in the small hours, my eyes lidded shut but I tossed and turned all night.

I woke up the next morning feeling like I'd been hit by a bus – I was so drained of energy. Thankfully Sam looked a lot calmer for spending the night in my bed. Will came bounding into my room as I was rubbing the sleep from my eyes.

'Are we going to see Chester now?' he asked anxiously.

I'd prepared my answer.

'We can see Chester this afternoon,' I told them.

The vet had said it was unlikely Chester would survive the night so there was no way I was going to risk the boys finding him dead. My mum was going to come with me to see him that morning instead.

I dropped Sam and Will at school and then Mum and I made our way to the field. We were armed with a Tupperware box full of stewed apples and the liquid paraffin that the vet had told me to inject into Chester's throat to soften his stools. I climbed out of the driver's seat and braced myself for the worst.

The hundred yards from the gate to the Wendy house was the longest walk of my life. Every footstep was weighed down with dread.

Please don't let him be dead, please don't, I prayed as we shuffled through the long grass.

As we neared the house, I could see Chester's trotters protruding from the door. He hadn't moved a centimetre since we'd left him the night before.

'Chester!' I called, willing him to let out his familiar grunt.

Nothing.

Oh God, no. I was certain he was dead.

But then, as we got closer to the trotters, from inside the Wendy house came a deep, breathless grunt. It was Chester – he was telling us that he was still with us.

'Oh Chester!' Mum and I cried in unison. We squeezed into Chester's den and gave him an enormous cuddle. He grunted weakly with a greeting and tried to lift his head to give us a kiss, but he was too sick.

'Just rest yourself, you poor sausage.' Mum stroked his sore belly.

There was no easy way to get around what we had to do next – we needed to prise open Chester's mouth to stuff all the goodness of the stewed apples and liquid paraffin inside him. He was too poorly to put up a fight; it was sad seeing our stubborn pig so lacklustre. I injected the paraffin and then Mum scooped up a handful of apple sauce and shovelled it down his throat. She literally used her hands to do this – it was the only way we could get the fruit inside him. We took turns to scoop up a handful of the apple sauce, and then each of us, one at a time, would put our upright hand inside Chester's mouth. We'd then turn it over, wiping the sauce off the palm of our hand by using his tongue. It was quite a tricky exercise because he was still lying on his side, and pretty disgusting, but we were so desperate to save him that we persevered.

Chester didn't like being force-fed one bit. 'It's for your own good,' we told him gently. We then tried to get him on to his feet. Poor Mum wasn't used to lifting such great weights. I told her to stop before she put her back out but she insisted on helping Chester.

There was a lot of groaning and grunting from all of us as

we levered him up and led him towards the door. Chester took a few steps forward, stopped, and then a few more. He managed to get half of his body out of his house and into the June sunshine. But after that huge effort, he was ready to collapse. We jumped out of the way as he came crashing down on to the straw.

I didn't like leaving him, but I felt a little less anxious than the day before. At least there were things we were doing to help him: administering the fruit and paraffin; making sure he got up on his feet at least a couple of times. The most promising thing was that he'd made it through the first night. If we could just get him moving, he might be OK. I gave the vet another call to give him an update on the patient's condition.

He asked me if we could observe Chester's toilet habits to see if he passed whatever had been obstructing him. In other words, the vet was politely asking me to wait for Chester to do a poo. *Lovely.*

That's one for the boys, I thought.

Our focus on getting Chester better brought us together as a family – we found strength in working as a team. Every morning, Sam took up his post by the stove in our kitchen; I found him a stepladder so he could reach the pan with his wooden spoon to stir the apples into a warm mush, mixing up Chester's 'medicine'. Will's job, once we got to Chester's field, was to keep his water bowl topped up and help with changing the straw.

Even though Darren was off on the rigs he also got involved, giving me a pep talk whenever I became sad about the possibility of Chester leaving us. If Darren thought I was being wet, he didn't show it. He just listened and tried to make me laugh by reminding me we were on 'poo watch'.

By day three, Chester was able to leave his house, though there was still no 'breakthrough' in his bowel movements. He wheezed hard as he tried to keep up with the boys. Sam and Will would stop and start in their chasing game, just as they had done around the apple tree all those months ago when Chester was a micro piglet. Their teasing was too much for Chester to resist joining in. Despite being so unwell, he found the strength to follow them along the path.

By day four, Chester could make it halfway across the field. As he and the boys gambolled in the distance, I funnelled my hands around my mouth and shouted from the Wendy house: 'Any poo?'

The boys shook their heads with dismay.

'No poo!' they shouted back.

We had to keep going with our mission: every morning and afternoon we had to get Chester on his feet until 'it' happened.

It was important to maintain the laughter because I knew there was something brewing with Sam. Even though he was putting on a brave face by helping look after Chester, I knew he was hurting inside. Every night Sam would climb into bed with me.

I don't think he really understood what death was, but he could sense things were serious. His uncharacteristic ability to feel empathy was now proving a mixed blessing. Part of me wished Sam wasn't empathic, because that way he wouldn't feel the pain if Chester didn't make it. I wanted to do everything in my power to shield my sons from hurt.

By now we were visiting Chester three times a day – I was making an extra trip up the hillside at lunchtime with my mum. Though it was possible Chester could have pooed without us being there, we never saw any sign of his stools and by day five Chester's tummy was enormous. It was like a balloon, ready to explode. He was wheezing like an old man as he huffed and puffed his way after the boys that afternoon. He managed to reach them and then, all of a sudden, he stopped in his tracks.

At that same moment, a cold breeze sailed down the hillside, sending a chill all the way down my spine. I had a feeling something terrible was about to happen.

'Come back!' I gestured to the boys to retreat to the Wendy house.

Sam and Will started bounding towards me, expecting Chester to be on their heels, but he was far behind. In fact, he hadn't moved a trotter since he'd stopped stock still. His head was hung low; his body was leaning to one side, as if ready to topple at any moment. The boys raced back to him, ready to catch him if need be. Chester then let out a long, low grunt – it was so loud and tortured I was certain it was his final breath.

'Hurry!' I screamed to the boys to reach Chester in time to stop him from keeling over.

But Chester wasn't dying – he was finally getting rid of his blockage.

'He's done a poo, he's done a poo!' the boys cheered, jumping in the air with joy.

I didn't think I'd ever been so happy to hear those words! I did a little celebratory dance and then I pulled my mobile out of my pocket and called Mum.

'Chester's done a poo!' was the first thing I said.

'Oh, thank God!' Mum breathed a sigh of relief. She understood that this meant Chester was going to live.

The passing of the blockage really had made Chester lighter on his feet. Almost at once, he rocketed through the long grass and flowers after the boys. Sam opened his arms wide and pretended to be a plane soaring through the sky. Chester squealed with delight as he gathered speed and the boys giggled with happiness as he gained on them. It could have been a scene from *Heidi* with the flowers and the sunshine and the bright blue sky.

But Chester's trotters were going too fast for his body . . . and he took off tumbling down the hill. I couldn't help letting out a scream as I saw him fall – an accident was the last thing he needed having only just recovered from a near-fatal blockage. Chester was perfectly fine, though. He staggered back on to his feet and chased Will and Sam all the way into his Wendy house.

As Sam and Will huddled around Chester, petting him fondly, I felt immensely proud. Our pig wouldn't have pulled through if it hadn't been for my boys – it was thanks to Sam getting up that little bit earlier every morning to stew apples, and thanks to both my sons for getting him back on his feet, that Chester was restored to health. Their love had given him back his life.

You could tell Chester was grateful to them by the way he wagged his tail and from his excited, breathless oinking. He also refused to leave Sam's side – if Sam stood still for even a moment, Chester would take the chance to lean his giant body against Sam's legs. 'Stop it, Chester,' Sam would say, giggling under the weight, although he didn't really want Chester to stop squashing him as he loved being smothered with his affection.

Becoming receptive to affection was something that had

changed in Sam since he had known Chester. The unconditional love Chester showed Sam had made him receptive to receiving love. The sad little boy who had wanted to be alone seemed to be long gone.

The scare with the barbed wire and then the blockage had made me realise that all that mattered now was bringing Chester home. Especially as I wasn't sure how he had come to eat a foodstuff that had bunged up his system so catastrophically. That was still an unsolved mystery and the sooner he was back home with us the better.

Darren was relieved to hear the good news when I spoke to him later that night.

Even though he liked to joke about how Chester was the most expensive pig in Devon, and that he could do without spending any more money on him, he admitted he'd had some sleepless nights as he too worried about Chester's survival.

'Why didn't you say?' I asked him. I was a person who wore my heart on my sleeve but Darren hadn't breathed a word about his concerns. He reminded me that he worked on an oil rig with macho men, so losing sleep over a pig wasn't really the thing to do! I burst out laughing and the stress of the past week felt as if it was receding as Darren and I both chuckled together on the phone.

The next day, I went to visit Chester by myself at lunchtime. I felt it was important for me to have a moment alone with him – I wanted to say thank you to him for helping my son. Nearly losing Chester had made me realise how precious he was. I didn't tell him how grateful I was enough and now the scare was over I wanted to take every chance I could to show him how very much he was appreciated.

I didn't panic when he wasn't at the gate to greet me – I thought he'd be in his Wendy house, probably still recovering from having a sore belly.

When he wasn't in his bed, I *did* start to panic.

'Chester, Chester!' I shouted across the huge field. The grass was waist-high in parts, so there was no way I could spot him easily.

It was then that I heard the noise. It wasn't the terrible rasping sound he'd made a week ago. It was deeper and slower, very much like . . .

SNORING!

I moved closer to the whistling grunts.

There he was, hidden in a patch of purple flowers. Chester was on his side, his big belly angled skywards to catch the sun. His mouth was slightly open, allowing the air to whistle as it passed in and out through his snout.

'Oh Chesty,' I sighed affectionately.

Chester always knew how to make himself comfortable. I thought back to all the times he'd taken over our living room. At times his size had been a massive inconvenience, but we were leaving all that behind now. Nearly losing Chester had made me realise what was important: bringing our pet pig home was all that mattered now. And, in good news for us all, our new house was ready and waiting for us at long last.

Home sweet home.

CHAPTER TWENTY

Home Sweet Home

FOR MOST PEOPLE, UNPACKING EVERYTHING IN THEIR NEW house would be a priority. But for us, making sure Chester was comfortable in his new home came first. We'd nearly lost him, and all we cared about now was bringing him back to be with us. Aside from our love and concern for Chester, it was crucial for Sam's wellbeing that we had our pig safely back in our care.

As timing would have it, the move fell during one of Darren's stints at home, but he had only five days before he had to be back on the rigs. We were all going to have to work at the speed of light again, packing, unpacking and, most importantly, making a pen for Chester.

It was 24 June 2010 when we followed the removal van through the country lanes to our new home, which was situated at the head of a coombe on the edge of Dartmoor National Park. It was everything I'd dreamed of when I'd planned our escape from Spain, with old cob walls, wooden beams, oak floorboards and a big open fireplace in the living room.

Built in 1610, the house was steeped in history and had once belonged to Lord Churchston's gamekeeper. The previous owners, who had lived there for forty-five years, had painted the outside pink, in keeping with how the cottage would have looked in the seventeenth century, when the locals used to mix the paint with the red Devon soil. Inside, the former owners had done little in the way of renovations, keeping the character of the place intact; the animal barn had been turned into a kitchen, but that was about all they had changed. When I stood in the living room and closed my eyes, I could imagine all the pheasants and venison hanging from the beams in front of the inglenook, as they must have done all those hundreds of years ago when it was a game-keeper's home.

Gorgeous as the house was, the garden was the main reason I'd fallen in love with the property. Spread out over half an acre, it was a haven of colours and sounds. There was a brook that meandered its way along the bottom – you could hear the sound of the water rushing over the pebbles from our bedrooms. There were apple and plum trees, a raspberry patch, a greenhouse ... and the previous owners had loved exotic flowers so, if you walked into the wooded area near the brook, you would discover an oasis of the most strange and unusual-looking plants.

The garden was important for two reasons. Firstly, I wanted a safe place where Sam could escape to have some alone time. The garden provided a sensual sanctuary for him and would keep him out of harm's way if he suddenly felt an urge to bolt, as some children with autism do when they are on the cusp of a meltdown. Secondly, I wanted somewhere big enough to make a nice home for Chester, that was far enough away from our neighbours not to annoy them!

So, as soon as we had assembled our beds on moving-in day, it was off to the DIY store to buy the posts and wire to make Chester a pen.

Darren and I debated where we should put him. I wanted to build the pen in the wooded area so Chester would have loads of room to roam around, but Darren pointed out that he would inevitably dig up all the beautiful flowers there.

Then I suggested the terrace, which was by the back door.

'No way, it's too close to the house,' Darren said, reminding me of all the work he'd had to do on the doors at our previous house.

Yet I reminded him that we were going to make Chester a pen that he *wouldn't* escape from, so the doors would be safe as houses.

'He'll get out, you wait . . .' Darren warned.

'No, he won't,' I said cheerily. Nothing could puncture my high spirits.

After talking it over, we settled on the bottom right-hand corner of the garden. Chester would be far enough away not to disturb us or destroy the house, but close enough for Sam to keep an eye on him. Sam would have a bird's-eye view of Chester's pen from his bedroom window.

The next big dilemma was how we were going to make Chester's pen escape-proof. We would have to do it in an old-fashioned way, by making a fence out of posts and wire and adding a stile for us humans to climb over – so we could get in and out but Chester couldn't.

Darren called on the boys to lend a hand. It was like building the Wendy house all over again, only by now Sam's upper body strength had improved so much he could help with the lifting. I watched Sam beam with pride as he handed Darren the posts and helped Will unravel the big roll of mesh wire, and I felt a flutter of relief that he was settling in so well. We had been lucky that the previous owners had been so understanding of his autism, letting us show Sam around the property half a dozen times in the lead-up to the move.

Showing Sam what was to come had made all the difference to his welfare as he could embrace the change rather than be terrified of it. He'd even drawn a picture of our pink cottage at school with the words 'This is my new home, I will be very happy here' written underneath. He carried the drawing with him everywhere.

Sam couldn't wait to have the pen finished so we could bring Chester home from his field, where our pig was still living. Every few hours he would ask, 'Can we get Chester?'

By the fourth day, we were finally able to say yes.

Darren had worked his socks off to get the pen finished before he left for the rig. Our new home was absolute chaos inside, with boxes piled high in every direction, but our pig's new pen looked like a palace. Yet it was a small price to pay to have Chester home safely.

We called on the old pig farmer, Mr Stephens, to help us move him again.

This time we led the convoy from the field through the lanes and up and down the vales and hills. How the Wendy house remained in one piece as it rattled around on the front of the tractor was anyone's guess. Once we'd arrived at our destination, Mr Stephens used pig boards and pignuts to lead Chester into his new palatial home. As soon as Chester and his Wendy house were inside, Darren boarded up the last segment of the fencing.

Chester seemed delighted with his new pad. He rummaged his snout through the grass, taking in the new smells, checking out what grubs and worms he might be able to root up.

'I give it a week before that's a mud pit.' Darren nodded at the rectangle of lush grass and clovers on which Chester was standing, merrily sniffing away.

The wonderful thing was, it didn't matter this time because it was *our* grass to dig up.

Sam leaned on the fence, resting his chin on his arms, soaking up the summer sunshine. Seeing him there, Chester spotted an opportunity to give his friend a pig kiss. He used one of the posts to lever himself up on to his hind legs, so his head was at the same level as Sam's. He grunted as he rubbed his nose against Sam's sun-kissed skin, just as he had done when they'd first met in the pen at Pennywell Farm.

'I love you, Chester!' Sam declared.

All the hard work had been worth it. Everything was so perfect and we really thought that day marked the end of all our dramas with Chester. Our family was complete again.

We celebrated by having dinner al fresco on our patio, watching the sun set. I made a big bowl of pasta and sauce; only at the last minute did I realise I hadn't a clue where I'd stashed the cutlery. We'd been so busy building Chester's pen I hadn't looked for it yet and we hadn't needed it until now as we'd mostly been eating picnic food. There was a mountain of boxes to work through, though, so in the end I settled on our using some big plastic salad ladles. The large serving spoons weren't ideal, but they made the boys laugh – they giggled away as they tried to stop the spaghetti slipping off the huge spoons.

We could see Chester from the terrace, and he could smell us – and the food. It wouldn't have been fair to leave him out so Sam brought him a plate full of goodies, but not including the pasta as we didn't want a repeat of the blockage scare.

As the 'cherry on top' of our sweet family reunion, it was about now, maybe a day or so later, that Sam sat down to draw a picture as usual – and sketched something very special indeed. Glancing over his shoulder as I pottered about, unpacking, I saw his artwork begin to take shape. He was sketching our cottage. He drew the brook which ran along-side the lane leading up to our new house, along with the stone bridge. And then, in his picture, the brook entered our land, weaving its silvery way along the bottom of our garden. In that garden, he drew a huge apple tree with twelve red apples, lots of green grass and flowers everywhere.

But it wasn't the lush, verdant vegetation that caught my eye.

Sam drew a boy and a pig playing in the garden.

It was the first time he had ever drawn Chester voluntarily. Lynda Russell had asked him to draw Chester at school before as part of a set task, but Sam had never *chosen* to draw his special pig before. It was an incredibly joyful picture and I liked to think it was confirmation that now we'd moved into our forever home, and moved Chester over from the field, Sam felt really secure, hence this drawing to express his happiness.

I was particularly sad to wave Darren off to the rig that time. Everything seemed so perfect and I just wanted him to be with us for a while longer while we made the house our own.

'Everything will be unpacked by the time you get back,' I promised him, reminding him of what he had to look forward to.

'And Chester will have destroyed his patch of grass!' Darren told me, in turn reminding me what *I* had to look forward to.

Darren was right about the grass: it took just under a week for our greedy pig to turf it up. But at least the grass was keeping him occupied – and the pen was keeping him in.

I was in the kitchen when *it* happened. I heard a roar of

laughter, followed by a series of loud grunts. I rushed into our living room to find Chester scuttling around, having a whale of a time sticking his snout in every nook and cranny. I winced as I heard the sound of his trotters scratching our oak floor.

'Chester, *out*!' I commanded, as I tried to herd him back into the garden.

But Chester wasn't anywhere near ready to go back in his pen. He wanted to check out what was in our bins. Let me tell you, attempting to separate a 15-stone pig from food is impossible. I tried pushing him, and pulling him, but he was determined to find out if there were any scraps worth rooting out in the kitchen bin.

All the while, the boys were sniggering in the background.

'Who let him in?' I demanded, annoyed at the chaos Chester was causing.

'It was me, Mummy,' Sam confessed with a mischievous grin.

Chester had somehow escaped from his pen and Sam, spotting him running free in the garden, had opened the back door to let him in. He'd obviously missed watching Chester misbehave!

I eventually managed to shepherd Chester away from the kitchen and tried to steer him back into the garden. He was too strong and quick for me, though; he bulldozed past my legs and ran back into the living room. In the blink of an eye, he had scampered across the room and jumped on top of his favourite green sofa.

It was the most ridiculous sight – a huge pig sitting on his haunches on the couch, grinning at us, while the bottom of the sofa sank straight to the floor under his enormous weight. Thank goodness it wasn't an expensive piece of furniture!

By now, the boys were doubled over with laughter. And even I could see the funny side. It really was hard to stay angry at Chester when he looked so adorable. In a way, too, I knew he just wanted to be back in the house with us – and who could blame him for that?

I felt a pang of guilt about Chester living out in the garden and decided I'd let him sit on the sofa for a while longer. What harm could it do?

As it turned out, quite a lot. Unsurprisingly, no more than five minutes later he was causing trouble – sticking his snout in the half-unpacked boxes and turning the chairs over. I'm sure he was looking for a reaction to his antics, just like a child craving attention.

'Right that's it, *out*!' I shouted.

Sam, Will and I all filled our hands with pignuts and rattled them around in our palms, trying to lure him out of the back door. Really, the food was unnecessary: all it took was Sam running into the garden for Chester to follow.

We headed for the pen. Darren – clever as ever – had, of course, foreseen just this sort of situation so his design for the pen had included some moveable horizontal slats of wood. I just needed to pull them out to create a temporary opening. Seeing the way made clear, Sam ran full pelt into the pen and Chester followed him in, enjoying the game. Quick as a flash, I locked our pig back into his pen, popping the wood back into place. Sam climbed back out over the stile into the garden.

'There, Mummy!' Sam showed me the hole in the wire on the far side, where Chester had made his escape.

You clever pig, I thought. It was the hedgerow side of his pen, which we'd simply covered with wire, thinking the hedgerow made a natural defence. I had to hand it to him: he'd spotted the weakest link. He must have spent the past week using his snout as a lever to lift the wire when we weren't looking. It was a testament to his determination. Chester's desire to be with us was stronger than any kind of Fort Knox we could build around him.

And, to be honest, I think that's why Sam let him in the house once he had escaped. Apart from the giggle factor of having his pig running riot, Sam could empathise with Chester's need for freedom. Sam also needed space to breathe – if things became too overwhelming, he liked to run into the garden to let off steam. His new 'flap' place was a strip of grass that ran parallel to Chester's pen.

I couldn't think how I was going to block the hole Chester had made so I grabbed the first thing that came to hand – the stepladder.

This should do the trick, I thought, as I lugged it across the garden and slotted it between the hedge and the fencing. Chester twitched his ears and nose simultaneously, as if to say, 'Do you really think that will stop me getting out?'

But it was going to have to do for now – I had other things to be getting on with, such as plenty of unpacking.

Incredibly, we then had a very quiet few months. Chester didn't break out again and Sam fed off his friend's calm mood – he was equally content with his new home. So much so, I felt confident enough to say yes to Lynda Russell when she suggested taking the children from the CAIRB on a camping trip on Dartmoor in November 2010.

Lynda was always encouraging the children to step outside their comfort zone and to have the same experiences that the children in the mainstream classes enjoyed. For this trip she picked four boys who she felt would be able to cope with two nights away from home in a tent. The fact that Sam, who was then nearly eight, was chosen showed how far he had come in just two years.

Like any nervous mum waving her charge off into the world, I must have checked Sam's rucksack for essentials three times over before I dropped him off at the school car park on the morning of the trip.

'He'll be fine,' Lynda reassured me as she placed Sam's bag carefully in the boot of her car. Luckily, I trusted her implicitly.

Sam clearly did too, for he wasn't the slightest bit nervous to be heading off on his great adventure. He didn't even look back as he jumped into Lynda's car. He knew exactly what was going to happen from Lynda's storybooks and was therefore at ease: Lynda had planned the camping trip with military precision. My mind, too, was set at rest by the knowledge that, as well as Lynda, there would be two teaching assistants on the moors with the children. Sam was going to be very well cared for so I gave him a big cheery wave as the car started up and the camping party set off for the moor.

As I turned for home, I reminded myself that as well as this being a great experience for Sam, helping him to learn independence, there was another beneficiary too. Sam's absence meant I could spend some quality time with Will. Even though Sam's little brother never once complained about the attention we gave to his sibling, I knew that moments like these were a fantastic opportunity for me to spend some real one-on-one quality time with my younger son and remind him how proud I was of him and how much I loved him.

I asked Will what he would like to do that afternoon – the world was his oyster. His answer surprised me. I'd thought he might say toy shopping, or even going to Pennywell Farm (our new house was only five minutes from the farm). But he said he wanted to spend time with Chester and me. I couldn't think of a better way for all three of us to be together than by mucking out our pig's pen, and Will was really enthused by the idea.

We hopped in the car and drove to Tuckers, a nearby farm supply shop. We bought a big bale of straw and more pignuts. The bale was too heavy to carry to the bottom of the garden so we put it in a wheelbarrow to transport it from the car – and then the fun really began. Will climbed up on to the bale of straw and we stuck a saucepan on his head as an improvised 'crash helmet'. Then I picked up the handles of the wheelbarrow and raced with my delighted passenger down to Chester's pen, deliberately 'crashing' into trees and obstacles as we went. Will gripped the sides of the wheelbarrow as he bounced around, squealing with laughter. He looked a real picture with the saucepan handle sticking out at a 90-degree angle from his head. Will loved every moment of that escapade, especially his impromptu 'helmet'!

Chester heard us coming and started grunting loudly in the deep, breathless oink he saved for when he hadn't seen us for a few hours. We took the precaution of wearing wellies, for Chester's 'back yard' now resembled a muddy swamp – just as Darren had predicted. Once we reached our destination Will leapt off the straw bale and helped me lift it into Chester's home.

Mucking out meant changing the water in Chester's trough, cleaning out his loo area (which he'd designated to be in the bottom right-hand corner of the pen), and changing his bedding straw. Chester always insisted on making his own bed. He loved nothing more than for us to place the bale of straw (string removed, of course) in his Wendy house so he could use his nose to spread it out. Watching him distribute the straw in the house reminded me of how you shake the feathers in a duvet before you spread it out over a bed. He was so clever, he even pushed a clump of straw in front of his front door, ready to cushion his trotters when he stuck them out later that night.

As Chester, Will and I transformed the pen, Will and I chatted easily with one another. My younger son was now six years old but incredibly mature for his age because of everything we had been through with Sam. He was still cheeky and mischievous but he was also caring and grounded. Because of Sam having autism, Will had essentially had to become a young carer; there are tens of thousands of them all across the UK and they don't get enough recognition in my opinion. Though Darren and I took the lead on caring for Sam, just living with his brother put Will in a position of responsibility. It was not easy for him but he has always been a brilliant brother to Sam. And as we swept out Chester's pen, Will revealed to me that his caring for Sam had recently taken on a new dimension. I'd known nothing about it, but Will now told me how he sometimes helped Sam to dress himself in the morning – by confiscating his brother's favourite Ben 10 figurine.

Will told me he would hide it behind his back, until Sam put his clothes on in the correct order. I was stunned for two reasons – firstly, that Will had come up with such an idea to help his brother, and secondly, that it had worked without sending Sam into a meltdown. Ordinarily, Sam became very distressed if he was separated from his favourite toys. It was a risky move, but one that had paid off. Sam might have reacted in the same positive way if I had tried this technique, but I knew I would never have thought to give it a go because sometimes I wrap Sam in cotton wool, trying to protect him from the meltdowns that are so distressing to us both. But Will didn't have the same instinct: instead, he wanted to push his brother, to show Sam that he could do more than he thought.

'I just want to help Sam,' Will confided.

It was reassuring – and incredibly moving – to realise how confident Will was in his ability to help Sam. I gave him a big hug, feeling so proud of him.

Sensing the mood, Chester wanted to share the moment too and waddled over to us, still with bits of straw sticking to his furry coat. He leaned against my legs affectionately, and both Will and I gave him a scratch behind his ears.

Suddenly, I had an idea – why didn't we use the broom as a belly-scratcher, just as Mr Murray had done with Pumbaa? Well, as soon as the bristles hit Chester's tummy, he dropped to the ground so we could get right in there. Will helped me run the broom back and forth over Chester's big hairy belly. With every scratch, Chester let out a grunt of happiness – there's nothing more satisfying than scratching an itch!

That evening, I played table tennis on the dining-room table with Will and cooked him his favourite meal of chilli con carne. We went to bed tired from our hard work in Chester's pen but very, very happy.

Halfway through the night, I woke up. There was a gale howling outside. My first thought was, of course: *is Sam OK?* It sounded pretty terrible weather for camping. I knew Lynda would be keeping everyone safe and sound, however, so I eventually managed to doze off, only to be woken again in the early hours by my mobile beeping, alerting me to an incoming message.

It was from Lynda Russell: 'A wild and windy night, everyone is safe, we are going to continue.' I'd known everything would be fine. And who knew? Maybe the 'adventurous' weather would add to the children's enjoyment of the trip.

I was right. When I picked Sam up at the end of the trip, he had a smile plastered all over his face as he ran to give me a hug. It just reinforced to me why leaving Spain for Devon had been the best thing I could have ever done for Sam.

Every week that passed, Sam became stronger and more confident. Most importantly, he became more able to regulate himself: to understand and react to the stormy moods caused by his condition and take steps to avoid a full-scale meltdown. If he was in class and needed to escape for a flap, he would show a card to one of his TAs (he had two: Mrs Short and Mrs Scull). If he was at home and needed to let off steam, he would run outside to his favourite spot next to Chester's pen.

But while Sam's outlook seemed sunnier by the day, the real weather didn't get any better. The windy wet night on the moors was a precursor to a bitter winter. And come the morning of the last day of term, 17 December 2010, all hell was let loose.

I didn't notice anything different when I first got up because it was still pitch-black outside. I went about my normal morning routine – switching the light on in the kitchen and leaning against the warm toasty Aga as I waited for the kettle to boil. The boys came down in their pyjamas, brushing the sleep from their eyes. I rubbed a hole in the mist on the window almost mindlessly, just looking out into the darkness as the whistle of the kettle started to build. But the lane outside looked somehow different than usual – although it was dark, the light spilling from the kitchen shone on to a differently textured path.

I switched on the outside light – and couldn't believe my eyes. The whole place was covered in a thick blanket of snow.

'Boys, it's been snowing!' I squealed in delight.

They came racing through the living room, heading straight for the back door. I had to stop them from stepping out in their bare feet. They'd seen the countryside dusted in a coating of snow the year before, but nothing as dramatic as this. I hadn't seen anything like it either – it was so deep that I couldn't drive the boys to school. Funnily enough, they weren't too disappointed by this news.

The boys spent the morning building snowmen and lying on their backs in the snow, making snow angels. Our garden was just as pretty white as it was green. The trees looked like they had been dipped in icing and Chester's Wendy house resembled a ski chalet, with the snow layered on the roof. I loved the sound of the snow on the ground crunching underneath my boots – it brought back happy childhood memories of snowball fights with my sister and skiing in the French Alps.

Chester was also delighted by the change in the weather because it meant that Sam and Will played by his pen all day long. He seemed to be handling the cold well, disappearing into his bed of straw whenever he needed to warm up. I wasn't too worried about him because I thought the snow would be gone by the next day.

I was wrong. It kept falling, and falling some more, until it was nine inches deep and we were well and truly snowed in.

It was fun at first because it brought the community together, but as the snow got deeper and deeper, not even the postman could make it up the lane. It was decided that he would leave all our cards and parcels with the people who lived in the cottage about a mile down the lane, and that our closest neighbour, James, who lived on the nearby farm, would fetch the post from that cottage and bring it to us on his sledge. When he arrived, he looked like Santa Claus pulling a sleigh full of presents. The whole scene was magical, with the sun bouncing off the snow and the glistening blue icicles hanging from the bare branches overhead. The boys were waiting for James in the lane, all wrapped up in their hats and scarves and mittens, barely able to contain their excitement at what the delivery might bring.

Luckily I'd already stocked up on all our Christmas food. We had fun delving into some of our supplies because we couldn't get out to the shops.

But by the fifth day of the snow, things got serious. We discovered when we got up that morning that Chester's straw had frozen overnight. The problem was the wooden Wendy house – the snow had seeped into the walls and floor, making the straw damp and soggy. It had then completely frozen as the temperature plummeted at night. Poor Chester had basically slept on a bed of ice.

I felt terrible thinking about how cold he must have been and dived into his pen to check he was OK. He seemed to be all right – he was a hardy animal – but I could feel him shivering as I stroked his back. I wrapped my arms around him, or rather as far around as I could reach given how large he was, and gave him a rubdown to try and warm him up. Seeing me at work, Sam and Will cottoned on to what I was attempting to do and joined in. With all three of us smothering him with affection, Chester perked up, grunting with delight as we rubbed his back and belly.

I wished I could bring Chester indoors for Christmas, but I knew if I did he would trash our new home. He'd caused such chaos the last time he'd broken out of his pen. No, sadly it wasn't an option. Instead, I was going to have to do my best to make his house as cosy and as warm for him as possible.

'Come on, boys, we've got to get Chester warm – this is not good for him.'

I fetched the pickaxe from the greenhouse and hacked away at the frozen straw, while Sam used the shovel to scoop it away; he insisted on being the one to clear the ice. Chester didn't make it easy for Sam as he spent the whole time leaning against his legs for warmth and comfort. But Sam merely giggled at his friend's touch as he soldiered on, shovelling the sludge into the wheelbarrow. Will then dumped it into the muddy part of the pigpen.

After two hours of hard slog, we eventually managed to clear all of it away. We had a fresh bale of straw ready for Chester and, knowing what was coming next, our pig started grunting even more loudly. I placed the bale in his house and cut through the pink string holding it together. Chester immediately started making his bed, spreading the straw around.

I was so worried about Chester's bed freezing again that I asked our neighbour and new 'postman', James, what I should do. The farmer very sweetly offered to dig a pit in his barn as a temporary home for Chester until the snow cleared, but if I took him up on this offer, I would have faced the problem of getting the pig movement papers signed – no mean feat given we were snowed in. I decided it would be easier, and better for Sam, if Chester stayed under our watchful eye – we would just have to make sure we checked his straw several times a day.

This would be easy to do over Christmas because an army of helpers was soon to arrive in the form of my sister, her boyfriend Simon and children Tom and Dan – and, of course, Mum also lent a hand. Fortunately, the snow didn't prevent them from getting to us: by the time they came, the tractors had carved paths through the snowy lanes.

It was an unforgettable white Christmas, not least because we had to resort to using the garden as a fridge-freezer; we only had a tiny one that the previous owners had left behind, but it was too small to store all our festive goodies. The boys loved being sent back and forth to the garden to fetch food as I prepared Christmas lunch. Thank goodness Chester didn't escape – if he had got out, we would more than likely have waved goodbye to our Christmas dinner!

Sam couldn't wait to wolf down his Christmas lunch – not because he was starving but because the sooner he finished eating, the sooner he could take some food to Chester. Sam was still wearing his paper crown as he ran out into the snow with a plate piled high with turkey, stuffing and veggies – we even treated Chester to a little bit of cranberry sauce! Before Sam had even reached the gate, Chester was on his hind legs. If a pig could drool, he would have been. Instead, he grunted so loudly that we could hear him from the dining room.

The one element that was missing from this magical Christmas, though, was Darren. He'd been contracted to work over Christmas so I had to wait until just before New Year to see him. I had a stockpile of presents from us all waiting for him under the tree, but he surprised me with his gift before we'd even got into the house.

We'd just pulled into the driveway after the journey from the airport and were sitting chatting as the bright winter sun streamed through the windscreen. I was about to climb out when he grabbed my arm. He suddenly looked nervous.

'Darren?' I asked uncertainly.

'Will you marry me?' he blurted out.

I wasn't expecting that! The breath left my lungs and caught somewhere in my throat so I couldn't speak for a few moments. Then a smile crept across my face.

'I'd love to!'

I guess it wasn't the most romantic proposal in the world, but it was the second time around for both of us, so it felt right that it was low-key. It certainly didn't detract from the love we had for each other.

At the time Darren proposed, we'd been together for three-and-a-half years. The heartache and hardship we'd suffered in Spain when Sam was so unwell were well behind us: we were at a stage where we were settled and Sam was doing well. Getting married felt like the icing on the cake to bring us together and make us an 'official' family.

I couldn't wait for the big day.

CHAPTER TWENTY-ONE

Wedding Bells and Pig Tales

I WANTED TO HAVE CHESTER AT OUR WEDDING. HE WAS PART of the family; it seemed only right that he be there. I imagined how cute he would look with a bow tie around his neck or a daisy chain on his head . . .

Then I remembered the house-warming disaster when he stole food from our guests' plates and peeled the wallpaper off the bathroom wall.

Darren, quite sensibly, was quick to point out all the other things that could potentially go wrong if I let our pig loose at the civil ceremony and reception we'd planned at a country house hotel in the nearby village of Gulsworthy. We'd agreed on a winter wedding because of the magical memories of our white Christmas when Darren had proposed. It was going to be a low-key occasion – only thirty-odd guests. But even I could see that Chester could not be among them. No: I was going to have to dream up another way to include him.

'I've got it!' I exclaimed as Darren and I were wedding-planning one day. 'Let's have Chester on our wedding cake!' Darren warmed to that idea and a plan was set in motion.

The next thing I knew, I was taking a photo of Chester to the bakery in Dartmouth that we'd chosen to make our wedding cake. They probably thought I was crazy for asking to include a pig in the design! I leafed through their brochure and spotted one particular cake design that summed up our topsy-turvy life perfectly. It showed the bride and groom lying on a four-poster bed with all their pets around them. I asked if they could make a pig out of icing, instead of the cats and dogs that were shown in the picture, and stick him at the end of the bed.

'Just leave it with us,' they said, trying to suppress their smiles at our peculiar pet.

Will was going to be best man and Sam would give me away. It was Darren's and my way of including the boys in our special day. We wanted it to be a celebration of how far we had come as a family.

Sam only had a few words to say in his role but it was going to be a massive deal for him to stand up and speak in front of all the guests. I knew he'd rise to the occasion, though, thanks to the confidence he'd gained in recent years. I'm sure it would have helped Sam to have Chester close by his side but I'd just have to remind him he was there in spirit – on the cake.

Sam wasn't the only one I spent time prepping before the wedding. I also warned the registrar that I had a son with autism who would be speaking during the ceremony to give me away. I wanted to know exactly what was going to be read out so I could run through the ceremony word for word with Sam beforehand. I didn't want there to be any nasty surprises that could upset him.

The big day finally arrived on 19 December 2011. You'd have thought I'd have been calm considering it was my second time around, but I found myself fretting over the tiniest details, such as the flower arrangements, the seating plan and the children's entertainment. I wanted everything to be perfect, right down to the little silver Christmas crackers that were our wedding favours and the italic handwriting on the place settings.

It was my best friend from school, Penny, who helped calm my pre-wedding nerves. As the boys got ready with Darren, she appeared in my hotel room with a bottle of champagne. Penny, who'd flown over from France with her two sons especially for our wedding, was a larger-than-life character. She looked like Cate Blanchett with her cropped blonde hair and toned physique. It was a real treat to have her there and even though we rarely saw each other, we fell back into our old friendship within seconds.

'Now, I'm going to ask you what my father asked me on my wedding day,' she said jokingly, filling my glass with bubbly. She paused for dramatic effect. 'Are you absolutely sure you want to do this?'

We both burst out into a fit of laughter.

'Yes, I'm sure!' I declared, still chuckling.

'Well, let's get on with business then,' she said, dialling room service and ordering me a cooked breakfast. 'You can't get married on an empty stomach!'

Penny helped me to slip into my ivory dress when the time came. I'd chosen a much less fussy wedding dress this time around; it was a simple halterneck. A team of pros did my hair and make-up, curling my long red tresses into ringlets and then letting them hang loose down my back. The finishing touch was the very pretty bouquet I carried, which was made up of heather from Dartmoor, pine cones, white roses, pussy willow and mistletoe – because it was Christmas – all threaded together with silver ribbon.

That was the colour theme of our wedding: silver and cream. I'd picked out silver bow ties and waistcoats for the boys to wear and as they came bounding into my room with their cousins Tom and Dan, just before the service, my heart leapt to see how wonderful they looked.

'Don't you all look handsome!' I exclaimed, straightening their bow ties in turn.

'Don't you start crying,' Penny warned me, conscious that any sentimental tears might mess up my carefully applied make-up.

She then ushered everyone out – everyone except Sam, because he was going to walk me down the aisle.

Sam, who would be eight in less than a month's time, stared up at me with wide eyes.

'Mummy, you look nice,' he said, stressing each word as he sometimes did. It was so sweet.

Our little moment was interrupted by a sharp knock at the door. The hotel owner popped her head around and said, 'Everyone's waiting for you now.'

A hundred butterflies fluttered through my stomach. This was it – I was about to marry Darren. I imagined everyone seated downstairs in the drawing room; Darren and Will would be waiting at the end of the aisle for us to appear.

'Come on, Sam, let's do this.' I took his little hand in mine.

Today, he was my rock, giving me strength and support. Both my father and my uncle had passed away and I needed Sam to be there for me. Our roles were reversed – I was leaning on him, rather than the other way around, for he was the man supporting me to the altar. And my little boy rose to the big occasion magnificently.

The photographer was waiting at the bottom of the stairs to capture us on camera. She teased me about how anxious I looked, but it wasn't because I was afraid of marrying

Darren – I could barely get down the stairs in my high heels as I was used to just wearing wellies! I gripped Sam's hand for dear life as I tottered from step to step. We made it to the bottom in one piece and both peered around the door of the drawing room at the same time. I could see Darren, nervously smoothing down his black velvet jacket with his hand. Will was also there, holding the cream leather bag containing the rings, and I spotted my mum in the front row.

Then the bagpipes started playing – a sound very close to Darren's heart. A lot of his colleagues on the rig were Scottish and they played the bagpipes as they walked around the helideck; he would often tell me on the phone how listening to the sound of the bagpipes drifting across the rig and out to sea gave him goose bumps, so he'd wanted the stirring instrument to provide the soundtrack to our ceremony. Listening to the haunting music, I could understand exactly why he found the pipes so moving.

I was still holding Sam's hand as we pushed open the double doors into the drawing room. The first thing to hit us was the scent of flowers: the room was filled with them. Then we felt everyone's eyes on us.

'You're doing so well, Sam,' I whispered.

As we walked down the aisle, Sam started to suck on his forefinger nervously, and his eyes were fixed on the ground. The guests were craning their necks so that they could get a glimpse of us. Sam's nervousness was palpable – I was so proud of him for managing to stay calm.

Darren couldn't resist looking back at me. A smile crept across his face.

'You look beautiful,' he mouthed.

A blush rushed up my neck and spread across my cheeks.

Sam was still sucking his finger as we came to a halt before the registrar. My eyes were darting between Sam and Darren.

'Well done, Sam,' I murmured.

As soon as the service started, my son stopped sucking his finger and gazed up at the registrar, eager to say his lines at exactly the right time. The registrar cleared his throat as he prepared for the big moment.

'And who gives Joanna away?' His voice boomed across the room.

The registrar looked down at Sam, trying his best to make my son feel important. Sam gazed back up at him with his beautiful angelic face. And everyone fell silent as they watched and waited for Sam to speak. It was so quiet you could have heard a pin drop.

'I do,' Sam said proudly.

A smile spread across the room from face to face, the pure joy impossible to resist. All our guests knew what a big deal it would have been for Sam to speak in front of everyone – yet he had done it.

I looked at Darren; both our faces reflected the same pride and love. Suddenly, it felt as though it was just the four of us – me, Darren, Sam and Will – alone in the drawing room. Everyone else seemed to fade into the background. For while it was just Darren and me up there saying our vows, the occasion signified a bigger union: the four of us coming together to be a proper family. As Darren and I exchanged our vows, the words weren't just about our love for each other, but our love for our children too.

The rest of the day went like a dream. The food was amazing, the atmosphere was incredible . . . I could not have wished for a more perfect wedding.

We'd done our best to include the children in the celebrations throughout the day. I'd wrapped up a load of presents for them in silver tissue paper and put them under the Christmas tree for them to open once the reception got going. As I stood chatting to my mum that evening, as the band played loudly in the background, out of the corner of my eye I could see the children tearing their gifts open. We'd given Sam some Lego, a toy he adores due to the ordered step-by-step construction, which appeals to his autistic brain.

As I kept half an eye on the boys, I saw Sam putting together his Lego toy. There was one piece left to go: the crowning glory. His cousin Tom, who was sitting close by, innocently leaned over and stuck the last Lego brick on to Sam's toy.

'Here you go, Sam,' he said cheerily, happy to be able to help.

Completing the toy meant nothing to my nephew – but it meant *everything* to Sam. The last piece of Lego going on meant the toy would be complete and perfect, and it was very important to Sam that he was the one to do it. Having Tom finish it off caused Sam huge frustration and this, coupled with the noise from the band, proved too much for him to cope with. It sent him over the edge.

Sam suddenly took to his heels and sprinted out of the room, crying. From my experience, I knew this meltdown could be serious and my first instinct was to keep Sam safe. I gathered up my wedding dress, kicked off my heels and chased after him. I ran up the sweeping staircase, along the corridor and into the library.

Smack! Smack! Smack! Sam was hitting himself in the

face. He was crying his eyes out, his little body heaving with sobs.

'Sam, stop,' I pleaded. Within a matter of minutes, my role had changed from that of the bride to being the mother of an autistic boy who needed my help.

I tried to give him proprioceptive input by throwing my arms around him, locking him into a cuddle. Proprioception is the concept of knowing where your body is in space and the ability to safely manoeuvre around your environment. By hugging Sam, I was attempting to bring him back to himself, so that he knew who and where he was and wasn't lost in his raging emotions.

The cuddle wasn't enough to calm him this time, though: he was too far gone and his mind was now in a state I considered to be dangerous to his wellbeing. He was fighting me, smacking himself, digging his nails in ... I wasn't strong enough to hold him and he escaped from my grip. He was so distressed that I was incredibly concerned he might hurt himself.

'Sam!' I pleaded, as he took off down the hallway again.

I sprinted after him, my heart pounding so loudly I could hear it in my ears. The music I'd been enjoying only moments earlier downstairs was now loud and intrusive. I wanted it to stop. I wanted Sam to stop.

He darted into our bedroom. *Come on, Jo,* I told myself, *you have to think on your feet.* As I wracked my brains for ideas to help Sam, I realised there was no alternative – I was going to have to apply more pressure than a simple cuddle could do.

I lay down next to him, using part of my body weight to apply deep pressure to his muscles, locking him in tight, essentially keeping him still and safe. I didn't lie on him completely, but I held him in a firm embrace to apply pressure and comfort. The music continued to pump through the ceiling and in my mind I willed it to stop, conscious that to Sam's sensitive ears it would have been an added overload to an already highly stressful situation.

'It's OK, Sam.' I tried to console him.

After about twenty minutes of me applying pressure to Sam's muscles, stroking his hair and covering his ears with the palms of my hands to block out the noise of the band, the door burst open and Penny appeared. Her face dropped with shock at the sight of us.

'It's OK,' I blurted, my voice muffled because my face was pressing into the sheets. She crept over to the bed, wanting to help but not really knowing how.

'I had no idea,' she said, referring to how unpredictable and out of hand things could quickly get when you had a child with autism.

But unless you live with it, you can't really know. Sam's meltdown was a reminder that, no matter how well he seemed to be progressing, his autism will always be a part of who he is. These kinds of episodes are inevitable if he becomes overwhelmed.

Luckily, slowly, the weight of my body on his nervous system worked. He stopped fighting me and I gently eased myself away from him. His breathing was deep and laboured as I stroked his hair and cuddled his exhausted body.

'Go downstairs, I'll look after him,' Penny said insistently.

'I can't leave him.'

Penny wouldn't take no for an answer, though. Eventually,

I gave in. By the time I finally slipped away, Sam was fast asleep in Penny's arms.

I pasted on a smile as I made my way downstairs because I didn't want to let on to my guests that anything was wrong. Inside I was crying, though. I was, after all, partly responsible for causing Sam to have his meltdown. It had been an incredibly busy and *different* day for Sam and, as much as I had tried to prepare him for what was going to happen, it had all been too much. I always hated seeing him in distress, but this time it felt worse than ever. This time, I felt guilty.

As I rejoined the party, Darren was quick to come to my side. He had noticed my long absence and my mum had told him I was with Sam. He came towards me with such a look of concern on his face, and I knew he had been as worried for Sam as he had been about me.

Seeing my new husband – dressed in his wedding attire, on this day when our family had become whole at last – was all I needed to feel my spirits start to rise a little again. Being Sam's parent was challenging, there was no denying it, but what had happened on this day – Darren and I becoming husband and wife – meant that I wasn't alone any more. Whatever the challenges of parenting Sam, Darren and I were a team and we would do it together now, whatever the future held for us all.

And not just the two of us. As Darren took me in his arms to twirl me around the dance floor on our wedding night, a very special pig looked on from his prime location atop our wedding cake. Though tonight had been a step back for Sam, Chester had helped him to make so many huge leaps forward – and I knew he would do so again in the future. It wasn't just Darren who had my back and Sam's back, Chester was there for us as well. In sickness and in health . . .

So while Sam's meltdown had been distressing, as the evening wore on I focused not on what he hadn't been able to manage that night, but on what he might manage in the years to come. For all of us – all us Bailey-Merritts, as we were now named – today was the first day of the rest of our lives. And I was excited to see what the future had in store.

CHAPTER TWENTY-TWO

Media Hog

NOT LONG AFTER SAM'S EPISODE AT THE WEDDING, HE BOUNCED back in a way that surprised us all. Darren and I went to pick him up from school one afternoon, and instead of coming out alone (he no longer needed Lynda Russell or a TA to hold his hand these days so he normally exited on his own), he ran to the gates with another boy in tow.

'This is Jack,' he said, proudly introducing his new friend.

We couldn't believe it; Sam had finally made a friend. I had honestly thought that this day would never come. It just showed how far my son had come: Sam had progressed from coming out of the school with Lynda or a TA, to leaving by himself, to now appearing with a friend.

While it was a landmark moment for my new husband and me, Sam and Jack seemed oblivious to what was going on around them. They were in their own happy little bubble, laughing constantly.

I looked at Darren with delight and he grinned back at me.

'Nice to meet you, Jack,' we both said.

Jack wasn't in the CAIRB but he did have special needs. That might have been what brought the boys together – an unspoken understanding that they were both a little different from the other children. They had met in one of the mainstream classes that Sam had been integrated into. They both shared a love of drawing: Jack would ask Sam to draw superheroes for him, which he did, and Jack would then enjoy colouring them in. From that moment on, Sam and Jack were inseparable.

Lynda Russell was gushing with stories of how they did everything together. One story that touched my heart more deeply than the others was how Lynda had once caught them chatting on the fallen oak tree in the playground.

'They were blind to all the other children playing around them – they just chatted and laughed until we had to drag them back to class,' she said, looking incredibly moved.

I couldn't help having a flashback to when I had helped out at Manor Primary and looked out of the window to see my boy all alone, running up and down the tree and flapping his hands, so isolated from the other children. Now he was sitting on that very same tree *with a friend*. What's more, he'd made this connection all by himself. He hadn't needed Chester to help him communicate. It showed how much he was improving and it made me think that maybe one day Sam might be able to fend for himself.

Darren and I really got a flavour of how close the pair had become at the school's annual sports day in the summer of 2012. Manor Primary has a unique way of approaching sports day so that the children don't feel under pressure to perform on an individual level, but are encouraged to work as a team instead. The children are put into groups and each group is set a different activity to do, so there are eight or nine different things going on simultaneously. The parents can follow the groups from activity to activity, which is really nice because you can cheer your own children on as they do each task.

Apart from in the running races, there is no emphasis on

who comes first, second or third. This was perfect for Sam, who struggled both to manage his coordination and to cope with his pressing need for perfection.

The teachers put Sam and Jack in the same group because they knew that they had become really good friends. The only drawback to this was that the boys were so busy laughing together, they forgot they had a sports day to take part in. Instead of joining in, they took themselves off to their favourite climbing frame of the fallen tree. While the rest of the school took part in sporting activities, Sam took part in something he'd never experienced before – having fun with a friend.

Neither Darren nor I had the heart to make them come back and join in. I think the teachers must have felt the same way, as everyone seemed to turn a blind eye.

It would have been nice to have Jack over to our house in the summer holidays but Sam was funny about having friends to stay over. It was a quirk with his autism – he compartmentalised everything. School was school and home was home, and the two should not be mixed. The only reason it had worked out when the children from the CAIRB had visited Chester was because all the teachers had been there too, giving a classroom feel to the experience. With Sam having no school friends to play with, it was down to Chester to be Sam's only buddy again until the new term started.

Chester was over the moon about having Sam back for the summer, and he was particularly happy because he had a new pad. The dilapidated Wendy house had finally collapsed and I had suggested we get Chester a proper home to sleep in so he wouldn't freeze in the winter. Darren's arm took some twisting, as the metal pig arks weren't cheap, but he came round in the end.

It would be fair to say that Darren wasn't Chester's biggest fan. Due to his job on the rigs, he didn't spend a great deal of time with him. But as fate would have it, Darren was handed a double dose of pig mischief one day while I was in town treating myself to an hour of reflexology.

When I left the house, Darren was peacefully working away at his vegetable patch, humming along to songs on the radio. By the time I got back, all hell had broken loose.

As I pulled into the drive, I saw Darren waving a big stick around – chasing after a scampering Chester. My husband's face was puce and he was sweating bullets of perspiration from his forehead.

'Darren, what are you doing?' I called out. I leapt out of the car and ran after the pair of them. Darren looked angry and when I caught up with him I saw that he was out of breath.

'I've been trying to get that pig back in his pen for an hour!' he raged.

Chester, who was just out of reach, stopped running and stared back at us with his cheeky grin. I knew exactly what was going on here – he thought this was a game. He'd been having a whale of a time having Darren chase after him, just as he loved the boys to do.

Sadly, I couldn't say the same for my husband.

'Did you throw some pignuts down for him?' I asked. It was a logical question but it infuriated Darren because he hadn't thought of doing that.

'No, I've just been chasing around after him,' he replied, a little shamefacedly.

Darren pointed to the ruins of the greenhouse: one of the panes of glass was smashed.

'Oh my God!' I exclaimed. 'What happened?'

Darren then explained how he'd been planting seeds when suddenly Chester had appeared by his side; the pig had escaped from his pen.

'I managed to lead him away from the veg patch back to his pen. I was just opening the gate when he suddenly veered to the left and darted off into the greenhouse. He wouldn't come out, no matter how much I called him, so my idea was to go in after him, get behind him, and shoo him out the door. But Chester went straight through the glass on the other side!'

As Darren told the story, his anger increased as he recalled the expensive damage and his fruitless chase after the pig. Meanwhile, I was doing my best not to giggle as I pictured the scene. I cupped my hand over my mouth to smother my laughter as I examined the shattered mess: the broken glass had gone all over Darren's vegetable patch.

'It's not funny, I've spent all day preparing that soil!' he snapped.

'What about Chester?' I asked. 'Is his nose OK?'

'Never mind about bloody Chester!'

Luckily, Chester was fine. He hadn't sustained a single scratch despite shattering the whole pane of glass. Darren had more to say on the matter. He shook his head as he glared at our pet pig.

'He's really crafty, he ran off every time I got close. It was stop, start, stop, start.'

I could easily see that the best thing I could do was to get Chester back in his pen before any more drama unfolded. I reached for the pignuts.

'Here, Chesty.' I rattled them around in my hand.

Chester lifted his twitching snout into the air. He then

obediently followed me back into his home. It took only a matter of minutes to lock him back up.

This didn't go down well with Darren, of course, given he had spent an hour trying to achieve the same goal. He stomped off into the house.

'Don't take it personally, Chesty.' I gave our pig a reassuring cuddle as we heard the door slam.

To be fair to Darren, that was the first time Chester had escaped when Darren was on his own. All the other times I'd dealt with it, so naturally I was the expert. The funny thing was, despite all his raging, I came down for breakfast the next morning to find Darren slaving over the Aga for Chester. He was making him a warm broth from all the leftover potato and vegetable peelings.

'What are you doing?' I teased him, knowing full well he was looking out for our pig.

'Well, I can't let Chester go hungry,' he said lightly, shrugging his shoulders. It was Darren's way of making it up to Chester for being so cross with him. And actually the duo went on to get on really well in the garden. Chester's pen was right by Darren's vegetable plot so they kept each other company whenever Darren was working on his patch. Chester would rest his big head on one of the wooden slats, grunting at Darren, and Darren would throw him weeds and sticks of rhubarb from the vegetable plot to chomp on. It was very sweet to watch!

A few weeks after the greenhouse disaster, the shoe was on the other foot when it was me on the receiving end of Chester's provocative behaviour.

By this time Darren had returned to the rig – but not before presenting me with a beautiful gift of two blueberry bushes; he knew they were my favourite fruit. I quickly set to work nurturing them in a sunny spot on the patio by the back door. As the bushes matured, I was able to saunter out on to the patio in the mornings, pick a few home-grown blueberries and throw them into my yoghurt. It was blissful country living at its best.

It was all going so well – until Chester decided to break out for a second time that summer. By chance, I spotted him escaping just as he bypassed Darren's vegetable patch and headed for our back door.

I ran out into the sunshine, ready to intercept him, yelling for the boys as back-up.

'Come quickly, Chester's got out!' I shouted.

I reached Chester just as he reached my blueberry bushes. They were enough of a temptation to make him pause before entering the house, which had been his Plan A. He hovered beside them, nose twitching. And then the greedy pig was upon them in seconds.

I pushed and pushed Chester as hard as I could, trying to move his snout away from the luscious fruit, but he was too big and too strong and already guzzling with such gusto, hoovering along the branches with such determination, that my efforts were in vain. He was making the desperate gobbling, grunting noise he saved for when he was devouring treats, such as when he stole the chicken feed from our former neighbours' garden. It was all over in seconds.

Chester, oinking with satisfaction, trotted past me into the house. I was left looking forlornly at my blueberry bushes, which now consisted of bare branches stripped entirely of their fruit. Meanwhile, the boys, as ever, were rolling about with laughter over Chester's naughty antics.

Of course, Chester's behaviour, as it had always been, was

a hot topic of conversation in the village – and beyond. So I suppose it shouldn't have been a surprise when the BBC got in touch one day to say they had heard about Chester (because news of our pig had spread far and wide) and wanted to film him for *Country Tracks*. But it was *definitely* a surprise! I didn't know what to say. The locals in our previous village had once joked that he would one day be a TV star but I never thought it would really happen.

Country Tracks wanted to make a programme about how our micro pig hadn't stayed micro. My first concern about this was how it might reflect on Mr Murray and Pennywell Farm. I worried that it might be bad business for them if it were to get out that Chester hadn't stayed miniature. So I rang the farm and Mr Murray said he'd be right over. It was the first time I'd ever contacted him about Chester's size, for I'd never wanted to complain about it. Chester was our pig and we loved him no matter what.

'Oh my goodness, he's *huge*!' Mr Murray exclaimed when he set eyes on Chester.

He scratched his head in bewilderment.

'I honestly can't explain it!' he said.

Mr Murray got in the pen with Chester and gave him a once-over as he tried to work out how his micro pig had ballooned to such an enormous size. Our pet pig was now 167cm long from snout to backside, but that didn't include his tail, which was 45cm long. And he was 80cm tall!

I kept telling Mr Murray that I didn't mind about it, but he insisted on giving me an explanation. In a roundabout way he said that Chester was a genetic 'throwback'. A throwback is an evolutionary term for when traits suddenly appear which had disappeared generations before. In the case of

Chester, a full-size pig had been born to two miniature pigs who'd been specially bred to be tiny. It was apparently something that could happen when farmers bred hybrids, although Mr Murray had never seen it before at his farm.

'I'm so sorry,' he kept apologising. 'You saw his parents, they are both tiny!'

'It's fine!' I kept on reassuring him.

Mr Murray was so worried that he'd let us down that he offered to swap Chester for a new piglet. The thought had never even crossed my mind.

'I wouldn't swap him for the world!' I exclaimed, glancing affectionately at Chester's smiley ginger face.

I explained to Mr Murray that Chester had transformed Sam's life, that our son would be devastated if we swapped him and that I'd be crushed to lose him too. I thought even Darren would be sad.

To his credit, Mr Murray insisted that I go ahead with the BBC programme to show the world how Sam's life had been changed thanks to an animal. I thought it was really decent of him not to put his own reputation first. And he also gave us some great advice for caring for Chester, warning us that we should part-cement Chester's pigpen as Chester had dug it up completely by this time and walking around in wet mud all day every day wasn't good for his trotters.

Darren arrived back from the rigs days before the filming was due to take place and his first job was, of course, to part-cement Chester's home. He went into classic Darren overdrive, trying to make Chester's pen look pristine for his starring role.

'He's got to look good; he's going to be on telly!' Darren insisted.

It was no small job. We had tons of wet cement delivered and had to put it to use while Chester was still in residence! It was a monumental battle keeping him out of the way as we spent the day transforming his pen, but hilarious fun.

Sam and Will jumped at the chance to turn their friend into a shining TV star with a pristine pad. They ran off to fetch the buckets and wheelbarrow and shovel and anything else they could think of to help Darren continue his mission to scrub up Chester's home. Together, the three of them replaced all the dirty straw with fresh straw and scrubbed at the ark, clearing away all the moss and dirt. Finally, Darren cut back the foliage that bordered the pen.

Darren even made Chester some toys from logs and branches he had chopped down in the garden! He formed them into a wigwam shape and then threaded a load of old wellies and plastic balls on to a string, which he hung between them. They dangled low enough that Chester could reach them with his snout. Darren spent hours and hours making the pen look incredible, which showed how much he really did care for Chester after all.

Chester loved every second of it; especially the part where he got a makeover. We brushed his thick ginger hair with the bristles of an outdoor broom. We braided the furry bit at the end of his tail. We even put moisturiser on his ears to make them look smooth. Grooming him was probably a harder job than clearing up his pen as he kept rolling on to the floor and putting his trotters in the air, desperate for his tummy to be rubbed. He looked very dapper by the end, though.

We arranged for the film crew to come at the weekend so the boys could star in the programme too. I was a lot more nervous than I thought I would be when three women with a very large camera showed up. They briefed us on the questions they wanted to ask us and how we should reply. I kept fluffing my lines and they had to keep doing retakes!

Sam, on the other hand, blossomed in the spotlight. He was a bit nervous when the crew first arrived – he went to have one of his moments down in the wooded area by the brook – but once he'd shaken the anxiety out of his body he transformed into a confident little boy. He led the crew down to meet Chester and he even advised them as to how he thought they should film his pig.

Will, Darren and I were speechless at his confidence and command of the situation.

'You weren't joking about him being big!' the women exclaimed when they clapped eyes on Chester.

Being a great performer, our pig rose to the occasion too. Chester levered himself up so that he was standing on his hind legs, his front trotters resting on the fencing. He wanted to make sure he shared the limelight.

The interview started with me and Darren explaining why we had wanted to buy a miniature pig. It was so fun watching Darren on camera, especially knowing his love/hate relationship with Chester. Darren was just as nervous as me and kept saying the word 'predominantly', which he never usually uses in his speech!

They then zoomed in on Sam.

Sam knew the camera was on him but he wasn't the least bit intimidated. He jumped into the pen with Chester and started grooming his pig and tickling his tummy. It was so sweet to watch them interact because you could tell Chester knew Sam needed him to be on his best behaviour. It was an inexplicable connection they shared – they seemed to know when they needed each other most.

As I watched Chester perform impeccably, I also thought to myself that it would never cease to amaze me how Chester could transform from being a hooligan pig to an angel pig in the blink of an eye . . .

The filming ended with a final question to Darren and me.

'Do you have any regrets?' the interviewer asked us, about getting Chester.

I glanced across at Darren with gritted teeth, apprehensive of what he might say.

But Darren leant back and announced cheerily: 'Wouldn't change him for the world!'

CHAPTER TWENTY-THREE

Chester to the Rescue

WE WERE SUCH A HAPPY FAMILY, THE FIVE OF US: DARREN, Will, Sam, Chester and me. And for Christmas 2013 Sam gave us all the best present: we discovered he could sing like a West End star. I'd had no idea of his hidden talent. I'd heard him hum in the bath, and sing to himself when he was drawing, but nothing like what I witnessed as I watched him belt out the songs for his end-of-year school production that winter. He was part of the choir for the World War Two musical *We'll Meet Again*, and his voice resonated above all the other children's. He had the voice of an angel.

'You can hear him above everyone else,' Mum whispered in my ear as we both proudly watched him sing his heart out.

I know every mum thinks her child is a star in the making, but at that moment I truly felt he was. My hair was standing on end; it was such a mesmerising performance. Inside, my heart felt as if it might burst with joy. I was overwhelmed at the sight of Sam standing on the stage, hogging the limelight and staring with such a passion into the spotlights, but most of all singing the lyrics to entire songs when he normally found language such a struggle – I just wouldn't have dared to imagine it might even be possible.

To top it all off, when the performance ended, all the other children stood there quietly, but Sam lifted his arm above his head to deliver a majestic bow, twirling his hand in front of him. Still looking to the front, he also turned sideways, spread his arms wide and wiggled his hands and fingers. He was the only one to do this and it made us roar with laughter! He was oozing confidence. Mum and I rose to our feet and applauded our wonderful boy.

Sam turned eleven in January 2014 and there was so much to celebrate. He had been fully integrated into all mainstream classes at primary school now. His speech had come on so much that he could say up to forty-five words in succession. Sam's autistic mannerisms had also massively decreased – he had stopped muttering sentences under his breath, and the flapping and bouncing had stopped altogether in public. He had made a best friend in Jack. He had also rekindled his friendship with his brother, much to my delight.

As we approached his final months at Manor Primary, I felt confident he was ready to make the leap to secondary school. I told myself it would be OK, that it would all work out.

Sadly, I couldn't have been more wrong.

The regression wasn't obvious at first. It started in June with small things, like Sam getting stroppy with his TA, Mrs Short. He complained that he hated her following him around to every lesson.

'Why does that woman have to be with me all the time? It's like I'm her husband or something!' he said bluntly.

He was also being rude to us: he'd arrive home and unleash a tirade of abuse. I didn't know he even knew swear words, but he certainly did. He started kicking doors and walls.

Next, Sam became afraid of the dark. He insisted on having the fairy lights around his bed on all night long and he wanted a torch by his bedside as a safety measure. Perhaps as a consequence of this new fear, he started sleeping in my bed, too. Many nights, as I was getting ready to go to sleep, I would hear his bedroom door creak open and then the quick succession of footsteps as he sprinted along the corridor as fast as his legs would take him. He would come crashing into my room and clamber into my bed. I'd then have a real job trying to get him to sleep as he was so agitated. It was exhausting for us both.

It was particularly distressing to watch his decline as only a couple of months earlier he had been that confident boy singing his heart out on stage. It was frightening because I began to feel I was reliving the horror of Spain all over again, when my little boy had started disappearing before my eyes.

The only advantage I had this time around was an understanding – I knew what was happening, and I could work out what was triggering him. It was the move to secondary school, of course, for Sam would be moving on from Manor Primary that September. Sam hated change at the best of times, let alone such a significant leap into the unknown.

I tried to keep calm and asked Mrs Short for help; Lynda Russell had by this time retired. Mrs Short advised that we did all we could to prepare Sam for his new school – South Dartmoor Community College. We'd chosen the school because it would allow Sam to stay in mainstream classes but there was also a CAIRB on site, on which Sam would be offered a place.

So that's what we did – I showed him pictures, Mrs Short made up storybooks, I took him back and forth to the uniform shop to give him an idea of what he would be wearing. But it didn't seem to help.

As we approached the last couple of weeks of term at primary school, Sam's new habit of sleeping in my bed was happening every night. It was exhausting for Darren as well, who was then home from the rigs, as Sam was hardly a little child any more who could cuddle neatly between us; he was a tall, lanky eleven-year-old who took up a lot of space. Sometimes one of us would have to creep out in the middle of the night to the spare room just to get some rest.

We pinned all our hopes on the week that had been earmarked to show Sam around South Dartmoor. Most children only spend a day, if that, looking around their new school; we spent a whole week showing Sam what was in store. Every morning either Mrs Short or Mrs Scull from Manor Primary took Sam to South Dartmoor. They started off by showing him the classrooms, the gym, the playing fields and the art room, where he'd be able to continue doing his wonderful drawings. He was slowly introduced to what day-to-day life would be like, and to the TAs who would help him at secondary school. By the end of the week, he was attending both morning and afternoon lessons, without either Mrs Short or Mrs Scull. So it went surprisingly well, despite all the anxiety he'd been displaying. But, as it had been so many times before, it proved to be just the calm before the storm.

Gradually, Sam got worse and worse. He refused to be alone – he wouldn't even go and see Chester by himself. Darren, Will or I would have to chaperone him into the garden. He refused to go upstairs – he would stand by the door, trembling, waiting for someone to take him. He wouldn't even go to the bathroom alone. He now wanted not just his fairy lights on, but also the main bedroom lights, his side lamp and his torch – he needed to be surrounded by light to feel safe. He was afraid and anxious.

'Mum, I can hear the animals.' He would clamp his hands over his ears as I tried to get him to go to sleep in his own bed. I knew his acute sense of hearing had been a problem at times, and he'd mentioned the noises of the foxes and the owls before, but this was different. In his mind, the animals had morphed into monsters and he was terrified they were coming to get him.

I could sympathise with how Sam might feel as the hooting of the owls could sound like ghosts calling to one another as their haunting voices echoed across the valley. So I made up a story about the owls – how they were a family having a chat at night, just like we did.

I tried to remind him of his drawing of the pink cottage: 'This is your home, this is where you are safe and happy.' I kept reiterating the word 'safe'.

But my words fell on deaf ears. Sam would burst into tears and mutter nonsensical words under his breath. He would then stop and beg me: 'Please don't leave me, Mum.' What could I say to that? I would take his hand and lead him into my bedroom for another night.

I had to stay strong and keep saying the right things to keep Sam calm, but it was hard not to panic. How bad was this going to get?

And then things went from bad to worse one day when we took a short car ride into town. Mum was in the front with me; the boys were in the back. As we drove the familiar route along the country lanes to the supermarket in Totnes, Sam started muttering. He was speaking under his breath so I couldn't decipher the words. He then suddenly blurted out very clearly: 'I can see them.'

Mum and I locked eyes. She gave me that look, that same

awful worried look I'd seen when things were at their worst with Sam in Spain.

'Sam, can you actually see anything?' I asked, trying to make sense of his thoughts.

Sam simply carried on murmuring again, and then he suddenly became very lucid. 'I can see black figures walking down the street,' he said, flickering his fingers in front of his eyes.

For a moment, Mum and I were shocked into silence. As soon as we'd parked up and got out of the car, Mum pulled me aside.

'My God, do you think he's seeing dead people?' Mum whispered to me, not wanting Sam to hear.

'No!' I didn't want to accept that was what he was imagining. 'Maybe he's got something wrong with his eyes,' I went on. 'Maybe he's got some black spots blocking his vision – floaters, I think they're called.'

I was determined to get this checked out. I hadn't come this far with Sam, only to see him regress so dramatically. Immediately, I booked Sam in to see an optician in town.

I had a little word with the optician before I brought Sam into the consultation room, just to explain what had been going on. Although I didn't want there to be something physically wrong with Sam, in a way I hoped there was, as that would have been better than the alternative – that my boy was imagining he could see the dead, or at least ghostly figures that were invisible to everyone else.

The optician was very caring. He took his time over Sam, making him feel special by explaining everything he was doing. He then handed me a folded piece of paper on which was written:

20/20 vision. Must be anxiety.

He had written it down as he didn't want Sam to hear his diagnosis and be upset by the news. Sam was old enough to understand what anxiety was. He was old enough, too, to understand he had autism – which we then discovered was what was really at the heart of the problem.

Throughout Sam's life, I had always made a point of making him understand that everyone in the world is different and told him not to worry about the fact that Will could do things he couldn't. I tried to educate Sam by telling him that while his autism did mean he struggled with certain things, that struggle in itself was completely normal, for we all struggled with different things ('I struggle with driving and Daddy struggles with eating seafood,' I would tell him). I told him over and over that autism was just a wonderful part of who he was and should be celebrated, for it allowed him to do some fantastic things, such as his drawing, which neurotypical people couldn't. And I told him never to allow his autism to define him because, at the end of the day, it was only a small part of who he was. Ultimately, he was Sam – not autistic Sam, or flapping Sam, but Sam who could draw brilliantly and liked pigs and happened to have autism. Autism was just a characteristic, I said, like his dark-brown hair or his passion for Ben 10.

As a young child, he probably only took about 5 per cent of all that in. He used to say proudly, 'I have autism,' not really knowing what it meant.

But the older Sam grew and the more he mixed with other children, the more he had become aware of his limitations and that he was actually 'different'. Now, as Sam geared up to change schools, he was seeing those differences in a negative light. His perspective of his autism was getting more skewed by the day.

Darren was back on the rigs when Sam's state of mind suddenly took a nose dive. I walked into his bedroom one morning to find him sobbing. He was muttering and flickering his fingers in front of his eyes, which was a sign of serious anxiety. I could feel the stress exuding from him.

'Sam, what on earth is the matter?' I asked, scooping him into my arms.

Sam just muttered words under his breath, over and over, so quietly I couldn't make them out. He did that when he was feeling distraught. Then he spoke clearly again – but the words weren't at all what I wanted to hear.

'Leave me alone!' He hid his face under his hands, but not before I saw his bottom lip was quivering and his face was drenched in tears. 'I hate having autism. I want to be like everyone else. *I wish I was dead!*'

Hearing Sam say that was the worst moment of my life. I'd never heard him say that he hated himself before, nor that he wished he was dead. It absolutely broke my heart.

After he shouted out the words, he sobbed – and it was a sob that came right from his belly, from his very soul. His whole body was shaking with sadness.

I gently rubbed his back as he buried his face in the duvet. It was clear that all he wanted was to make himself disappear. I took a deep breath. After years of dealing with distressing situations like this, I was used to putting my emotions to one side and giving Sam the response he needed to hear. Even though his words had shocked me, I knew how to respond and wasted no time in reassuring my devastated little boy.

'No, Sam, autism isn't bad, it just means you see the world differently,' I told him softly, rubbing his back. 'We are *all* different. I'm different to you; Daddy's different to Will. Autism is a good thing – because wouldn't it be boring if we were all the same?' I felt a lump rising in my throat as I spoke. And my words didn't have the desired effect: Sam crossed his arms over his face, sobbing and sobbing.

I kept going, doing my best to bring him back to me.

'There are so many great things about autism! Look how wonderful your hearing is, and your eyesight, which makes you brilliant at drawing. We can't draw like you, and that's because you can see things in so much more detail than we can.'

'Will doesn't sleep with the lights on.' Sam kept on criticising himself.

'Sam, that's OK. We're all different and we all have different needs, each and every one of us.'

I kept rubbing his back. I kept trying to show him how much I loved him.

'Mummy, I hate myself!'

'But, sweetie, what is it about the autism that you don't like, when it's given you so many gifts?'

Sam looked up at me, his eyes red and puffy from all the tears.

'People are going to laugh at me in my new school,' he cried. 'My autism makes me flap.'

'It doesn't matter if you flap,' I told him. 'And if people laugh at you *because* you flap, then that doesn't make them very nice people, so why worry about them?

'But if you don't want to flap, we can work out ways of helping you to manage it better.'

There was no point in telling him how far he had come

with his self-regulating, because he couldn't see it. I needed to reassure him he would be OK, that there was a future. As Sam got older I'd be able to explain to him why he felt the need to flap, as well as all the other terms I knew, but, for now, I told him we would simply work on ways to manage his flapping.

'We'll learn to control it,' I promised, kissing his tear-soaked face.

Eventually, he calmed down enough that I could get him to school that morning for his last day of term; his last-ever day at Manor Primary.

As soon as I got home from dropping him off, I called Darren. I didn't know what time it was for him – he was now stationed in the Gulf of Mexico – but I was so concerned about Sam that I just picked up the phone and dialled his number.

I was redirected through his office in Scotland. Every second I was on hold, my heart was beating louder. I needed to hear his voice more than ever.

'Is everything OK?' Darren was suddenly on the line.

'No, it's Sam,' I told him, my voice cracking as I said the words. I explained everything that had happened and told him how incredibly distraught Sam had been.

'I don't know what to do!' I cried out. 'I'm losing him again.'

But Darren replied calmly: 'We'll get him through this; it's going to be OK.'

Darren told me to ring the mental-health team. He said we couldn't take any chances if Sam was saying things like he wished he was dead. My boy had already shown us through the years that he had no compunction about hurting himself physically.

We had been assigned a social worker through the NHS, through whom I could access this service for Sam. Strengthened by Darren's sensible advice, I wasted no time in picking up the phone and calling her. It was the first time I'd really needed her help.

'Something terribly harrowing happened to me this morning,' I told Sam's social worker.

I recounted everything Sam had said to me, trying my hardest to control my emotion. I was desperately worried about him. She told me to sit tight, that she was going to refer us for further assistance from the mental-health team. I knew it was really difficult to get a referral so I felt incredibly lucky, and somehow both reassured and anxious about the fact they were taking it so seriously. Several days later, a nurse from the mental-health team and a psychiatrist came to the house to assess Sam.

Sam was in the garden, running up and down the stretch of lawn that he'd worn down from all his flapping. I watched him for a moment, his anxiety obvious in every pounding step, and then called him over.

'Sam, come and say hello.'

I didn't tell him that one of his visitors was a doctor as I didn't want to make him even more stressed than he already was.

Unusually, Sam didn't answer me. His eyes were on the ground and he was muttering to himself. He clearly didn't want to come over.

'I won't be a moment,' I excused myself. I walked over to where Sam was flapping and crouched down on one knee. 'Sweetie, please come and say hello to our guests.'

Sam wouldn't look me in the eye. But he would let me lead

him, so I gently took his hand in mine and brought him inside.

'Would you like a drink?' I asked them all, gesturing to the nurse and psychiatrist to congregate in the kitchen. I thought Sam would be more likely to engage with the professionals if he could see it was an informal gathering.

'Hello, Sam,' the doctor said in a very gentle voice.

Sam wouldn't respond. He continued to flicker and weave his fingers in front of his eyes.

My own anxiety levels were rising as I watched the scene unfold. For how would the doctor ever be able to help Sam if he wouldn't communicate? How could she fix him if my son wouldn't tell her what was wrong?

'Sam, say hello.' I encouraged him again to engage.

Nothing.

I looked at the doctor and nurse in despair. I wanted to scream at them to do something, to help us – but I needed to stay calm for Sam's sake.

Suddenly, a solution dawned on me. The answer had been staring me in the face all along. In fact, the answer was sitting out in our back garden!

Chester.

Chester had been the key to helping Sam build his confidence, to making him laugh, to easing all the symptoms of his autism. Chester had helped Sam find his voice before . . . so maybe he could help my son now?

I took Sam by his shoulders and said, 'Sam, why don't you show Chester to our visitors?'

Sam looked up at me and smiled. My heart leapt: his eyes were suddenly alive again. I explained to the nurse and doctor who Chester was and, once they'd got over their initial surprise that we had a pet pig, they gamely rose from their chairs and prepared to follow Sam out into the garden. Sam started to flap his hands with excitement as he led them through the back door, across the terrace and towards Chester's pen. Chester heard the footsteps and started grunting furiously in excitement.

I didn't follow them into the garden. I knew how important it was to give Sam his space. Instead, I ran up to his bedroom, so I could watch them out of the window. I was praying that Sam would start talking, that he would open up to the psychiatrist. As his mother, there was only so much I could do – I needed the help of professionals now.

Peering through the window, I observed Chester rushing out of his pig ark, wagging his tail. I couldn't hear any of the noises – but it was amusing to watch the reactions of the two women as they both took a step back! I then watched with delight as Sam started pointing at Chester and interacting with the professionals. A huge wave of relief washed over me. Things were finally moving in the right direction.

Twenty minutes later, they all came back into the house and I ran down the stairs. I hovered in the background, busying myself in the kitchen as they occupied the living room. I was trying to listen in to what was going on, but I couldn't hear everything that was being said clearly. I could tell that Sam was speaking and I heard him say: 'Chester is my pet pig. He used to live in the house with us before he got too big.'

I couldn't help but smile. Bless my little Sam, talking about his friend and all the dramas we'd had with Chester. And then the doctors called to me – they'd had an idea. Since Sam still struggled with his speech, but excelled with his drawing, what if he illustrated how he was feeling for them?

It was a great idea. I fetched paper and Sam's treasured collection of felt-tip pens.

'Sam, can you draw some pictures of yourself, and describe each one to me?' asked the nurse.

Without any hesitation, Sam got to work. The channels of communication had been opened thanks to Chester, and now Sam was trying to tell them how he was feeling through his artwork. I nervously stepped away, leaving them alone for the second time, though every now and again I would pop my head around the kitchen door to see how he was doing. And Sam was calm, he was speaking, and he was trying to do the best job he could with his pictures. I felt a little bit of hope spark inside me.

An hour later, they finally emerged.

'Look at this amazing drawing Sam has done,' the nurse said as she rolled the artwork across the carpet.

Sam had drawn five faces, and written a word underneath each one. My face fell as I saw that three of them were negative: *Silly. Stupid. Sad.*

It shouldn't have come as a shock, considering how down he was on himself, but seeing his simple self-portraits really emphasised his lack of confidence. *My poor boy*, I thought.

I looked to the nurse for reassurance.

'This is great,' she said brightly, beaming at me. She told me it was a very positive sign that Sam was communicating his feelings so well. She told me I wasn't to worry about how negative they might seem.

As Sam headed back out into the garden to see Chester, his running steps seeming lighter already, the women brought their visit to an end. They told me that they would be keeping a close eye on Sam but from what they had witnessed, and from what Sam had communicated to them, there was no imminent danger. It was such a relief to hear trained professionals tell me that.

As they left, I felt as though a weight was lifting from my shoulders. I went to Sam's bedroom window again and watched Sam and Will playing with the pig. Sam seemed calmer and happier in his own skin. He wasn't flickering his hands in front of his face, and from that point on he seemed less anxious to be alone.

It wasn't an overnight recovery, but once Sam had expressed how he was feeling to the mental-health workers, he started to improve. And the catalyst for it all had been Chester. Talking about his pig had opened up Sam's channels of communication again. Just as Sam had rescued Chester when he'd been ill and close to death, Chester had reciprocated by rescuing Sam from the dark place he'd found himself in.

I owed so much to that pig.

As July crept into August, Sam was able to go and see Chester on his own once more. I'd spy on him from the top of the garden as he fed his friend pignuts and tickled his tummy with the broom, just to reassure myself he was OK. And, when I glanced across the lawn to see Darren also looking up from his veg patch and gazing thoughtfully at the two friends, I could tell that he was thinking the same thing as me: we were so lucky Sam had Chester in his life.

Bit by bit, day by day, all the tension that had been building over the past few months eased. Sam was now happy to walk around the house by himself and he would play in his bedroom if Will was there too. The last thing to come was sleeping in his own bed at night – but he was getting there. When he did make it through the night in his own bed again, we made such a fuss over him and I bought him a little present as a reward.

By the time it came to starting secondary school in September 2014, Sam was almost back to his usual self. He still wouldn't sleep without the lights on, but he'd made an incredible recovery.

In fact, as the big first day approached, he seemed a lot calmer than I was – though, of course, I didn't let on. This next stage for Sam was a landmark, and I'm not ashamed to admit that, like many mothers, I found myself a bit concerned about him moving to 'big school'. I fretted about him getting lost, being bullied or having a meltdown when there was no one there to help him. He was moving from a school with 275 pupils to one with 1,400, so it was a huge step up.

On the plus side, a lot of provisions had been made to help Sam. He would have two TAs looking out for him at all times. He would be taken out of class and back to the CAIRB just before the bell rang, so he could avoid the hustle and bustle and the noise of the corridors. Devon County Council had even assigned him a taxi service to take him to and from school. His TA would be there to meet him when he arrived at the start of the day and would put him in the taxi when it was time to come home.

Before the big day, I emailed the TAs, who I'd met during the week we had shown Sam around the school, to make sure they would be there to meet him from the taxi. Once I had their reassurance, I ran through with Sam what he should do if for some reason they didn't show up. It was ridiculous, I know, but I was so concerned about Sam regressing again and I knew all it could take to tip him over the edge was one bad experience; and that one bad experience would then become implanted in his brain like a phobia. It might mean he would never want to go back to that school again.

Sadly, Darren wasn't there to see Sam off on his first day. Will was, though, and joined in helping Sam get dressed in his new uniform of a black blazer and trousers, white shirt, and a red-white-and-black striped tie.

I handed Sam his lunchbox before he left for the day. I'd prepared his favourite sandwiches and also, tucked way at the bottom, I'd included a postcard of a pig. I wanted Sam to know Chester was with him in spirit! It was something familiar, something to make him smile. On the back of the card I'd written:

> *Dear Sam,*
> *I hope you're having a lovely day at school.*
> *Just wanted to let you know how proud we all are of you.*
> *Lots of love, Mum, Dad, Will and Chester XXX*

Being the proud mum that I was, I pulled out the camera as the children and I waited for the taxi to arrive. I snapped away as I wanted a lasting memento of the moment.

'And together!' I directed the boys to stand by the flower-beds so I could get a photo of the two of them.

I was in the middle of my impromptu photo shoot when the taxi pulled into our drive. The windows were steamed up, so I couldn't see who was inside. I was expecting maybe one or two other children, but the door slid open and there were five in there.

I panicked momentarily, thinking that so many new faces might be too much for Sam.

And then I made a big mistake. Sam got into the taxi and *I put his seatbelt on for him.* As soon as I'd done it I regretted it, thinking that Sam might be picked on for me helping him like that. I told myself sternly that I had to stop mothering him. He was nearly twelve, after all.

As the taxi did a three-point turn, Sam rubbed a hole in the condensation on the window so I could see through to him. He smiled and waved enthusiastically, and I breathed a sigh of relief. He was fine. He was more than fine.

I walked back to where Will was patiently waiting on the front step for me to drive him to school ... and promptly burst into tears. Will wrapped his arms around me.

'Don't cry, Mummy, he'll be OK.'

Will was being so mature about it all, and there I was, cry-ing! We'd all been through so much that I think, as I said goodbye to Sam that morning, all the emotions that had been building up over the last few months suddenly came out. I felt as if I was letting go.

It was a peculiar day. I must have checked my emails and phone dozens of times, just in case Sam or the school had rung and needed me to go and pick him up. But there was nothing: no messages, no calls, no cries for help. Just silence.

By the time the taxi pulled into the drive after school, my heart was in my mouth as questions rattled through my head. *Has Sam had a good day? Is he happy?* I wanted that more than anything: just for my son to be happy.

It was almost as if everything was happening in slow motion as the back door of the taxi opened – first I saw Sam's shoes, then his legs, and then the rest of him appeared with his satchel on his back. He bounced over to me.

'I *love* my school, I've had the best day!' he boomed. I burst out laughing. All that worry over nothing!

'I'm so glad, Sam.' I gave him a hug and a kiss.

Someone else had also heard Sam arriving home.

'Chester!' we chorused together. He was calling out for us to go and see him, probably hoping we would throw him some pignuts while we were there.

I put my arm around Sam as we wandered down to the end of the garden to see our pig – the pig that had changed my son's life.

The pig that had brought happiness to all of us.

Chester, the larger-than-life pig!

Epilogue

Devon, April 2015

SEVEN MONTHS AFTER SAM HAD STARTED AT HIS NEW SCHOOL, a letter arrived in the post.

It was springtime and I was weeding the flowerbeds near Chester's pen when the postman pulled into our driveway. He handed me a bundle of letters and I leafed through them, expecting the usual mix of bills and junk mail, but one of them stood out. It had the logo of Sam's school stamped on the front and was addressed to: 'The parent/carer of Samuel Bailey-Merritt'.

My stomach lurched with apprehension. *Oh God, what's happened?* was my first thought. Sam had seemed really happy of late – was there something wrong at the College that he hadn't told me about? The boys were at school that day so he wasn't there to ask – I just had to open the letter and find out.

I tore open the envelope in a rush. My legs were a little shaky so I sat down by the back door. As I read the words on the page, tears welled in my eyes.

Although the boys were at school, luckily I wasn't alone; my mum was with me and had popped indoors for a break from the gardening.

'What is it, love?' she asked me as I joined her on the sofa in the living room.

I clutched the letter in my hand and took a deep breath. 'I've just received this from Sam's school.'

Mum looked pensive but alert at my words, ready to hear what I had to say.

I cleared my throat and began to read the letter aloud to her. As I did so, I felt tears pricking at my eyes again and the words on the page blurred . . .

Dear Mr and Mrs Bailey-Merritt,

I am pleased to inform you that Sam is invited to attend a cele-bration tea on Thursday for his continuing hard work and success within Fox Tor [Sam's house at school]. He was one of only two students selected by me from the entire house. They were chosen in recognition of their approach to their studies and their ability to use a range of the emotional, social, thinking and strategic learning habits we wish the young people of the College to develop.

Sam's friendly, courteous and reliable nature has won him many friends and made him a pleasure to have within the house. His endeavours to succeed will ensure he makes the most out of his future, and South Dartmoor benefit greatly from having someone like Sam within the College.

I would like to congratulate him and to share his success with you as his parents. We wish Sam continued success.

Yours sincerely,
Jamie Morrison-Hill
Performance Leader, Fox Tor

By the time I'd finished reading, Mum was stunned into silence.

'Sam has made some friends!' I exclaimed. Every single

word in that letter was wonderful, but the part about Sam making friends meant the most to me. It was almost unheard of for children with autism to make friends, and one of my biggest concerns about Sam starting secondary school had been that he wouldn't have any friends and would be bullied, so to hear this meant *everything* to me.

'Oh, Jo, that is wonderful.' Mum beamed with happiness. She grasped for my hand and squeezed it, her face suddenly serious. 'I cannot express how proud I am of *you*. I have not known another mother to do for her child what you have done for that boy.'

It was wonderful to hear her words and they made me reflect on everything the whole family had done to 'save' Sam when we'd moved from Spain to start our new life in England. But that battle seemed a world away now. For when Sam had first been diagnosed, my fight for him wasn't simply to ensure he had the best opportunities and the best teachers; I'd actually believed that early intervention and the right help could rewire his brain; that he could literally be 'saved' from something I then saw as a negative. It was wrong of me, but I think many parents think like that when they first receive a diagnosis of autism for their children.

But, of course, I now knew that no manner of techniques would make Sam neurotypical – and I was very, *very* glad of that fact. Autism was part of Sam and I loved him for who he was; I now celebrated his differences rather than thinking they were something from which he needed 'saving'. He was not a tragedy. He was Sam!

So while Mum may have been proud of me, I knew this wasn't my victory. This was all about Sam – and I could not have been prouder of my boy.

And pride became a familiar feeling as time went by. For Sam went on to succeed not just at school, but in other ways too. In the spring of 2016, life came full circle when Sam was offered a volunteering job at Pennywell Farm. Mr Murray was so accommodating about it and said he'd be delighted to have Sam on board: one of the team helping with the next generations of miracle-working micro pigs.

I will confess that my own, personal hope is that, after a couple of years of volunteering, when Sam turns sixteen, he will know the ropes well enough and be confident enough to perhaps land a summer job at the farm, at the very least. It would be an incredible achievement and I know such a job would make Sam very, very happy. What could be more perfect for him than working with the pigs he loves so much?

But all that is for the future. And while Sam loves *all* the Pennywell pigs he works with, there remains one pig who is snout and shoulders above the rest. Chester, of course! The pig who started it all, who set Sam on the path to living a full and happy life – the pig I owe my life to, too.

The not-so-little ginger pig has transformed my boy over the years. Chester showed him friendship and proved to Sam that he could be loved, *just the way he was*. From the moment the two buddies bonded, first at the farm where Sam now volunteers, and then beneath our dining-room table in their den, my son blossomed. When I look at him now, it's just incredible – he is succeeding, he is communicating and he is living the life I always dreamed for him.

And I know he could never have done it alone.

Sam and Chester still play together frequently, chasing each other round and round the garden, Sam howling with laughter as Chester dodges and dives and simply delights. As

Epilogue

I watch them gambolling about, two friends doing what they love best – being together – I often raise a toast to them in my mind, as I give thanks for that special bond they share, which has made such a difference to my son.

Won't you join me now in celebrating them?

To Sam and Chester.

Acknowledgements

This book would not have been possible without the help and support of many wonderful people, whom I'd like to thank here:

The National Autistic Society, who provided me with so much information when I began to research schools in the UK and who pointed me in the direction of all the Devon CAIRBs.

Chris Murray, for introducing us to Chester and for very kindly welcoming Sam to volunteer at Pennywell Farm.

Ruth Kelly, my co-author, for giving me the chance to tell my story. It has been a real pleasure working with you. For the record, you are one of the few people brave enough to get up close and personal with Chester! Also Susan Smith of MBA Literary Agents, who has guided me through this entire process with such professionalism. I have felt very safe in your hands and for that I am extremely grateful.

The fantastic team at Transworld Publishers for having faith in the story which we hope will inspire and bring hope to many others. A very special thank-you to Editorial Director Michelle Signore, who has been an absolute joy to work with, and to Sophie Christopher and Josh Crosley – particularly for the delightful goody bag you brought Chester all the way from London! Thanks also to Richard Ogle, who designed the cover, and to Nicola Wright, Josh Benn and Louise Jones.

Kate Moore, who worked with me through the final edits. It was a real honour and such fun!

All our lovely friends in Devon whose lives are touched by autism and special needs: Scott and Dawn Miller, Jo and Lee Lawton-Cook, Chris and Juliet Boardman, Rebecca Sadler, Lesley Mcgill, Tony and Sue O'Leary, Sandra Hart, Tamsin Summers, Simon Skinner and Sarah Morgan. You truly are some of the most resilient and resourceful people I have ever met.

Our fantastic neighbours, who have embraced the boys and Chester and welcomed us to their little hamlet with open arms: James, Debs, George, Jack, Sally and Rowan.

I am unable to list you all, but the *entire* staff at Manor Primary – an outstanding school that has given the boys an excellent start in life. Especially Ian Hemelik, Karen Dixon, Julie Solomon, Rob Wills, Sue Parker, Jo Chandler, Ian Rowland, and the fabulous ladies in the office.

The outstanding CAIRB team at Manor Primary. What an extraordinary bunch of wonderful women you are – Clare Ellison, Lisa Tomlinson, Catherine Macmilllan, Gayner Bennett and Gill Steele. And a very special mention to Sam's amazing hands-on TAs, whose dedication throughout his primary years was just incredible – Nikki Short, Kay Scull and Jane Sharp.

All the professionals who have worked with Sam and me over the years – with a special mention and huge thank-you to two exceptional women, Ronni Hale and Marie Mills.

Acknowledgements

The staff at South Dartmoor Community College, especially Fiona Goodchild and Wendy Waters. All the CAIRB staff who do excellent work with not-so-easy teenagers on the spectrum; your dedication to the job is quite remarkable and I am so grateful for the support you offer Sam – Sue Nicholson, Monica Hannaford, Bev Fulford, Rachael Mitchelmore and Ian Karkeek. Also Hugh Bellamy and Jamie Morrison-Hill.

Dan Chapman, Sam's enabler from Care & Support South West Ltd, who does amazing work with Sam every single weekend. You are a fantastic role model for my son and an absolute joy to work with. Thanks also to Khya, Chelsea and Matt.

All the friends and family who rallied round in the early days, and who helped me to build my case to bring the boys home; I really couldn't have done it without you – the Walldens, especially Matthew and Vanessa, Alex McCann, Fran Yule, Timothy Wall, Carole Heinen, Andrea Yule and Antonio Reyes.

Andy Despard, our wonderful builder, who, no matter how far away, downs tools to come and get Chester back into his pen on the occasions I am unable to. Thanks also to Andy's sidekick, Colin Bovey, for the daily treats you bring Chester whenever you are working at the cottage!

All our friends, old and new, for their continued love and support, and in particular our very special friends, Flora and Richard Bowler, John and Helen Butler, Lucy and Mike Wheeler.

The amazing Penny Wall, who has been there for as long as I can remember, for all the incredible support, advice and love you have given me and the boys over the years. Your friendship means everything to me.

My friend Lynda Russell – I am truly indebted to you. Thank you for all the support and encouragement I needed when I wanted to bring Sam home. The progress that the CAIRB children made under your care at Manor was inspirational and a testament to all your hard work, dedication and unfaltering belief that all-inclusion for these amazing children was the only way to go.

My wonderful in-laws, Dave, Marilyn, Tree and Olivia, Ian and Rose, for welcoming the boys and me into your family with such love and support.

My lovely sister, Sarah, and Simon, for all the laughter and the good times we have shared and for all the love and help you have given Sam and me over the years. And the coolest nephews any aunty could wish for – Tom and Dan! You boys are really special young men and you have helped Sam more than you can imagine. I am so proud of you both.

My amazing mum, who insisted I took Sam to see someone in those early days. Thank you for your ongoing love and support and for teaching me that in life the only failure is to give up trying. I can only hope I have acknowledged sufficiently within the pages of this book how very much you have done and still do for me.

My wonderful husband, Darren, for your wicked sense of humour, patience, kindness, and unconditional love. Life with you is such fun, you are an amazing father to the boys and we love you the world!

Acknowledgements

William, my happy-go-lucky chatty man, of whom I am so immensely proud. Sam is a very lucky boy to have a brother like you and both Dad and I feel so very proud to have a son like you. You bring us all such joy each and every day.

Chester, what can I say? He may be the most expensive and mischievous pig in Devon but he has filled our lives with joy and laughter. We hope his wonderful, smiley face continues to greet us each morning for many years to come – preferably not from the sofa.

And, last but not least, Sam: my special, special boy, who is so honest and pure and beautiful inside and out, thank you for showing me every day what life is really all about. I wouldn't change you for the world, but if I could, I would certainly change the world for you.

Jo Bailey lives in Devon with her husband, Darren, and two sons, Sam and William. Moving to the UK from Spain in 2006 to find help for Sam, their lives were changed the moment they met Chester. Thanks to this lovable, larger-than-life pig, Sam has blossomed into a happy and confident teenager. Through Chester, he has learnt the value of friendship.

Ruth Kelly is an award-nominated journalist, who has ghosted a string of *Sunday Times* bestsellers including entrepreneur Michelle Mone's autobiography, *My Fight to the Top*, *Out of the Darkness* by Tina Nash and *You Can't Hide* by Tina Renton. Ruth has ten years' experience in print journalism and television.